An Introduction to the Works of Peter Weiss

The plays and prose works of the German writer, director, and political activist Peter Weiss (1916–1982) have been immensely influential in the shaping of European modernism in the second half of the twentieth century. Weiss's writings are driven by the desire to find creative responses to the question of how an artist and writer who makes use of a wide variety of techniques of artistic expression can also participate in political activism. Combining exploratory aesthetic openness with an uncompromising ethical drive, Weiss's literary works, especially the plays *Marat/Sade* (1964), *The Investigation* (1968), and *Hölderlin* (1971) as well as his novel *The Aesthetics of Resistance* (1975–81) continue to provide vital points of reference for any discussion of culture and politics in our times. Olaf Berwald's study serves as a comprehensive introduction to Weiss's work and vision. The introductory chapter outlines Weiss's life and work in exile. Three chapters provide detailed discussions of Weiss's theater work, from his early grotesque plays and the documentary dramas from the 1960s that address Auschwitz, Angola, and Vietnam, to his most complex plays, in which intellectuals are staged as outsiders. The subsequent four chapters discuss Weiss's prose works, which include his autobiographical novels from the early 1960s, essays and notebooks on art and politics, and his summum opus, *The Aesthetics of Resistance*, one of the most important European novels of the twentieth century.

Olaf Berwald is Assistant Professor of German at the University of Tennessee.

Studies in German Literature, Linguistics, and Culture

Edited by James Hardin
(*South Carolina*)

AN INTRODUCTION TO THE WORKS OF
Peter Weiss

Olaf Berwald

CAMDEN HOUSE

First published 2003
by Camden House

Camden House is an imprint of Boydell & Brewer Inc.
668 Mt. Hope Avenue, Rochester, NY 14620 USA
and of Boydell & Brewer Limited
PO Box 9, Woodbridge, Suffolk IP12 3DF, UK

ISBN: 1–57113–232–5

Library of Congress Cataloging-in-Publication Data

Berwald, Olaf.
  An introduction to the works of Peter Weiss / Olaf Berwald.
    p. cm. — (Studies in German literature, linguistics, and culture)
  Includes bibliographical references and index.
  ISBN 1–57113–232–5 (alk. paper)
    1. Weiss, Peter, 1916 — Criticism and interpretation.   I. Title.
  II. Series: Studies in German literature, linguistics, and culture (Un-
numbered)

  PT2685.E5Z578 2003
  832'.914—dc21

                                                      2003001570

A catalogue record for this title is available from the British Library.

This publication is printed on acid-free paper.
Printed in the United States of America.

Contents

Acknowledgments

I WOULD LIKE to thank the editors, Jim Hardin and Jim Walker, for their patience and their generous feedback throughout the writing process. I have thoroughly enjoyed our productive dialogues. The University of Tennessee has supported my research with a Professional Development Award. Thanks are also due to the friendly staff at the Academy of the Arts' Peter Weiss Archive in Berlin. At the University of Tennessee, I am very fortunate to work with colleagues with whom I share symphilological friendships, both in and beyond the Department of Modern Foreign Languages and Literatures. Amy Billone, Department of English at the University of Tennessee, has read a final version of the manuscript. I want to thank her for her kind suggestions and for our conversations.

I am very grateful for the trust and support of my teachers and mentors during my formative years in Germany and the United States: Joachim Knape, the late Paul Hoffmann (Eberhard-Karls-Universität Tübingen), the late Robert Asch (Tufts University), Helga Bister-Broosen, Alice Kuzniar, Siegfried Mews (all University of North Carolina at Chapel Hill), and Klaus Weimar (Universität Zürich).

Finally, this book is one small way to thank Wilhelm, Frieda, Jörg, and Manuela Berwald, as well as Luciana Camargo Namorato, meu amor.

O. B.
Knoxville, Tennessee
June 2003

Introduction

IN SEARCHING FOR AN ART OF writing capable of confronting the violent beginnings of the new millennium, it is indispensable to study the literary oeuvre of Peter Weiss (1916–1982), whose plays and narrative works have helped to shape European modernism in the second half of the twentieth century. Weiss's literary works explore how a writer can assume social responsibility while working toward multifaceted modes of artistic expression. Combining aesthetic openness with an uncompromising ethical drive, Weiss's literary works, for example his plays *Marat/Sade* (1963) and *Die Ermittlung* (1965, The Investigation), and especially his novel *Die Ästhetik des Widerstands* (1975–81, The Aesthetics of Resistance), provide vital reference points for any discussion of culture and politics in our times.

Peter Ulrich Weiss was born during the First World War, on November 8, 1916, in Nowawes, near Potsdam. He was the son of Eugen Jenö Weiss (1885–1959), a Slovak Jewish textile entrepreneur, and the Swiss actress Frieda Franziska Weiss, née Hummel (1885–1958). In 1917, the Weiss family resided in Przemyśl (Galicia) but returned to the Potsdam area the following year. In 1919 his family moved to Bremen, and lived there until moving on to Berlin in 1929, where they remained until 1934.

In August 1934, Weiss's sister Margit Beatrice Weiss died in a car accident, an event whose impact permeates much of Weiss's visual art and literary works. He immigrated with his family to England in 1935 to escape Nazi persecution. Until 1936, they lived in Chislehurst, near London. In 1936, Weiss studied at the Polytechnical School of Photography in London. In a storage room in Little Kinnerton Street, Weiss, together with his friends Ruth Anker and Jacques Ayschmann, organized an exhibition of his paintings in 1936. Later that year, the Weiss family left England and moved to the Czech town of Warnsdorf, where Weiss's father had been offered a lucrative business position. Weiss studied painting at the Art Academy in Prague from 1937 to 1938 under the noted artist Willi Nowak (1886–1955). Seeking a career as a painter, Weiss participated in an exhibition hosted by the Prague Art Academy in 1938.[1]

From 1937 until 1962, he corresponded with the German writer Hermann Hesse (1877–1962), who had left Germany in 1912 and settled in Montagnola, Switzerland. In the late 1930s, Weiss visited Hesse several times and contributed illustrations to some of his minor works, including the novella "Kindheit des Zauberers," which was published with Weiss's illustrations in 1974.[2] Hesse's prose, which earned him the Nobel Prize for literature in 1946 and gained worldwide cult status among young readers throughout the second half of the twentieth century, not only explored the suffocation of individual desires by authorities and the resulting alienation from society, in such novels as *Unterm Rad* (1906, Beneath the Wheel) and *Steppenwolf* (1927), but also provided room for imaginative journeys. Hesse invented harmonious societal as well as personal maturation processes in his novels *Siddharta* (1922) and *Das Glasperlenspiel* (1943, The Glass Bead Game). In a letter to Weiss from January 1937, Hesse suggested some poetological principles whose impact on Weiss's literary works were considerable and remained evident even in his final writings. Hesse recommended exercises in stylistic precision and soberness, and admonished the twenty-year-old writer that every word had to be able to stand for itself and that a writer was responsible for each of his words. While dissuading Weiss from absorbing stylistic and thematic influences, Hesse emphasized the constructive and experimental character of the writing process, which he likened to drawing and building.[3]

Because it was impossible to gain a permanent visa in Switzerland, Weiss returned to Berlin. In January 1939, he joined his family in Swedish exile in Alingsås and worked for his father, who now owned a textile factory. He moved to Stockholm one year later and hosted an exhibition of his paintings.

Weiss's paintings from the 1930s included *Selbstporträt zwischen Tod und Schwester* (1935, Self Portrait between Death and Sister), *Das große Welttheater* (1937, The Great World Theater), *Gartenkonzert* (1938, Garden Concert), *Im Hof des Irrenhauses* (1937–38, In the Courtyard of the Mental Institution), *Jüngling am Stadtrand* (1938, Young Man on the Outskirts of the City), *Der Hausierer* (1940, The Peddler), *Jahrmarkt am Stadtrand* (1940, Fair on the Outskirts of the City). Many of his paintings were destroyed or disappeared during the escapes from the Nazis. In 1941, Stockholm's Mässhallen showed an exhibition of Weiss's paintings.

German-Jewish emigrants were not received warmly in Sweden, and the material conditions for survival were very limited. Weiss worked as a farmhand and as a lumberjack in northern Sweden before he began to work as a graphic designer in his father's factory in 1943. In the same year, he engaged in productive dialogues with Swedish modernist poets who formed the "Fyrtiotalisterna" ("writers of the 1940s") circle. Between 1944 and 1946, Weiss's paintings were shown in five exhibitions in Stockholm.

Weiss's personal relationships with women during the 1940s were short-lived. His marriage to the painter Helga Henschen, with whom he had one daughter, Randi Maria, lasted only from 1943 to 1944. For several years, Weiss lived with the Danish artist Le Klint. In 1949, he married Carlota Dethorey, the daughter of a Spanish diplomat, when she became pregnant. Weiss divorced her in the same year, soon after the birth of their son Paul. Since 1952, Weiss lived with Gunilla Palmstierna, a Swedish artist and stage designer whose parents were psychoanalysts. Her Russian-Jewish mother had studied with Freud. Palmstierna spent most of her childhood years in Rotterdam and managed to board a flight from Berlin to Sweden at the end of the Second World War. Weiss spent the rest of his life with her. They married in 1964, and their daughter Nadja was born in 1972. Gunilla Palmstierna-Weiss was responsible for the stage design of most of Weiss's plays. Their creative teamwork lasted until Weiss's death.[4]

Immediately after the end of the Second World War, Weiss's paintings, for example *Obduktion* (1944, Autopsy), *Apokalypse* (1945), *Der Krieg* (1946, War), and *Der Reiche und der Arme* (1946, The Rich and the Poor Man), addressed the themes of death and destruction in an intensified manner, with a new focus on social contexts of violence. Some paintings from this time period, such as *Adam, Eva und Kain* (1946) and *Odysseus* (1946) make free use of mythological and biblical configurations. Cain forces his parents to pull a plow, and Odysseus, exhausted and mourning, rests for a moment in the face of debris, a dead woman, or a fallen statue of a woman, sculptured heads whose eyes seem to be alive and in fear.

In 1945, Weiss contributed several illustrations to a poetry volume by Gunnar Ekelöf (1907–1968), an influential poet of Swedish modernism who encouraged Weiss's art and writing.[5] Weiss spent part of the year in Paris. His first book, the Swedish prose poem volume *Från ö till ö* (From Island to Island) was published in 1947. Having received Swedish citizenship in 1946, Weiss visited Berlin one year later as a journalist for a Swedish newspaper and wrote a series of articles about the destroyed city. He also visited Paris again in 1947. In 1948, Weiss wrote his first major work in German, *Der Vogelfreie* (The Outcast). German publishers, among them Peter Suhrkamp, rejected the manuscript, and

Weiss privately published a Swedish version in 1949, which served as a film script for his movie *Hägringen* (1959, The Mirage). Under the pseudonym "Sinclair," an allusion to Isaak von Sinclair, Friedrich Hölderlin's friend, and to Hesse, who had used the same pen name for his novel *Demian* (1919), *Der Vogelfreie* was published under the title *Der Fremde* (The Stranger) in 1980. In 1948, Weiss's Swedish prose collection of haunting impressions of postwar Berlin, *De Besegraden* (The Defeated), was published. His Swedish short stories "Ur anteckningar" (Journal Notes) and "Den anonyme" (The Anonymous Man) were published in 1948 and 1949. In the same year, *Rotundan,* an unpublished Swedish version of Weiss's first play, *Der Turm* (The Tower), whose original German text was published in 1963, premiered in Stockholm. In 1953, Weiss privately published his Swedish narrative *Duellen* in Stockholm.

In close cooperation with Palmstierna, Weiss began to produce, direct, edit, and sometimes even act in sixteen mostly short, experimental movies, which, like his literary works, address the unconscious as well as social issues and put into question sharp distinctions between surrealism and a documentary style. He co-founded the "Arbetsgruppen för film" (Working Group for Film), the most important Swedish avant-garde film group. His films include *Studie I / Uppvaknandet* (1952, Waking up), *Studie II / Hallucinationer* (1952), *Studie III* (1953), *Studie IV / Frigörelse* (1954, Liberation), *Studie V / Växelspel* (1955, Interplay), *Ansikten i skugga* (1956, Faces in the Shadow), and *Ateljéinteriör* (1956, The Studio of Dr. Faust), his only color movie. *Ingenting Ovanligt* (1957, Nothing Unusual) was commissioned by an insurance company and documents a traffic accident, which echoes the lethal car accident of his sister, the traumatic childhood event that Weiss repeatedly worked through in his early paintings. Other movies from the 1950s include *Enligt Lag* (1957, In the Name of the Law), a documentary collage of a juvenile prison, and *Vad ska vi göra nu da?* (1958, What should we do now?), a work that was commissioned by the Swedish Social Democrats' youth organization. Weiss's only full-length movie, *Hägringen* (1959), was based on his novel *Der Vogelfreie*. His last documentary short films are *Bag de ens facader* (1960, Behind the facades), a documentary about new apartment developments in Denmark, *Två Kvinnor* (1960/61, Two Women), which approached the theme of lesbian love, *En Narkoman* (1960/61, A Drug Addict), and two film essays on Swedish artists, *Anna Casparsson* (1960) and *Öyvind Fahlström* (1960).[6] Weiss also wrote a concise narrative on the history and theory of experimental film. In 1956, his Swedish book *Avantgardefilm* was published.

In the same year, Weiss wrote the Swedish novel *Situationen,* which remained unpublished. In 2000, a German translation made the work accessible to German readers. In 1960, Weiss published *Der Schatten des Körpers des Kutschers* (*The Shadow of the Coachman's Body*). Written in 1952, this experimental prose work employed a collage- or filmlike style. Weiss illustrated this book with his own collages, which incorporated medical scenes and disembodied limbs. In the same year, Weiss's paintings were exhibited in Aleby. In 1960, Weiss wrote the poetic essay "Der große Traum des Briefträgers Cheval" (The Great Dream of Cheval the Mailman), which densely describes and interprets an eclectic and phantasmagoric architectonic experiment as a manifestation of the unconscious.

In 1961, Weiss's autobiographical novel *Abschied von den Eltern* (*Leavetaking*) appeared, together with collage illustrations, in which a shipwreck, wild animals, naked bodies, and agitated survivors as well as onlookers form tableaus of ambivalence. His novel *Fluchtpunkt* (*Vanishing Point*), which many read as a sequel to *Abschied von den Eltern,* was published in 1962. In the same year, Weiss wrote an essay and speech on August Strindberg, "Gegen die Gesetze der Normalität" (Against the Laws of Normalcy) and participated in a meeting of the influential German postwar writers' group, "Gruppe 47," in Berlin.

In 1963, the narrative *Das Gespräch der drei Gehenden* (The Conversation of the Three Walkers) and the play *Nacht mit Gästen* (Night with Guests) were published, and Weiss's paintings were exhibited in Berlin. Weiss and Italo Calvino shared the Charles Veillon award for their experimental prose works. In 1964, he traveled to Auschwitz and regularly attended a trial against Auschwitz officials in Frankfurt, during which he took extensive notes in preparation for a drama. His most famous play, *Die Verfolgung und Ermordung Jean Paul Marats dargestellt durch die Schauspielgruppe des Hospizes zu Charenton unter Anleitung des Herrn de Sade. Drama in zwei Akten* (The Persecution and Murder of Jean Paul Marat Performed by the Acting Group of the Hospital in Charenton Directed by Mr. de Sade), premiered in Berlin in 1964. In the same year, Peter Brook directed the play in London, and one year later on Broadway.

In 1965, the City of Hamburg's important Lessing Prize and the Swedish Workers' Movement's Literature Prize were awarded to Weiss. He published several poetological essays in which he outlined his view of the role of a politically alert and undogmatic writer, including "10 Arbeitspunkte eines Autors in der geteilten Welt" (10 Practical Guidelines for an Author during the Cold War), "Laokoon oder Über die Grenzen der Sprache" (Laocoon, or On the Boundaries of Language), which he delivered as his Lessing Prize acceptance speech, and "Gespräch über Dante." In the same year, Weiss wrote the Auschwitz essay "Meine Ortschaft" (translated as "My Place," 1967) and his drama about the Auschwitz trial in Frankfurt, *Die Ermittlung. Oratorium in 11 Gesängen,* premiered simultaneously in East and West Germany. Throughout his life, Weiss maintained an ambivalent relationship to his Jewish heritage. Not only did he refuse to see himself as a victim, but he rejected the importance of any national or ethnic categories for his personal identity.[7]

In the same year, Weiss provided an illustration for a volume by the Swedish author Artur Lundkvist (1906–1991). This collage depicts an anonymous nocturnal cityscape with a winged female mythological figure, which is observed by a lunar eye.

In 1966, the prestigious Heinrich Mann Prize was awarded to Weiss, and Peter Brook directed the movie version of *Marat/Sade.* Also that year, Weiss's drama *Die Versicherung* (The Insurance), written in 1952, premiered in Sweden, and he gave an autobiographical and antimilitaristic speech in English, "I Come out of My Hiding Place," at Princeton University. In 1967, *Gesang vom Lusitanischen Popanz* (Song of the Lusitanian Bogey) premiered in Stockholm. This play was aimed against colonialism in Angola. In the same year, Weiss received the Carl-Albert-Anderson Prize in Stockholm and traveled to Cuba with a group of French artists and writers, including Marguerite Duras and Michel Leiris.

Together with Jean-Paul Sartre and others, Weiss actively participated in the Russell tribunals against international war crimes. To show his solidarity with the Vietnamese people, Weiss traveled to communist Vietnam in 1968. In the same year, Weiss's play *Diskurs über die Vorgeschichte und den Verlauf des lang andauernden Befreiungskrieges in Viet Nam als Beispiel für die Notwendigkeit des bewaffneten Kampfes der Unterdrückten gegen ihre Unterdrücker sowie über die Versuche der Vereinigten Staaten von Amerika die Grundlagen der Revolution zu vernichten* (Discourse on the Progress of the Prolonged War of Liberation in Viet Nam and the Events Leading Up to It as Illustration of the Necessity for Armed Resistance against Oppression and on the Attempts of the United States of America to Destroy the Foundations of Revolution) premiered in Frankfurt. Throughout the 1960s and 1970s, a large number of open letters by and interviews with Weiss, in which he vehemently criticized the war in Vietnam, appeared in international newspapers.

The play *Wie dem Herrn Mockinpott das Leiden ausgetrieben wird* (How Mister Mockinpott Was Cured of His Sufferings) premiered in Hanover in 1968, and Weiss's "Notizen zum dokumentarischen Theater" (The Material and the Models. Notes towards a Definition of Documentary Theatre) were published in the same year. Weiss, who joined the Swedish Communist Party in 1968, nevertheless refused to confine his critical remarks to centers of capitalism. In open letters from 1967 to 1977, he attacked socialist countries for attempting to silence critical intellectuals and artists such as the Czech playwright Pavel Kohout (b. 1928) and the East German songwriter and poet Wolf Biermann (b. 1936), and he protested against the violent end of the "Prague Spring." In 1970, Weiss offered his play *Trotzki im Exil* (Trotsky in Exile) as his contribution to the socialist countries' celebration of Lenin's birthday. The play premiered in Düsseldorf and earned him the status of persona non grata in East Germany, since Trotsky, Lenin's designated successor who was forced into exile and killed in Mexico, still was a taboo subject for official communist historiography.

Weiss suffered a heart attack in 1970. During the period of recovery, he wrote the journal *Rekonvaleszenz*, in which he juxtaposed political alertness and unconscious fears and desires. Parts of these autobiographical reflections were first published in Weiss's *Notizbücher* (1981–82). In 1971, Weiss had controversial discussions with GDR officials. Refusing to hold back his criticism of dogmatic fossilizations in the GDR and other socialist countries, he insisted on the nonconformist role of art. In the same year, his drama *Hölderlin* premiered in Stuttgart. In 1972, his daughter Nadja, who was named after the protagonist in André Bréton's novel *Nadja* (1928), was born. In preparation of what would become his novel *Die Ästhetik des Widerstands,* Weiss conducted a series of interviews with resistance fighters and their families throughout Europe. In 1972 and 1973, Weiss participated again in the Russell tribunal. This public forum investigated war crimes that had been committed in the Vietnam War. In the same year, Weiss visited the World Youth Games in East Berlin.

One year later, Weiss traveled to Spain, Amsterdam, Paris, Zurich, and Lisbon and joined a writers' conference in Moscow. In 1975, he visited East Berlin in order to gather material for his last novel, *Die Ästhetik des Widerstands,* whose first volume appeared in 1975. That year, Weiss also visited Paris and Amsterdam and attended rehearsals of his play *Der Prozeß* (The Trial), which premiered in Bremen and Krefeld. In 1976, Weiss met with his colleagues Martin Walser and Max Frisch in Zurich. Between 1976 and 1980, exhibitions of Weiss's paintings, drawings, and collages were organized in Sweden, Germany, Switzerland, and France. In 1977, he visited an exhibit of his works in Munich.

In 1978, the second volume of *Die Ästhetik des Widerstands* was published. Weiss received the Thomas Dehler Prize from the West German government. In his acceptance speech with the programmatic title "Verständigung" (Peaceful Communication), he sharply criticized West Germany's anticommunist laws, which led to the unemployment of thousands of left-wing intellectuals. In the same year, Weiss met with his fellow writers Max Frisch, Christa and Gerhard Wolf, and Hans Magnus Enzensberger in Stockholm. He traveled to Paris in 1979 and in 1980. In 1981, the final volume of *Die Ästhetik des Widerstands* was published, and the Cologne Literature Prize was awarded to Weiss. In 1982, Weiss rejected honorary degrees from both East and West German universities. His last play *Der neue Prozeß* (*The New Trial*), dedicated to Franz Kafka, premiered in Stockholm, under the direction of Weiss and his wife. On May 10, 1982, Weiss died in Stockholm.

In the year of his death, Weiss was honored with four literary awards: the Bremen Literature Prize, the Georg Büchner Prize, the De Nios Prize, and the Swedish Theater Critics' Prize. In 1982 and 1983, exhibitions of his paintings were shown in Switzerland, Germany, and Sweden. In 1998, Fredric Jameson and his colleagues organized a Peter Weiss Conference in which Gunilla Palmstierna-Weiss participated. During the conference, most of Weiss's experimental films were shown, his collage works were exhibited, and his last play, *Der neue Prozeß,* premiered in English.

Weiss's main work, *Die Ästhetik des Widerstands,* has a complicated reception history. Like the dramatist and novelist Hans Henny Jahnn, a major author of European modernism whose emphasis on sexuality and the body had a major impact on his work, Weiss found himself bewildered by a Cold War dilemma of reception mechanisms in both East and West Germany. East Germany often exercised censorship on theater performances of Weiss's plays and hesitated to publish his books, while West German newspaper critics often attacked his texts because of the author's political convictions.[8]

Weiss's literary works, which have been translated into many languages, in France, for example, by the philosopher Jean Baudrillard, are increasingly becoming more accessible to a worldwide readership. Some of his plays continue to enjoy international success. Except for *Die Ästhetik des Widerstands,* all of his major works have been translated into English. Weiss inspires readers and theater audiences to expose themselves to political and psychological questions without seeking refuge in conventional ways of fabricating easy answers. For Weiss, a committed fight against regimes of torture and oppression is never dissociated from intellectual and aesthetic curiosity that dares to think and feel without any prescriptions. Weiss's works bring politics and creative projects into a mutually challenging dialogue.

Notes

[1] Raimund Hoffmann, *Peter Weiss: Malerei. Zeichnungen. Collagen* (Berlin: Henschel, 1984).

[2] On Hesse's influence on Weiss, see Matthias Richter, "'Bis zum heutigen Tag habe ich Ihre Bücher bei mir getragen': Über die Beziehung zwischen Peter Weiss und Hermann Hesse," in *Peter Weiss,* edited by Rainer Gerlach (Frankfurt a.M.: Suhrkamp, 1984), 32–56.

[3] Hesse's letter to Weiss from January 21, 1937, is published in Raimund Hoffmann, *Peter Weiss: Malerei. Zeichnungen. Collagen* (Berlin: Henschel, 1984), 163: "[. . .] das möglichst genaue, präzise, nüchterne Nachzeichnen durch Worte [. . .] bis jedes Wort feststeht und Sie für jedes Wort einstehen können. [. . .] ein verantwortliches Dichtertum [. . .] mit grosser Strenge im Wort, und grosser Vorsicht im Anlehnen an Vorbilder. [. . .] ein richtiges Zeichnen und Bauen mit den Worten probieren, so bewusst und nüchtern wie möglich, man lernt da nie aus, die Aufgabe ist mit jedem Satz wieder neu."

[4] See Arnd Beise, *Peter Weiss* (Stuttgart: Reclam, 2002), 18.

[5] For the impact of Swedish intellectual life on Weiss see the important monograph by Anne Bourgignon, *Der Schriftsteller Peter Weiss und Schweden* (St. Ingbert: Röhrig, 1997).

[6] See Hauke Lange-Fuchs, *Peter Weiss und der Film: Eine Dokumentation zur Retrospektive der 28. Nordischen Filmtage Lübeck vom 30. Oktober bis 2. November 1986* (Lübeck: Nordische Filmtage Lübeck, Senat der Hansestadt Lübeck, Amt für Kultur, 1986). See also Andreas Schönefeld, "Die filmische Produktion des multimedialen Künstlers Peter Weiss im Zusammenhang seiner künstlerisch-politischen Entwicklung in den späten 40er und 50er Jahren," in *Peter Weiss: Werk und Wirkung,* edited by Rudolf Wolff (Bonn: Bouvier, 1987), 114–28.

[7] Weiss's ambivalent relationship to being a Jewish writer is carefully examined in three recent articles. See Irene Heidelberger-Leonard, "Jüdisches Bewußtsein im Werk von Peter Weiss," in *Literatur, Ästhetik, Geschichte: Neue Zugänge zu Peter Weiss,* edited by Michael Hofmann (St. Ingbert [Germany]: Röhrig, 1992), 49–64; Ingo Breuer, "Der Jude Marat: Identifikationsprobleme bei Peter Weiss," in *Peter Weiss: Neue Fragen an alte Texte,* edited by Irene Heidelberger-Leonard (Opladen: Westdeutscher Verlag, 1994), 64–76; Julia Hell, "From Laokoon to Ge: Resistance to Jewish Authorship in Peter Weiss's Ästhetik des Widerstands," in *Rethinking Peter Weiss,* edited by Jost Hermand and Marc Silberman (New York etc.: Lang, 2000), 23–44.

[8] *Notizbücher 1971–1980. Band 2* (Frankfurt a.M.: Suhrkamp, 1981), 758–59: "Der komplizierte, paradoxe Prozeß, in den ich mit meiner Arbeit, seit Jahren in wachsendem Grad, verwickelt bin: in der BRD, wo ich eine starke gesellschaftskritische

Position einnehme, können meine Bücher erscheinen [. . .] manche Läden führen meine Titel nicht [. . .] und auch die meisten Theaterleiter verschließen sich vor meinen Stücken [. . .] In der DDR, wo ich bei aller Kritik immer noch nach einem Ausgleich suche [. . .] kann die 'Ästhetik' noch nicht erscheinen. [. . .] In der DDR, wo es ein großes Leserpotential für dieses Buch gäbe [. . .] wird diese meine Hauptarbeit dem Publikum vorenthalten [. . .]" Compare Hans Henny Jahnn's letter to the poet Peter Huchel from September 4, 1952, in: Hans Henny Jahnn, *Werke in Einzelbänden. Hamburger Ausgabe. Briefe. Zweiter Teil,* edited by Ulrich Bitz and Uwe Schweikert (Hamburg: Hoffmann und Campe, 1994), 736: "Es ist doch sehr traurig, daß man mich einen Dichter nennt, im Westen nicht kauft und im Osten nicht zulässt. Dieses doppelte Gewicht der Verneinung [. . .]"

1: Subversive Slapstick: The Early Plays
Der Turm, Die Versicherung, Nacht mit Gästen, and *Mockinpott*

D ER TURM, PETER WEISS'S first drama, was written in 1948 and premiered in a Swedish version on a small stage in Stockholm two years later.[1] In the German-speaking countries, it first appeared as a radio play in 1962, before its first production, directed by Irimbert Ganser, took place in Vienna in 1967. Detlef Heusinger's opera *Der Turm* (1988), whose libretto is based upon Weiss's play, premiered in Bremen in 1989.[2]

The topos of the tower as a scenic construction of painful passivity has a long literary history, including Calderón de la Barca's "comedia seria" *La vida es sueño* (1630) and Hugo von Hofmannsthal's drama *Der Turm* (1923–1928). Weiss's *Turm* displays strong thematic and stylistic affinities to German romanticism as well as to August Strindberg's dramas and Hermann Hesse's works.[3] The play implies but never fully reveals a preceding story of a young man's imprisonment and desperate outbreak.

Pablo, the protagonist of Weiss's *Der Turm,* lived and worked in the tower of a circus company in his childhood, where he was kept against his will and forced to perform balancing acts. He returns to the tower to overcome his fear of his past by reenacting it rather than by running away from it (13).[4] In his prologue to the radio play version, Weiss highlights the necessity for Pablo to work through his traumatic past in a detached manner to overcome it.[5] Pablo does not seek the rapture of a sudden dismissive break with his past. Instead, he employs the strategy of consciously approaching psychological constraints that had been imposed on him by a circus director, his wife, and a magician. Realizing the frailty of these characters that used to terrorize him, Pablo hopes to be capable of departing calmly this time.

Operating under the pseudonym "Niente" (Nothing), Pablo tries to reinvent his youth. He applies for a position at the tower circus. Instead of building on his former expertise in the performance of balancing acts on a ball, he presents himself as an "Entfesselungskünstler," an escape artist, an apt choice that reflects a shift in his perspective on the tower inhabitants. Rather than balancing his desires and allowing his employers to domesticate him, Pablo/Niente embarks on the project of self-liberation. He has experienced that there is a world outside of the tower, and his temporary return serves him to find out whether he is capable of leaving through any tower's gate by his own will.

Reminiscent of the life-affirming masked gentleman who prevents a teenager from committing suicide in Frank Wedekind's controversial drama *Frühlings Erwachen* (1891, Spring's Awakening), which examines the impact of an oppressive educational ideology on young adolescents, an anonymous yet vigorous and positive voice addresses Pablo directly and repeatedly in moments of acute danger. The voice reassures Pablo of the unalterable fact of his inner freedom and encourages him to disentangle himself from the rope (30–32).[6]

Pablo's antagonist is an enigmatic, cruel, and cunning magician who tried to lure the young boy into guilt-driven suicide during his first stay in the tower. The magician is the only tower resident who does not seem to work at all. He is also the only character who recognizes Pablo despite his pseudonym Niente. The magician's main occupation consists in whispering hypnotic, seductive, suicidal insinuations into Pablo's/Niente's ear, reminding him of the violent death of a young woman for whom he had romantic longings.[7] The magician also attempts to convince the protagonist that another escape is impossible or that, as he is gloating, the key is outside (26).[8]

But there are cracks and identity crises within the monolithic structure and the captivating organs of the tower prison. Usually echoing and subservient to the magician, a dwarf experiences a momentary disorientation crisis during which he desperately approaches Pablo and asks him about his own identity and about the meaning of his surroundings in a hoarse and whispering voice (20).[9] Freedom, in this play, is also the product of a painful generational conflict, even though those who are in control of the circus company are not members of Pablo's/Niente's physical family. Formerly dominating figures of authority who used to paralyze Pablo with fear and isolation are subjected to aging and appear to be rather unthreatening, fragile, and ridiculous to their returning victim.

A stylistic detail contains the protagonist's struggle in a concentrated and disturbing form. Although the German language is full of reflexive verbs, "ausbrechen" (to break out, to escape) is not one of them. Weiss, however, employs the verb in an unusual, reflexive manner, when Pablo/Niente says: "Ich bin hier, um mich auszubrechen," and "Einer bricht sich immer aus" (13; 32).[10] The reflexive turn of self-liberation thus receives an aggressively physical connotation of breaking and hammering oneself, or rather one's self, out of the debris of oneself, or vice versa. This idiosyncratic usage does have famous parallels and predecessors in twentieth-century German and Austrian literature. In the first part of Robert Musil's (1880–1942) novel *Der Mann ohne Eigenschaften* (1930, The Man without Qualities), Clarisse insists: "Man muß sich aus sich herausarbeiten!" In one of his *Prosaische Fragmente* (Prosaic Fragments) from 1948, the poet Gottfried Benn (1886–1956) suggests a corresponding repeated praxis of the craftsmanship of self-liberation, of breaking out of personal contexts and dividing oneself into blocks: "brechen Sie sich immer wieder heraus aus Ihren eigenen Zusammenhängen."[11]

The self-invented escape artist Pablo/Niente summarizes his unbridled desire for autonomy and independent insight in a concise aphorism:

> Man muß schon frei sein, bevor man anfängt. Das Ausbrechen ist dann nur eine Beweisführung. (10)

According to the protagonist, self-liberation is a mere a posteriori side effect that only becomes noticeable after an act of radical self-realization has taken place. But is Pablo alive at the end of the play, does he hang himself, or does he drown like the permanent tower circus residents? The enigmatic voice of freedom has the last word in the play and slowly announces that the rope is hanging down from him like an umbilical cord (33).[12] Is this laconic remark part of an unfinished autopsy report, or does it indicate a successful cut, Pablo's separation from his past passivity? It remains an open question whether the comforting yet neutral voice announces that Pablo has mastered the art of escape by consciously exposing himself to the terror of his childhood again.[13] Providing a quick and decisive answer to this question would require constructing yet another circus tower of forceful and impatient interpretation.

Emphasizing the psychological vein in Weiss's early work, the writer Wolfgang Koeppen highlights the ambiguity of the term "Widerstand" when he observes that Weiss's narrators took an active part in the struggle for resistance but that the object of their resistance was the trauma of being born and its aftermath.[14] *Der Turm* can, among other possible conclusions, be read as staging a metaphor for writing as a conscious return to suppressed and forgotten injuries. Integrating the psychological and the political and trying not to reduce the one to the other remains an open-ended project that Weiss pursued throughout his literary career. Should Pablo's/Niente's liberation, successful or not, be read as psychological or political, or both? Forceful interpretive decisions, rather than elucidating this play, might even blur the reader's view. As Kleinschmidt emphasizes, the text neither unequivocally embraces social critique nor individual introspection. One reading should not exclude its alleged opposite.[15] Like each of Weiss's works, *Der Turm* can be understood as an experiment with, and as an attempt to endure, conflicts of and between rational and unconscious realms. The drama simultaneously calls for and examines correlations between social protest and individual maturation.

Written in 1952, the drama *Die Versicherung* (The Insurance) was rejected by theaters in Sweden and Germany for many years. The student theater at the University of Göteborg put the play on stage in 1966.[16] The first German performance was directed by Hansgünther Heyme in Cologne in 1969. Hans Werner Henze, arguably the most prestigious contemporary German composer, had planned to compose an opera based on *Die Versicherung* and had already begun to write a libretto for the 1972 Olympic Games in Munich when the plan was dismissed by the Olympic Games Committee.[17] In 1999, Jan Müller-Wieland's opera *Die Versicherung. Traum in zwei Phasen* premiered in Darmstadt. In his reflections on the play from 1968, Weiss highlights his openness for modifying the setting of *Die Versicherung* as well as the names of the characters and suggests the possibility of transporting the play into an American context.[18]

Initially, Weiss had envisioned the integration of filmic components. In a commentary to the play, Weiss writes in 1968:

> Ich wollte einen vielschichtigen Eindruck hervorrufen: Sprecher, und dazu überlebensgroße gefilmte Gesichter; kleine Handlungszellen, und dazu eingeblendete Bilder aus der Großstadt; das Eindringen der Außenwelt in den Bühnenraum; von Schauspielern begonnene Aktionen, die sich im Film erweitert fortsetzen; Leuchtreklamen, dokumentarische Bilder von Straßenunruhen und Naturkatastrophen. (260)

Remnants of the original plan of an avant-garde synthesis of film and drama can still be found in the seventh scene, in which segments of advertising movies promote everything from plates to custard powder, and in the twelfth scene, where a newsreel juxtaposes, among other current events, a dog competition and a diplomatic reception (54; 64).[19]

The storyline of this one-act play in nineteen scenes unfolds as a grotesque social satire on human helplessness, greed, cruelty, and the obsession to be overprotected. The play begins with a celebration in the household of a successful model citizen who is responsible for maintaining law and order in his town. Alfons, chief of police, is hosting a party during which he festively and with repetitive phrases announces that he, as a responsible "Vater, Gatte, Hausbesitzer und Bürger," is going to sign insurance contracts in the face of growing threats of catastrophes and revolutions (40).[20] Throughout the play, Alfons suffers from intervals of convulsive crying and displays regressive behavior. Two insurance company representatives are among the guests. It is no coincidence that Kafka worked for an insurance company and that Weiss directed a movie for an insurance company.

All party guests wear exaggerated make-up, and their gestures and conversations are likewise forced and artificial. The party is staged as a celebration of helpless hypocrisy. When Alfons declares the meat buffet open and cuts out pieces with his pocketknife, the guests do not restrain themselves any longer and politely fight over the best parts of the food. Alfons's dog, played by an actor, has full access to the buffet. He is attacking one guest, Frau Burian, who lies unnoticed under the dinner table, bleeding and choking. Alfons even stamps on her hand when she reaches out for help, unable to speak.

Offering medical assistance to Frau Burian in his private clinic, Dr. Kübel, whose name denotes a liquid-manure container, invites everybody else to come along with them. However, the free examination offer turns into an imprisonment. Kübel subjects the party guests to an extended electroshock therapy and locks them up in his clinic. Involuntary patients who protest too loudly, for example a casino owner, are thrown into a dungeon where they have to live with goats. In brief, wordless interludes of dreamlike scenes, first Alfons, and then Dr. Kübel, all of a sudden alone, display their helplessness, disorientation, and fear amidst a night of thunder, lightning, and heavy wind (48; 51).

But it is impossible to distinguish victims from aggressors clearly in this play. Most characters indulge in filling both complementary functions. Hulda, for example, is raped by Kübel's assistant Grudek. However, right after the act of violence, she appears to stay with him voluntarily, and at the end of the play, she joyfully humiliates Alfons, who, in another scene of regressive oral dependence, whiningly demands Hulda's breast and acts like an unweaned infant. Dr. Kübel, while in control of his involuntary patients, suffers from a miserable domestic routine and is disgusted not only by his wife's burned pudding but by his marriage. Leo, an unemployed and egocentric young man with a strong sexual interest in married women, seizes all opportunities for material gain without hesitations. It is one of the paradoxical features of this play that the opportunistic Leo, who cynically humiliates women and who is responsible for the grotesque death of a husband, later acts as a revolutionary fighter for human rights.

Both Kübel and Alfons eventually succumb to their insecurities and repeatedly retreat to the habit of whining. Several characters play a mean trick on Alfons by stripping him of his identity. He is arrested by police officers who do not believe him when he declares that he is the chief of police. Only one girl, a shy worker in a textile shop, feels compassion and displays an impulse to help Alfons during his arrest. However, a colleague holds her back, and the scene, which is superimposed on Alfon's violent disappearance, shows Hulda and Grudek taking an idle, pseudo-romantic walk (87).

Die Versicherung is a burlesque with strong affinities to Kafka and Brecht. While neither reducible to a clearly definable message nor to a playful arrangement of intertextual correlations, the play can be read as a scenic exaggeration of complacent passivity. The characters' need for being fully covered by insurances runs parallel to a desire to be comforted by constant reassurance.[21] In an age marked by a renewed fear of terrorism, *Die Versicherung* takes on an unexpectedly timely new dimension.

Nacht mit Gästen (Night with Guests) was written in 1963 and premiered the same year in Berlin's Schiller Theater under the direction of Deryk Mendel.[22] During the 1960s and 1970s, the play was performed in at least twenty different European cities. Reinhard Febel's opera version of the play premiered in Cologne in 1990.

This burlesque play, announced by Weiss as a first attempt toward revitalizing the theatrical form of the show booth, experiments with stylistic elements borrowed from Japanese theater traditions and from puppet plays.[23] As Weiss outlines in a comment on the play, the Punch play interested him as a way to display the aggressive and the horrible behind the mask of humor, while the Kabuki theater inspired him to experiment with the artificiality of movements and with estranging uses of the voice.[24] According to the stage directions, the play is to be continuously accompanied by instruments reminiscent of a fair, drawing acoustic parallels to the fair and circus motif of Weiss's paintings.[25]

The storyline of this brief play in simple rhymes, which is not divided into acts or scenes, revolves around violence and cunning methods of survival. A family is visited by a stranger who threatens to stab all of them to death. Weiss is not interested in portraying the family as mere victims. Instead, the play highlights their submissive opportunism. Not only the parents, but also the children, who act like adults, hypocritically try to please the robber. The children even pretend to want him as their new father (100). The family promises the robber access to a treasure box that they allegedly possess and have hidden in a lake. Each family member, except for the father, tries to survive at the cost of the others. Weiss explicitly notes that he wants to stage the fakeness and the spiteful, fearful, and sly characteristics of a normal family.[26] This haunting "Moritat" (street ballad) illustrates the complicity of violence and its passive acceptance. The victims of this play, including the surviving children, are neither more likeable nor less wicked than the intruder who kills the father.

Wie dem Herrn Mockinpott das Leiden ausgetrieben wird. Spiel in 11 Bildern (How Mister Mockinpott Was Cured of His Sufferings: Play in 11 Scenes) was drafted in 1963 and completed in 1968.[27] The play premiered in Hanover in 1968 under the direction of Horst Zankl. In 1977, the play was performed in Paris. *Mockinpott* can be read as a satirical rhyme version of the Hiob story in its mocking of passivity and obedience. Mockinpott complains about his seemingly undeserved misfortunes without ever questioning the societal order that he still takes for granted.

In the opening scene, the protagonist finds himself in a prison cell. Since he is convinced that he has always been a good citizen, he is desperate about the apparent injustice. The guard accepts a bribe and gives Mockinpott access to legal help. A greedy lawyer who always mispronounces his client's name, giving room to humorous wordplays such as "Koppimpott," helps Mockinpott to an expensive release. Mockinpott even has to pay for his stay in prison, not only for his release. At the end of the scene, two angels comment on Mockinpott. They maintain that he needs to go through a series of humiliating experiences and that he should not be spared any misfortune in order to understand his suffering (119).[28]

After leaving prison, Mockinpott encounters a potential friend, Wurst, who repeatedly mishears Mockinpott's words and is more interested in eating and drinking than in continued sympathetic conversation. Every other scene is ironically titled "Im Freien," which can be translated as "outside" or "in the open, in the realm of freedom," and depicts an interlusive conversation between Mockinpott and Wurst. In the third scene or "Bild," Mockinpott is forced to confront the next surprising disillusionment. Returning home, he is not welcomed by a loving wife but kicked out of the house. His wife is not only blaming him for wasting money and betraying her, she has in the meantime invited a new lover into their home. The two angels reiterate their litany of life-threatening suffering (128).[29]

Mockinpott visits his employer to report that he is back. The employer pretends not to recognize him, calls him a beggar, and kicks him out. Having lost both his home and his job, he meets Wurst again, who suggests that he visit a doctor. The doctor and Wurst examine Mockinpott's brain and stomach and declare that they have fixed those damages that can be repaired by surgery.

During their next conversational interlude in the open, Wurst urges Mockinpott to find the government administration. When Mockinpott reports to government officials, most of whom are engaged in conversations about exquisite food and clothes, that he has been subjected to unjustified police violence, one official responds by thanking Mockinpott for illustrating the laudable fact that the police follow their orders to ruthlessly suffocate any signs of rebellion (143).[30] He is benevolently dismissed with a mechanical staccato of political phrases on steadfastness, unity, and responsibility (145). Mockinpott's last conversation with Wurst is accompanied by a government proclamation via loudspeakers. Repetitive fragments highlight the meaninglessness of political rhetoric.

Finally, Mockinpott and Wurst pay a visit to God, whose depiction as a not-so-self-assured cigar-smoking businessman shares, as Karnick has noted, many affinities with Blaise Cendrars's text *La fin du monde filmée par l'Ange N.-D.* (1919, The End of the World, Filmed by the Angel N.-D.).[31] Mockinpott accuses (149).[32] Eventually, God loses all of Mockinpott's respect. The protagonist gives up his former role of an obedient inquirer. Angrily, he shouts that he has had enough of this game of betrayal (152).[33] God, now a sad and broken man, leaves the stage. Mockinpott, who finally also manages to put his shoes on correctly, has been liberated by his own anger. The last scene takes its repeated title "Im Freien" to its truth. The angels do not mock Mockinpott anymore. They call him "good" without any trace of irony, and they claim that he is now capable of gaining orientation. With his feet firmly on the ground and each shoe on the foot on which it belongs, Mockinpott is going his way, like a dancer or skater in joyful circles, while Wurst is asleep, snoring peacefully (152–53). Celebrating the importance of tying one's own shoes while indulging in onomatopoetic wordplays, Weiss's slapstick farce is not without a didactic impetus. It teaches the necessity of productive and liberating anger.[34]

Notes

[1] All following excerpts and quotations from this play refer to the following edition: *Der Turm* in Peter Weiss, *Werke in sechs Bänden. Vierter Band,* edited by Suhrkamp Verlag in cooperation with Gunilla Palmstierna-Weiss (Frankfurt a.M.: Suhrkamp, 1991), 7–33.

[2] See Detlef Heusinger, *Material zum Werk von 1978 bis 1998* (Bad Schwalbach: Edition Gravis, 1998), 32–34.

[3] Antonio Pasinato, *Invito alla lettura di Peter Weiss* (Milano: Mursia, 1980), 39: "[. . .] un lavoro in cui si intessono, oltre al chiaro riferimento a Hermann Hesse e, per la forma drammatica, a Strindberg, rinvii alla poetica del romanticismo e alla teorizzazione estetica dell'idealismo [. . .]" A psychologizing reading of the play is certainly justified, and Cohen's claim that *Der Turm* is a "dramatisierte Psychoanalyse" can lead to productive insights, see Robert Cohen, *Peter Weiss in seiner Zeit. Leben und Werk* (Stuttgart, Weimar: Metzler, 1992), 69. Falkensteins's formulas of identification, however, give way to authorial fallacies that preclude careful examinations, see Henning Falkenstein, *Peter Weiss* (Berlin: Morgenbuch, 1996), 60: "Weiss selbst erscheint verwandelt als Pablo, Margit als Nelly, die Eltern als Direktor und Verwalterin."

[4] "Langsam hinauszugehen. Nicht blind hinauszustürzen. [. . .] Ruhig aus dem Tor zu gehen —"

[5] *Werke* 4, 259: "Nur wenn er es wagt, noch einmal tief in den Turm einzudringen und sich mit seiner Vergangenheit auseinanderzusetzen, kann er sich vielleicht befreien."

[6] "*ganz frei und offen* [. . .] Pablo, du bist frei! Du mußt heraus aus dem Seil! [. . .] Du mußt raus! Du bist frei! [. . .] Du bist frei, Pablo!"

[7] See the stage directions, 12; 22: "*Mit lockender, hypnotisierender Stimme* [. . .] *nah — flüsternd* [. . .]"

[8] "*schadenfroh* Der Schlüssel ist draußen!"

[9] "Wo bin ich — wo bin ich? [. . .] Was geschieht hier — was geschieht denn hier?"

[10] Compare Weiss's narrative *Der Vogelfreie/Der Fremde* (1948), in *Werke* 1, 188: "Was würde geschehen, wenn man sich aus dieser Existenz herausbräche [. . .]"

[11] Robert Musil, *Der Mann ohne Eigenschaften. Roman,* edited by Adolf Frisé (Reinbek: Rowohlt, 1988), 658. Gottfried Benn, *Sämtliche Werke. Band V,* edited by Gerhard Schuster (Stuttgart: Klett-Cotta, 1991), 244.

[12] "[. . .] *ganz langsam, sachlich, kühl* Der Strick hängt von ihm herab wie ein Nabelstrang —"

[13] On the ambiguity of the drama's final scene see Erich Kleinschmidt, "*Der Turm,*" in *Peter Weiss' Dramen: Neue Interpretationen,* edited by Martin Rector and Christoph Weiss (Opladen and Wiesbaden: Westdeutscher Verlag, 1999), 9–24. Here: 20: "Ob Pablo die Befreiung gelingt, was in der Logik einer zu Ende gebrachten Initiation läge, oder ob er sich doch möglicherweise stranguliert, läßt sich nur schwer entscheiden."

[14] "Peter Weiss' erzählendes Ich engagierte sich im Widerstand. Er versuchte zu widerstehen dem Geborenwerden und seinen Folgen," in Wolfgang Koeppen, "Der Moralist glaubt an den Teufel," in *Gesammelte Werke in sechs Bänden. 6: Essays und Rezensionen,* edited by Marcel Reich-Ranicki (Frankfurt a.m.: Suhrkamp, 1986), 410–13. Here: 410. First published in: *Frankfurter Allgemeine Zeitung,* November 5, 1976. Koeppen alludes to Friedrich Nietzsche's, Martin Heidegger's, and E. M. Cioran's variations on the Greek, Hindu, and Buddhist topoi of birth as a source of discontent and despair.

[15] "Ob sie ganz allgemein gesellschaftskritisch zu verstehen ist oder ob sie als chiffrierter Ausdruck eines sehr persönlichen, psychischen Befreiungsprozesses ihres Autors funktionalisiert werden sollte [. . .] Der Text selbst liefert dazu keine gesicherten Anhalte." Erich Kleinschmidt, *"Der Turm,"* in *Peter Weiss' Dramen: Neue Interpretationen,* edited by Martin Rector and Christoph Weiss (Opladen and Wiesbaden: Westdeutscher Verlag, 1999), 9–24. Here: 10.

[16] All following excerpts and quotations from this play refer to the following edition: *Die Versicherung. Ein Drama,* in Peter Weiss, *Werke in sechs Bänden. Vierter Band,* edited by Suhrkamp Verlag in cooperation with Gunilla Palmstierna-Weiss (Frankfurt a.M.: Suhrkamp, 1991), 35–87.

[17] See *Spiegel* 19/1990, 251.

[18] *Werke* 4, 260: "Die Handlung kann z.B. in die Vereinigten Staaten verlegt werden, wobei auch die Namen amerikanisiert werden können."

[19] "[. . .] ein paar kurze Reklamefilme [. . .] Anpreisungen von Tellern und Gläsern, von Küchenherden, vom Kleidungsstücken und Puddingpulvern. [. . .] Projektion einer aktuellen Wochenschau. Kurze Szenen von einem Hundewettbewerb mit Preiskrönung, einem diplomatischen Empfang, von der Einweihung eines neuen Wohnviertels, einer Modeschau usw. Keine kriegerischen Ereignisse."

[20] "[. . .] sich Katastrophen und Revolutionen verbergen, will ich den Gedanken in die Tat umsetzen, meiner Verantwortung als Vater, Gatte, Hausbesitzer und Bürger bewußt [. . .]"

[21] Hofmann provides a very concise overview of the play. At times, however, his interpretive conclusions run the risk of becoming too stagnant and formulaic. By operating with terms such as "the fundamental intention," Hofmann prestructures and prepackages hermeneutic ingredients and prophylactically reduces internal tensions in the text. See Michael Hofmann, *"Die Versicherung,"* in *Peter Weiss' Dramen: Neue Interpretationen,* edited by Martin Rector and Christoph Weiss (Opladen and Wiesbaden: Westdeutscher Verlag, 1999), 25–42. Here: 27: "Die grundlegende Intention der *Versicherung* liegt in der Entlarvung bürgerlicher Normalität, hinter deren Fassade sich latente Strukturen von Gewalt und Unterdrückung verbergen." While this political impetus certainly permeates the play, only the question of the text's and its theatrical realization's imaginative and cognitive surplus would mark the first step toward a thorough and self-aware textual analysis.

[22] All following excerpts and quotations from this play refer to the following edition: *Nacht mit Gästen. Eine Moritat,* in Peter Weiss, *Werke in sechs Bänden. Vierter Band,* edited by Suhrkamp Verlag in cooperation with Gunilla Palmstierna-Weiss (Frankfurt a.M.: Suhrkamp, 1991), 89–111.

[23] *Werke* 4, 262: "[. . .] einer Theaterform, die ich wiederbeleben möchte: der Schaubude. 'Nacht mit Gästen' ist der erste Versuch in dieser Richtung."

[24] *Werke* 4, 262: "Als Inspirationsquelle für eine Inszenierung können das Kabuki-Theater sowie die volkstümlichen Kasper-Spiele dienen. Vom Kasper-Spiel wäre hier das Grobschlächtige, Possenhafte zu entnehmen, die starken Effekte, das laut Herausgerufene, oft falsch Betonte, das Aggressive und Grauenhafte unter der scheinbaren Lustigkeit. Vom Kabuki-Theater die akrobatische Beherrschtheit der Bewegungen, das Unnaturalistische, die verfremdete Stimmenbehandlung [. . .]"

[25] *Werke* 4, 263: "Sehr wichtig ist die Musikbegleitung. [. . .] Am besten wäre eine durchgehende Komposition mit jahrmarkthaften Instrumenten, wie Drehorgel, Schalmei, Hirtenflöte, Trommel."

[26] *Werke* 4, 262–63: "[. . .] vielmehr soll das Böse, Gehässige, Geängstigte und Verschlagene herauskommen [. . .] Auch soll das Falsche, Einschmeichelnde hervorgehoben werden [. . .]"

[27] All following excerpts and quotations from this play refer to the following edition: *Wie dem Herrn Mockinpott das Leiden ausgetrieben wird. Spiel in 11 Bildern,* in Peter Weiss, *Werke in sechs Bänden. Vierter Band,* edited by Suhrkamp Verlag in cooperation with Gunilla Palmstierna-Weiss (Frankfurt a.M.: Suhrkamp, 1991), 113–53.

[28] "Miserere Miserere / daß es sich ihm noch viel mehr erschwere / Sehet nur sehet unsern guten Mann / der sein Leiden nicht verstehn kann / Miserere Miserere / daß er auch kein einziges Unglück entbehre."

[29] "Miserere Miserere / daß sich ihm alles gründlich verheere / Sehet nur sehet unsern guten Mann / der sein Leiden nicht verstehen kann / Miserere Miserere / daß ihn sein Unglück gänzlich verzehre."

[30] "Was sich an Aufruhr zeigt vor unsern Blicken / haben die Gendarmen rücksichtslos zu ersticken / es freut uns besonders von Ihnen zu erfahren / wie dieselben das Land vor Gefahren bewahren."

[31] See Manfred Karnick, "Peter Weiss' dramatische Collagen: Vom Traumspiel zur Agitation," in *Peter Weiss,* edited by Rainer Gerlach (Frankfurt a.M.: Suhrkamp, 1984), 208–48. Here: 241.

[32] "Lieber und ehrwürdiger Herr Gott / [. . .] / bitte ergebenst weil es mich interessiert / was wird an mir eigentlich ausprobiert."

[33] "[. . .] ich krieg eine Wut / [. . .] von diesem Betrug / hab ich jetzt ein für alle Male genug."

[34] For the most recent research contribution to *Mockinpott,* see Alexander Honold, "*Wie dem Herrn Mockinpott das Leiden ausgetrieben wird,*" in *Peter Weiss' Dramen: Neue Interpretationen,* edited by Martin Rector and Christoph Weiss (Opladen/Wiesbaden: Westdeutscher Verlag, 1999), 89–107.

2: The Choreography of Documents: *Die Ermittlung, Gesang vom Lusitanischen Popanz,* and *Viet Nam Diskurs*

IN HIS NOTEBOOKS FROM THE 1970s, Peter Weiss invents a poignant auctorial job description that disregards conventional generic distinctions between documentary and poetic works: "Dante, der Reporter."[1] Weiss's productive juxtaposition of Dante's poetic techniques and historical documents concerning crimes against humanity in the twentieth century has been thoroughly examined by Christoph Weiss, who makes frequent use of unpublished fragments in which Weiss approaches what he envisions to become his "DC (Divina Commedia) Projekt."[2] Weiss is by far not the only writer who employs Dante's construction of hell in order to address organized killings in the twentieth century. In "Herrn Dante Alighieri," a short prose text that was written in 1948–49 but not published until 1989, Arno Schmidt (1914–1979), one of the most innovative German postwar writers, draws parallels between Dante's *Inferno* and the Shoah from a polemical perspective. In a fictional letter to Dante, a public official from the Defense Ministry's "Abteilung: Einrichtung von Lagern" (Department for the Construction of Camps) thanks the "Meister" and praises the usefulness of his "Inferno. Handbuch für KZ-Gestaltung" (Inferno: Handbook for Concentration Camp Design).[3] Arno Schmidt's bitter satire implies a sharp rejection of any aesthetic replication of organized oppression and torture. Dante's *Inferno* has also been used as a structural model and imaginary background for politically engaged literature in the United States. Arguably the most influential example is the African-American writer and Civil Rights activist Amiri Baraka's prose volume *The System of Dante's Hell* (1963).[4]

In his essay *Das Material und die Modelle: Notizen zum dokumentarischen Theater* (1968), Peter Weiss vehemently argues against any mystification of historical events. But how can the Shoah be documented on stage or in any form of cultural production without reducing it to a commodity that is designed for convenient consumption? Bertolt Brecht, in his *Gespräche mit jungen Intellektuellen* (1948–49), writes that he considers the Shoah to be incompatible with any description in literary form.[5]

Weiss, however, was looking for aesthetic means to address the mass killings. The reluctance to persecute Nazi criminals remains one of the most outrageous scandals of postwar German and Austrian history. The West German justice system did not investigate the Shoah until 1958. Finally, the "Strafsache gegen Mulka und andere," the first trial against Auschwitz officials, was conducted in Frankfurt from December 1963 until August 1965. Having attended the trial in 1964, Weiss wrote *Die Ermittlung. Oratorium in 11 Gesängen* (The Investigation: Oratorio in 11 Cantos) between 1964 and 1965.[6] The play simultaneously premiered in East and West Berlin and in several other German cities in October 1965. While in East Berlin, politicians and artists recited the text, and Erwin Piscator directed the play in West Berlin, with music composed by Luigi Nono. In the same year, the drama was also performed in more than thirty European cities, including Peter Brook's London production, and it was often played by radio and public television channels in both East and West Germany. Peter Schulze-Rohr directed a film version of the play in 1965. The play soon was performed worldwide, for example on Broadway in 1966, in Moscow, Buenos Aires, and Montevideo in 1967, and in Tel Aviv in 1968. As productions in the United States and Italy in 2001 and spontaneous readings in Germany in 2002 have shown, the play is still widely performed throughout the world, partly in order to counter new occurrences of racist violence. For example, actors visited schools in Cottbus in 2000 and performed passages from Weiss's play in order to act against the emerging juvenile ethnic hatred in that city.[7]

As Weiss's handwritten margins on the galley proofs show, he was hesitant about the title and thought of alternatives such as "Das Lager" (The Camp), "Die Beweisaufnahme" (Taking Evidence), "Das Tribunal" (The Tribunal), and "Die Besichtigung" (The Inspection).[8] However, the title choice *Die Ermittlung* provides access to a wider spectrum of connotations, from the concrete trial to a more comprehensive philosophical examination of the fragility and possibility of truth ("Wahrheit ermitteln, ausmitteln"). Weiss is interested in creating tensions between aesthetic form and thematic concern. As the subtitle emphasizes, the drama is, in spite of its content, an "Oratorium in 11 Gesängen." Each canto consists of three parts, paralleling the numeric canto structure of Dante's *Commedia*. Christoph Weiss's recent monograph about *Die Ermittlung*, a new point of departure for any future research on the play, not only comprehensively documents its reception history, but also reconstructs its place within Weiss's Dante project, which was never fully realized.[9]

The list of the tripartite scenes or "Gesänge" alone already accentuates and problematizes the juxtaposition of a traditional art form and the detailed documentation of violence. The cantos include: "Gesang von der Rampe" (Canto of the Loading Ramp), "Gesang von der Schaukel" (Canto of the Swing, a Torture Instrument), "Gesang vom Phenol" (Phenol Canto), and "Gesang vom Zyklon B" (Cyclone B Canto).[10]

In his preface to the play, Weiss rejects any aspiration to reconstruct the Auschwitz trial, an endeavor that in his view would be as impossible as representing the camp on stage.[11] Based on court transcripts from the Frankfurt Auschwitz trial from 1964, the play includes eighteen defendants, who represent authentic persons and keep their real names, and nine nameless witnesses, who represent alternately the many anonymous witnesses (8–9).[12]

The drama reduces the use of adjectives to a minimum and produces emotional responses by carefully arranging detailed descriptions of facts.[13] As Walter Jens wrote in 1965, *Die Ermittlung*, far from merely rendering raw documents, has to be recognized as a minutely stylized aesthetic product, which operates with a wide register of rhetorical techniques.[14] A text collage in rhythmical prose, the play condenses the witnesses' detailed descriptions and the defendants' apologetic and cynical outlines of medical experiments, torture, and murder. Reading this play, or experiencing it on stage, is emotionally demanding for the very reason that Weiss's text collage, while providing rhythmical help, does not add any text to the court transcripts' wordings. The audience or reader is confronted with a drama that refuses to offer any conventional plot supplies or the convenient moral satisfaction of a Hollywood version. Several passages of Weiss's oratorio highlight the economical implications of the Shoah and the continuity of inhuman pursuit of power and profit in postwar Germany. At the very end of the play, a defendant echoes the popular postwar ideology of selective memory and the widespread refusal of Germans to face their crimes.

Only the fifth scene, "Gesang vom Ende der Lili Tofler," makes a modest concession to the conventional expectations of a reader or an audience, the interest in an identifiable human being. The story of the courage and death of an individual Shoah victim emerges. The trial gathers information about Lili Tofler, a secretary in the camp who had written a letter to a prisoner and who had been interrogated and subjected to physical and psychological torture before she was killed. She did not give away the prisoner's name (93).[15] Lili Tofler is the only victim whose personality is at least rudimentarily outlined when a witness characterizes her as a woman who never lost her inner strength (105).[16]

Using a redundant jargon of public service and duty, the defendants play down their role in the camp or plainly deny their guilt. At times they ridicule the victims. As Weiss hints at in his play and accentuates in an open letter, some of the witnesses participated in the crimes and were never persecuted.[17]

In the wake of Weiss's aesthetic and political use of documents as material for a text collage, Heimrad Bäcker uses documents from the Nazi bureaucracy and fragmentary quotations from Shoah victims in his gripping textual montages *Nachschrift* (1986) and *Nachschrift 2* (1997). In recent German literature, Thomas Lehr's *Frühling* (2001) stands out as an engaged and self-reflexive poetic prose text that addresses the Shoah without transforming it into a piece of cultural commercialism.[18]

Weiss's drama *Gesang vom Lusitanischen Popanz. Stück mit Musik in 2 Akten* premiered in Stockholm in 1967 under the direction of Etienne Glaser.[19] Later in the same year, Karl Paryla directed the first German production in Berlin. Adapting the play to promote civil rights in the United States, the Negro Ensemble Company performed it in New York. The play was performed more than fifty times worldwide until the mid-1970s. Its most recent production was realized in Bochum in 2000.

The *Popanz* drama criticizes Portuguese colonialism in Africa, more specifically in Angola. Portugal's Salazar regime, in power since 1932, was supported by the Western nations, especially since it joined NATO in 1949. In 1951, Salazar renamed the colonies that were from then on officially referred to as overseas provinces in order to preclude anticolonial protest.[20] The military conflicts in Angola had not ended yet when Weiss wrote the play. Postcolonial Angola is still torn by civil war today.[21] An example for anticolonial literature that was written by Angolan resistance fighters during the independence war is Pepetela's novel *Mayombe* (1980).[22]

Weiss's stage directions, which call for constant brightness on stage, a lighting instruction that also applies to his drama *Viet Nam Diskurs,* exhibit an acute awareness of the inherent danger of stereotyping blackness. Since only seven actors are filling all roles of the play, the question of how to signal a change of character becomes urgent. Weiss dismisses the use of masks or make-up in order to indicate the ethnic identity of a character. Regardless of their skin color, Weiss requires the actors to alternate between European and African characters (202).[23]

The bogeyman, a large construction made of sheet metal whose clattering indicates that it is approaching a time of obsoleteness and replacement, utters monotonous sets of ideological phrases about morality, values, and the sanctification of power. The fact that his speeches on moral values are disingenuous is not only indicated by the ridiculing rhyme scheme, but also by the bogeyman's occasional yawning. At times, he even transforms them into an aria (204–5; 207).

Similar to the focus on the character of Lili Tofler in *Die Ermittlung*, Weiss inserts concrete female figures, Juana and Ana, into the *Gesang vom Lusitanischen Popanz*, to prevent the theatrical documentation from becoming too abstract and depersonalized. Juana works as a housemaid in the home of a Portuguese couple who pride themselves on being progressive and modern, all the while ordering Juana around (208).[24] In a monologue, Ana lists her daily duties in detail. Her workday usually lasts from five in the morning until after midnight (208–9). When Ana, a maid in Angola who is six months pregnant, asks for permission to go home after twelve hours, her employers call the police and accuse her of disobedience. The police take Ana away from her family. She is relocated and detained, and her husband is unable to attain any information about her whereabouts. At the end of the first act, a sympathetic chorus offers to help Ana, who has lost her baby in the meantime due to the violent treatment by the military regime (229–31). Another woman, a nameless laborer on a cotton plantation who, like Ana, has been torn from her family, describes her life and despair in a monologue. Her husband was taken away and forced to work in asbestos mines, her teenage sons were subjected to forced labor in fish factories, and her daughters disappeared. The systematic strategy of separating families demanded that no family member was informed about the fate of the others (223–24).

The play highlights parallels to the Nazi regime's vocabulary of an industrial use of human beings by having the oppressors complain that their "Menschenmaterial" does not spontaneously satisfy the market demands (221).[25] The second act continues to criticize colonial crimes against humanity. When a group of fathers requests that a new school be built, they are rounded up at night by troops and transported away on trucks (239).[26] While a representative of the regime expresses his satisfied view that everything was quiet in Angola (239), the chorus reports that the remains of the regime's victims are thrown into the ocean from airplanes:

> Ein Flugzeug brachte das / was von den Männern übrig war / hinweg zum Meer in Säcken / Nach Tagen schwemmte dann die Flut / was übrig war zum Strand zurück / Arme Beine Rümpfe. (239)

The documentation of the colonial regime's torture practices and murders is often immediately preceded or followed by cynically euphemistic official statements about an economic boom, the humane and noble purposes of colonialism, and the population's "freundliche und dankbare Gesichter."[27] The play puts its final focus on the growing force of a movement marked by solidarity. A chorus that consists of everybody on stage announces that a carefully planned liberation is near (247; 265).

Weiss's documentary and poetic, choreographic translation of Vietnam's liberation and defense wars into a stage production, his *Diskurs über die Vorgeschichte und den Verlauf des lang andauernden Befreiungskrieges in Viet Nam als Beispiel für die Notwendigkeit des bewaffneten Kampfes der Unterdrückten gegen ihre Unterdrücker sowie über die Versuche der Vereinigten Staaten von Amerika die Grundlagen der Revolution zu vernichten* (Viet Nam Discourse) premiered in Frankfurt in 1968, under the direction of Harry Buckwitz.[28] Peter Stein, who directed the play in Munich in the same year, temporarily lost his job because he attempted to collect donations for the Viet Cong after the performance. Ten days after the West German premiere, an East German production of the play premiered in Rostock, under the direction of Hanns Anselm Perten. Only about a dozen performances were given in subsequent years.

Before it addresses U.S. warfare, the play sketches the history of Vietnam over the last 2000 years. Having been occupied by French colonial troops in the nineteenth century, Vietnamese armies successfully ended French and Japanese occupation after a long liberation war, which lasted from 1941 to 1954, when Vietnam was divided. The war, however, continued, and the United States emerged as communist Vietnam's main enemy until 1975. Despite their technologically much more advanced military machinery, which not only heavily bombed the whole country for years, but which also committed war crimes against civilians, the United States lost the war. It should be noted that Weiss's partisan perspective prevented him from addressing the fact that both sides committed war crimes. In 1976, Vietnam was reunited.

Weiss is not the only playwright who wrote a drama about the Vietnam wars while they were still continuing. For example, the French writer Armand Gatti, a Holocaust survivor, wrote the play *V comme Vietnam* in 1967.[29] In his introductory remarks to *Viet Nam Diskurs,* Weiss insists on dramaturgic simplicity and argues that a display of exoticism in costume, stage design, and instrumentation would be counterproductive. Continuing a feature of his previous documentary plays, he demands that the actors have numbers instead of names and that stage effects be used sparsely (271).[30] Echoing the stage directions concerning the lighting for the *Gesang vom Lusitanischen Popanz,* the *Viet Nam Diskurs* also suggests an alert visual and cognitive perception of the play and its political impetus by requiring the lighting to remain constantly bright (270).[31]

Two poetic folk songs, or rather two versions of the same song about a rice field, which is compared to a pregnant woman, echo each other across different temporal layers of the play. They negotiate the desirability and fragility of nonviolence. In the second scene, a chorus instructs workers about the art of careful harvesting and demands respect for the anthropomorphized rice field. The song emphasizes the duty to nourish the fields and to keep them free of brutality (288).[32] The gentleness and respect toward nature that is expressed in this song also connotes ethical values such as dignity and a sense of codependence between man, woman, and nature. The precariousness of beauty is highlighted by the emphasis on compassion that nourishes the bond between a rice field and a pregnant woman. Toward the end of the play, however, the song is significantly revised and has shifted its focus to the necessity to fight back at any given moment, even while carefully harvesting rice (454).[33]

The dignity of the Vietnamese people and the superiority of its cultural values to the Western nations' aggressive actions also become apparent when a Vietnamese man speaks about future hardships. This scene at the end of the play realizes Weiss's programmatic claim that, while the personal should not become the center of a political play, the characters should not appear too abstract (269).[34] In a low voice, an exhausted Vietnamese man utters a disillusioned prognosis about the United States' aggressive role in Asia (456).[35] This passage contains a moving sign of inner strength and an awareness of one's own fragility. The soft-spoken Vietnamese man does not appear to embody aggressive fanaticism but plainly summarizes the relentlessness of a superpower's warfare. These unassuming words, in their laconic simplicity, formulate a warning and a conviction that carry an immense weight. Throughout the final part of the play, choruses express a continued realistic assessment of American military power. However, often a chorus nevertheless calls for courageous optimism and small yet efficient countermeasures (456–58).

At times, observations by a chorus in Weiss's *Viet Nam Diskurs* can be seamlessly integrated into today's discussions of terror and national interest in the age of globalization. For example, Weiss polemically questions the use of the economic term "surplus," which euphemistically points at an abundance of goods and profits, while it also serves as a code word for the desirability of new funding for continued destruction:

Ja / Wir sehen / was ihr / aus dem Überschuß macht / Kampfflug-
zeuge / Raketen Bomben / Napalm und Gas / Panzer Automobile /
Fernsehgeräte / auf deren Bildschirmen ihr / uns zeigt bei Tag / und
bei Nacht / Generäle und Stars / brennende Dörfer / Leichenhaufen /
Ruïnen und Schrott / Ja / wir sehen / was ihr aus dem Überschuß
macht. (452)

This list juxtaposes economic booms, warfare, and media coverage,
themes that continue to be subjected to more and more complex variations in our century. Another passage points toward the future. In it, an
American official admits the political and moral superiority of the Vietnamese people but maintains that, from his administration's perspective,
the Vietnam War merely serves as an exercise for possible future threats
posed by underprivileged parts of the world (447–48).[36] Like Weiss's
other documentary plays, *Viet Nam Diskurs* still encompasses and addresses many locations today, and its intricate choreographic arrangements have explored new dramaturgic directions.[37]

Notes

[1] *Notizbücher 1971–1980. 1. Band* (Frankfurt a.M.: Suhrkamp, 1981), 85.

[2] See Chistoph Weiss, *Auschwitz in der geteilten Welt. Peter Weiss und die "Ermitt-
lung" im Kalten Krieg* (St. Ingbert: Röhrig, 2000); Christoph Weiss, "Die Ermitt-
lung," in *Peter Weiss' Dramen. Neue Interpretationen,* edited by Martin Rector and
Christoph Weiss (Opladen and Wiesbaden: Westdeutscher Verlag, 1999), 108–54.
For a discussion of Weiss's Divina Commedia project, see also Arnd Beise, *Peter Weiss*
(Stuttgart: Reclam, 2002), 110–16.

[3] Arno Schmidt, "Herrn Dante Alighieri," in *Arno Schmidt's Wundertüte. Eine
Sammlung fiktiver Briefe aus den Jahren 1948/49,* edited by Bernd Rauschenbach
(Bargfeld/Zurich: Arno Schmidt Stiftung im Haffmans Verlag, 1989), 6–9.

[4] Amiri Baraka (Leroi Jones), *The System of Dante's Hell* (New York: Grove Press,
1963). A 1965 version is also published in *The fiction of Leroi Jones/Amiri Baraka*
(Chicago: Lawrence Hill, 2000), 15–126.

[5] Bertolt Brecht, "Gespräche mit jungen Intellektuellen," in Bertolt Brecht, *Werke.
Band 23: Schriften 3. Große kommentierte Berliner und Frankfurter Ausgabe,* edited
by Werner Hecht, Jan Knopf, Werner Mittenzwei, and Klaus-Detlef Müller (Ber-
lin/Weimar/Frankfurt a.M.: Aufbau/Suhrkamp, 1993), 101: "Die Vorgänge in
Auschwitz, im Warschauer Ghetto, in Buchenwald vertrügen zweifellos keine Beschreibung in literarischer Form. Die Literatur war nicht vorbereitet auf und hat
keine Mittel entwickelt für solche Vorgänge."

[6] All following excerpts and quotations from this play refer to the following edition:
Die Ermittlung. Oratorium in 11 Gesängen. In Peter Weiss, *Werke in sechs Bänden.*

Fünfter Band, edited by Suhrkamp Verlag in cooperation with Gunilla Palmstierna-Weiss (Frankfurt a.M.: Suhrkamp, 1991), 7–199.

[7] The most recent productions of *Die Ermittlung* include Baltimore (2001), Newton, Massachusetts (2001), Torino (1998–2001), Prato (1998), Veroli (1996), Parma (1996), and Milano (1995). In January 2002, celebrities and politicians joined for a public reading of *Die Ermittlung* in Potsdam.

[8] See the reprint in Christoph Weiss, *Auschwitz in der geteilten Welt: Peter Weiss und die "Ermittlung" im Kalten Krieg. Teil 1* (St. Ingbert: Röhrig, 2000), 123.

[9] Christoph Weiss, *Auschwitz in der geteilten Welt: Peter Weiss und die "Ermittlung" im Kalten Krieg* (St. Ingbert: Röhrig, 2000). See also Christoph Weiss, "Die Ermittlung," in *Peter Weiss' Dramen: Neue Interpretationen,* edited by Martin Rector and Christoph Weiss (Opladen and Wiesbaden: Westdeutscher Verlag, 1999), 108–54; Burkhardt Lindner, *Im Inferno. "Die Ermittlung" von Peter Weiss: Auschwitz, der Historikerstreit und "Die Ermittlung"* (Frankfurt a.M.: Frankfurter Bund für Volksbildung, 1988); Erika Salloch, *Peter Weiss' "Die Ermittlung": Zur Struktur des Dokumentartheaters* (Frankfurt a.M.: Athenäum, 1972); Gerd Weinreich, *Peter Weiss: Die Ermittlung* (Frankfurt a.M.: Diesterweg, 1983).

[10] The other cantos are entitled "Gesang vom Lager," "Gesang von der Möglichkeit des Überlebens," "Gesang vom Ende der Lili Tofler," "Gesang vom Unterscharführer Stark," "Gesang von der Schwarzen Wand," and "Gesang vom Bunkerblock."

[11] 9: "Bei der Aufführung dieses Dramas soll nicht der Versuch unternommen werden, den Gerichtshof, vor dem die Verhandlungen über das Lager geführt wurden, zu rekonstruieren. Eine solche Rekonstruktion erscheint dem Schreiber des Dramas ebenso unmöglich, wie es die Darstellung des Lagers auf der Bühne wäre."

[12] "Angeklagte 1–18 stellen authentische Personen dar [. . .] Sie tragen Namen, die aus dem wirklichen Prozeß übernommen sind. [. . .] Zeugen 1–9 stellen abwechselnd die verschiedensten anonymen Zeugen dar."

[13] Compare Arnd Beise, *Peter Weiss* (Stuttgart: Reclam, 2002), 124.

[14] Walter Jens, "*Die Ermittlung* in Westberlin," in *Über Peter Weiss,* edited by Volker Canaris (Frankfurt a.M.: Suhrkamp, 1970), 92–96.

[15] "Lili Tofler wurde vernommen / Sie sollte den Namen des Häftlings nennen / Boger leitete die Verhöre / Auf seinen Befehl / wurde sie in den Bunkerblock gebracht / Dort mußte sie sich viele Male / nackt zur Wand stellen / und es wurde so getan als sollte sie / erschossen werden."

[16] "Jedesmal wenn ich Lili traf / und sie fragte / Wie geht es dir Lili / sagte sie / Mir geht es immer gut."

[17] "Antwort auf eine Kritik zur Stockholmer Aufführung der 'Ermittlung.'" Swedish original version in *Dagens Nyheter,* March 18, 1966. German version in *Rapporte 2* (Frankfurt a.M.: Suhrkamp, 1971), 45–50. Here: 46: "In dem Stück treten immer wieder Zeugen auf, die auf seiten der Angeklagten tätig waren, doch heute unbescholten in der westdeutschen Gesellschaft leben. Warum sitzen sie nicht auf der Anklagebank?"

[18] Heimrad Bäcker, *Nachschrift* (Graz/Vienna: Droschl, 1993; first edition: Linz/Vienna: edition neue texte, 1986); Heimrad Bäcker, *Nachschrift 2* (Graz/Vienna: Droschl, 1997); Thomas Lehr, *Frühling. Novelle* (Berlin: Aufbau, 2001).

[19] All following excerpts and quotations from this play refer to the following edition: *Gesang vom Lusitanischen Popanz. Stück mit Musik in 2 Akten*. In Peter Weiss, *Werke in sechs Bänden. Fünfter Band,* edited by Suhrkamp Verlag in cooperation with Gunilla Palmstierna-Weiss (Frankfurt a.m.: Suhrkamp, 1991), 201–65.

[20] See Peter Hanenberg, "*Gesang vom Lusitanischen Popanz,*" in *Peter Weiss' Dramen: Neue Interpretationen,* edited by Martin Rector and Christoph Weiss (Opladen and Wiesbaden: Westdeutscher Verlag, 1999), 155–75. Here: 158. For a discussion of Weiss's responses to colonial warfare see Rüdiger Sareika, "Peter Weiss' Engagement für die 'Dritte Welt': *Lusitanischer Popanz* und *Viet Nam Diskurs,*" in *Peter Weiss,* edited by Rainer Gerlach (Frankfurt a.m.: Suhrkamp, 1984), 249–67.

[21] For concise historical analyses of Portuguese colonialism in Africa, see David Birmingham, *The Portuguese Conquest of Angola* (London/New York: Oxford UP, 1965); David Birmingham, *Portugal and Africa* (Hampshire, London, New York: MacMillan / St. Martin's Press, 1999); Linda Heywood, *Contested Power in Angola, 1840s to the present* (Rochester, N.Y.: U of Rochester P, 2000).

[22] Pepetela (Artur Pestana), *Mayombe* (Lisbon: edicões 70, 1980); English translation by Michael Wolfers (London / Ibadan / Nairobi: Heinemann, 1983).

[23] "Auf keinen Fall dürfen mit Schminke und Maskierung Wechsel von europäischer zu afrikanischer Rolle, und umgekehrt, gezeigt werden. Die Schauspieler, gleich welche Hautfarbe sie haben, sprechen abwechselnd für Europäer und Afrikaner. Nur in ihrer Spielweise nehmen sie Stellung zu den Konflikten. [. . .] Die Beleuchtung konstant hell."

[24] "Natürlich bin ich als fortschrittlicher Mann / dafür daß jeder sich entwickeln kann / Juana die Zeitung [. . .] / [. . .] Natürlich kenne ich als moderne Frau / die Rechte meiner Angestellten genau / Juana mein Haar bürsten."

[25] "Das Menschenmaterial kommt nicht spontan / dem Angebot entgegen."

[26] "Bei Nacht umzingelten die Truppen das Dorf / [. . .] / und jeder mußte antworten mit seinem Namen / Dann wurden sie auf Lastwagen verladen."

[27] See for example 261; 254.

[28] All following excerpts and quotations from this play refer to the following edition: *Diskurs über die Vorgeschichte und den Verlauf des lang andauernden Befreiungskrieges in Viet Nam als Beispiel für die Notwendigkeit des bewaffneten Kampfes der Unterdrückten gegen ihre Unterdrücker sowie über die Versuche der Vereinigten Staaten von Amerika die Grundlagen der Revolution zu vernichten*. In Peter Weiss, *Werke in sechs Bänden. Fünfter Band,* edited by Suhrkamp Verlag in cooperation with Gunilla Palmstierna-Weiss (Frankfurt a.m.: Suhrkamp, 1991), 267–458.

[29] Armand Gatti, *V comme Vietnam* (Paris: Éditions du Seuil, 1967).

[30] "[. . .] daß bei der Aufführung des Stücks größte Einfachheit gelten soll. Der Verzicht auf Kostümierung und die Beschränkung auf sparsamste dekorative Einzelheiten weisen darauf hin, daß die Spieler Wort, Gestik und Gruppierung zum zen-

tralen Gegenstand der sinnlichen Wahrnehmung machen müssen. [. . .] Die Instrumentalbegleitung [. . .] auf keinen Fall exotisch."

[31] *"Die Beleuchtung ist gleichbleibend hell."*

[32] "Das Reisfeld ist eine schwangere Frau / Erschreckt den blühenden Reis nicht / Keine Axtschläge keine Rufe auf den Feldern / Nennt nicht die Toten und Dämonen / Der blühende Reis verlangt nach Nahrung / Tragt Früchte und Wasser in die Felder / Erschreckt den Reis nicht wenn ihr ihn erntet / haltet das scharfe Messer auf dem Rücken versteckt / Bückt euch tief und schneidet unmerklich / Achtet daß die Sonne nicht aufblitzt / in der Schneide des Messers"

[33] "Das Reisfeld ist eine schwangere Frau / Im Erschrecken welkt der blühende Reis / Ein Dröhnen und Bersten auf den Feldern / Wir rufen laut die Namen der Toten / Der blühende Reis verkohlt im Feuer / Bringt neue Saat in die Felder / Seid ohne Furcht wenn ihr erntet / Tragt das geladne Gewehr auf dem Rücken / Schneidet den Reis schnell eh sie kommen / Achtet daß euch die Sonne nicht blendet / beim Heben der Gewehre."

[34] "Wenn auch Figuren in diesem Stück nicht ihre persönlichen Eigenheiten und ihren privaten Werdegang aufzeigen, so darf ihr Wesen doch nicht abstrakt erscheinen; vielmehr sollen die Schauspieler sich bemühen, sie als solche zu zeigen, die als handelnde, mit lebendigem und faßbarem Ausdruck, die Veränderungen in der Geschichte bewirken."

[35] "Dieser mächtige Feind / tritt an die Stelle / aller früheren / Unterdrücker / Seht diesen Feind / wie er sich müht / die Kraft der Revolution / zu brechen."

[36] "Viet Nam ist für uns / die Probe aufs Exempel / Wie können wir / an jedem beliebigen Ort / einen Gegner besiegen / der militärisch schwach / uns aber politisch / überlegen ist / [. . .] / Wir erlernen dort nur die Methoden / für den Tag / an dem es einmal wirklich geht / um Leben und Tod."

[37] See Arnd Beise, *Peter Weiss* (Stuttgart: Reclam, 2002), 140.

3: Staging Writers as Outcasts: *Marat/Sade, Trotzki im Exil, Hölderlin, Der Prozess,* and *Der neue Prozess*

THIS CHAPTER DISCUSSES five plays that simultaneously advocate radical political uprisings and criticize hierarchical structures of orchestrated change. These plays examine to what degree economic and political systems can obliterate the dignity of the individual as well as creative thought.

Weiss's most famous play, *Die Verfolgung und Ermordung Jean Paul Marats dargestellt durch die Schauspielgruppe des Hospizes zu Charenton unter Anleitung des Herrn de Sade. Drama in zwei Akten* (Marat/Sade), first written in 1963 and constantly revised until 1965, premiered in Berlin in 1964, under the direction of Konrad Swinarski.[1] Peter Brook's productions of the play in London (1964) and on Broadway (1965), as well as his film version (1966), have earned the play worldwide success and have led to Weiss's reputation as one of the twentieth century's most important playwrights, along with Beckett and Brecht. Inmates at the prison of Volterra have performed the play from 1993 to 1997 in various cities throughout Italy.[2] Recent productions in Boston (2001), as well as in Berlin, Minneapolis, and Hollywood (2000), document the fact that *Marat/Sade* is still one of the most played contemporary dramas.[3]

Marat/Sade integrates divergent theatrical traditions of the twentieth century, including Brecht's belief in theater as an incentive to rational political thinking, Beckett's stagings of existence as grotesque and monotonous, and Artaud's concepts of total theater and theater of cruelty.

The boundaries between levels of theatrical reality that are both superimposed on and conflict with one another remain porous and permeable throughout the play. The audience is exposed to an intricate configuration of plays within plays, or, to use the French technical term, mise-en-abîme. We are thrown into abysmal disorientation of reflecting theatrical mirrors. Actors play prisoners and mentally ill patients who are allowed to enact a play about the French Revolution. Marquis de Sade (1740–1814), imprisoned at Charenton, a mental institution that also served as a prison for political opponents, is allowed to direct some of his plays. While it might have been intended to form a therapeutic distraction for participating patients and prisoners, it also became a popular form of entertainment for Napoleonic members of the ruling class to visit plays by the Charenton inmates. This dramaturgical scenario is based on historical documents. However, the historical Sade never wrote or directed a play about the end of Jean Paul Marat (1743–1793). He did, however, give the funeral speech at Marat's grave. Therefore, there is a historical link between the two protagonists. The audience of this hospital theater is also part of the play within and beyond the play, as are the guards of the mental institution, its director and his family, and ultimately the real audiences.

Apart from Sade and Marat, whose philosophical disputes on inertia and change provide the core of the play, the character of the inmate who plays the most radical protagonist of the play, the former priest Jacques Roux (1752–1794), inhabits, and endeavors to extend, a precarious place of freedom, even though he is constantly confined by a strait jacket. The announcer, who guides the fictional and actual audiences through the play, reports that Roux is not played by a mentally disabled patient but by a radical monk who was sent to Charenton as a political prisoner during the time of Napoleon's dictatorship, when the play in the play is produced. The announcer also tells the audience that much of Roux's text had to be cut due to censorship regulations (162).[4] Jacques Roux comes closest to succeeding in breaking through the multiple transparent walls of silencing, censorship, and historicized distances that the play installs. Even though, after a few seconds, such dangerous behavior is brutally interrupted and punished by the nurses and guards, the nervousness of Coulmier, the institution's director, still indicates that Jacques Roux is the only real threat to the saturated spectators of Sade's show. Roux and the inmate who plays him form the only potential source of unpredictable challenge to the layers of control that encapsulate human dignity in *Marat/Sade*. They attempt to open the confinements of theatrical containment. Marat's elaborate exclamations and dialogues, on the other hand, are already historical events for Sade's players. Their task will be to reenact Marat's death in his bathtub by the hands of Charlotte Corday (1768–1798). Corday is played by a somnambulist patient who throughout the drama is guided and combed by two nurses (157).[5]

The richness of Weiss's complex plot on the production and performance of a theater play is highlighted by the fact that it remains unclear whether everything that Roux says and does in the play within the play precisely follows Sade's script. Sade never interrupts Roux. Therefore, it even remains open whether he is really opposing Marat's claim for the necessity of change that Roux demands in a much more radical manner. When Roux, in the sixth scene of the first act, which is titled "Erstickte Unruhe" (Suffocated Unrest), all of a sudden begins a series of not only rhetorical questions, but concrete challenges, asking who owns the land that was supposed to be distributed to the people, a nurse is pulling him backward. Sade is not surprised at all. He is either the author of Roux's fragmentary speech, then he might have calculated the interruption by the nurse, or he is content that his play is open for radical improvisation. When Coulmier, the director of the prison and hospital, is shouting in protest that only pure reason and beauty should be put on stage and that Roux's acting should not be tolerated, Sade simply ignores him. His work of art has gained force and has provoked the control mechanism to unfold its brutality. The male nurses function as guards who try to domesticate their inmates with violence, while the female nurses sing a litany to lull the excited and unruly patients into a more passive mood (167).[6]

Charlotte Corday's disoriented questions for the audience upon her arrival in Paris in scene 10 can also be understood as a poem apart from the dramatic plot. Like many other passages in Weiss's works, this series of parallel perceptions that Corday utters against the background of a danse macabre that the inmates perform, interrupted and enhanced by their involuntary convulsions, can be taken out of its context and stand on its own as a poetic manifestation of disoriented despair:

> Was ist dies für eine Stadt / in der die Sonne kaum durch den Dunst dringt / und es ist kein Dunst von Regen und Nebel / es ist ein warmes dickes Dampfen / wie in Schlachthäusern / Was johlen sie so / was zerren sie da hinter sich her / was tragen sie da auf den Spießen / was hüpfen sie so was tanzen sie so / was ist das für ein Lachen das sie so schüttelt / was klatschen sie so in die Hände / was kreischen die Kinder / was sind das für Klumpen um die sie sich raufen / Was ist dies für eine Stadt / in der das nackte Fleisch auf den Straßen liegt / Was sind das für Gesichter. (174)

In the eleventh scene, the patients and inmates excessively enjoy their pantomimic depiction of a series of executions. When Coulmier stands up, the second prisoner in Sade's play is beheaded, and the institution's stage becomes the venue of a brief ballgame. Sade again ignores Coulmier's protest (175–76). The following scene, titled "Gespräch über Tod und Leben," shows the first dialogue between Sade and Marat. Sade postulates the cruel indifference of nature towards any form of violence, from murder and torture to the possible complete eradication of mankind. He states that he hates nature's immobile, icy, and voyeuristic face and that he attempts to overcome it with its own weapons (177).[7] Offering an illustration of prolonged cruelty, Sade describes the death of Robert François Damiens. Damiens had attempted to assassinate the French king Louis XV and was slowly tortured to death in 1757. Weiss's Sade alludes to Giacomo Casanova's memoirs that describe how aristocratic voyeurs watched the torture and execution of Damiens from their windows and enjoyed it as a form of erotically stimulating entertainment. Sade then goes on to predict mass killings and regrets the loss of death's individuality. When Marat rejects these arguments by identifying the alleged indifference of universal life as the projection of Sade's own personal apathy, the Marquis responds that compassion had become a quality that could not be achieved by the nonprivileged and that emotions were nothing but symptoms of pettiness. Marat does not accept Sade's conclusions and claims the importance of inventing alternatives and of intervening forcefully to work against the omnipresence of indifference (178–80).[8] In scene 15, Sade continues his critique of Marat's impetus to reinvent society. Sade maintains his view that everything is transient, and this skeptical perspective makes it impossible for him to divide the world with any certainty into what he perceives as the outdated and illusionary static categories of good and evil:

> Um zu bestimmen was falsch ist und was recht ist / müssen wir uns kennen / Ich / kenne mich nicht / [. . .] / und nie sind andere Wahrheiten zu finden / als die veränderlichen Wahrheiten der eigenen / Erfahrungen / Ich weiß nicht / bin ich der Henker oder der Gemarterte / [. . .] / Ich bin zu allem fähig und alles füllt mich mit Schrekken. (184)

Marat, on the other hand, affirms the necessity of a radical praxis even though, he admits, the first concrete steps might remain unavoidably uncertain attempts (187).[9] Sade rejects Marat's plea for practical measures by pointing out the bloodshed that has been practiced by adherents of all political convictions. In scene 18, he denounces all patriotism and nationalism as a mask and an excuse for excessive violence.[10]

Jacques Roux interrupts the play with impromptu speeches, or maybe Sade has instructed him to perform these seemingly spontaneous declamations. Many patients gather around Roux when he condemns warfare and patriotism:

> Ein für alle Mal / muß der Gedanke an große Kriege / und an eine glorreiche Armee / ausgelöscht werden / Auf beiden Seiten ist keiner glorreich. / Auf beiden Seiten stehn nur verletzte Hosenscheißer / die alle das gleiche wollen / Nicht unter der Erde liegen sondern / auf der Erde gehn / ohne Holzbein. (200)

Coulmier protests vehemently, and Roux is strapped to a bench and brutally beaten. It can be argued that the violence of the nurses and guards was also calculated by Sade since the reactions of the institutional authorities were predictable. Sade's play forces the hierarchical system to display its mechanisms and its desperate clinging to the status quo. Always ignoring Coulmier's attempts to talk with him, Sade addresses Roux instead and praises him as the embodiment of a timely and successful strategy of camouflage (201).[11]

In scene 21, Corday acts as a dominatrix who lashes Sade during his reflections on the horror of violence that he was not able to prevent in his function as a judge during the French Revolution. Repeatedly interrupted or punctuated by Corday's whippings, Sade describes the disgust and pain that he felt when he had to witness the endless executions and the violence of common people on the streets.[12]

These experiences lead Sade to the conclusion that any participation in political events equals a corrupt alliance with sanctioned killings. He longs for a radical retreat from society and for his death. He wishes to become unidentifiable:

> Und wenn ich verschwinde / möchte ich alle Spuren / hinter mir auslöschen. (206)

The last scene of the first act, titled "Marats Gesichte" (Marat's Visions), far from focusing on Marat's political values and projects, is built around a series of his nightmares. People in his life who have hurt, ridiculed, and rejected him appear as ghosts. One by one, from his teacher and his parents to the philosopher and playwright Voltaire and the scientist Lavoisier, everybody who has deprived him of respect as a human being, as a writer, or as a physicist comments on him and expresses his or her contempt (217–23). This dance of death, which might offer the temptation to psychoanalyze and depoliticize Marat's radicalism, is interrupted by Roux, who, not unlike Marx in Weiss's play *Hölderlin*, defends the protagonist by emphasizing his courageous attempts to think through and beyond a petrified social system. Roux laments:

> Wehe dem Andersgearteten / der es wagt nach allen Richtungen / gegen die Begrenzungen anzudrängen / um sie zu erweitern und zu durchstoßen / überall aufgehalten und angepöbelt / von den scheuklappenbehängten Sicherern / alter Positionen / Du wolltest Helligkeit. (223)

While it is still a matter of debate among scholars whether Marat or Sade wins the ideological dispute that they perform against each other in Weiss's play, it should not be forgotten that there is no animosity on the part of Sade. He appears as someone who earlier in his life had adopted a view that was similar to Marat's unchanging perspective. Rather than engaging in ideological debates about a favorite dramatic character, readers and audiences of the play are invited to recognize the extent to which Marat's and Sade's insights are compatible. Sade's distanced view, far from being cynical, can be read as the result of his experience with historical developments and the palinodic mechanisms of praise and blame. At the end of the first scene of act two, Sade gives a laconic yet compassionate prognosis of the reception history of Marat:

> Einen werden sie finden / auf den sie alles abladen können / und sie werden ihn ernennen zu einem blutgierigen Ungeheuer / das in die Geschichte eingehen kann / unter dem Namen Marat. (232)

In scene 30, shortly before Charlotte Corday stabs Marat to death in his bathtub, Sade postulates the priority of an individual, inner revolution (245).[13] Weiss changed the play's epilogue several times, shifting the weight of arguments back and forth between Sade and Marat. In the first draft of the epilogue, Sade claims that he is still confronting an open question and that he neither finds himself at home in Marat's theses nor in the individualistic visions of self-annihilation that he himself has brought forward in his dialogical exchange with Marat (253).[14] However, the final words, which can be read as a new beginning, are exclaimed, or rather screamed, by Roux, who addresses not only the characters of the play as well as the institutionalized patients and inmates with their nurses, guards, and spectators within the play, but also the theater audience outside of the play, if there is such a thing as an outside of the stage of *Marat/Sade*:

> Wann werdet ihr sehen lernen / Wann werdet ihr endlich verstehen. (255)

Roux throws himself in front of the ecstatically marching patients, while the male nurses fight the uncontrollable theater group with excessive violence. Standing on a chair and watching his production dissolve in this tumultuous manner, or perhaps enjoying his production of dissolution, Sade is laughing triumphantly (255). In comments on his play's political implications and in the light of productions in countries of different political systems that usually championed either Sade or Marat's perspective, Weiss rewrote the parts of *Marat/Sade* many times in order to maintain its dialectical ambivalence. In interviews, he advocated an interpretive openness towards the play and insisted that possible forms of dramatic realizations were inexhaustible.[15]

Trotzki im Exil. Stück in 2 Akten premiered in Düsseldorf in 1970, under the direction of Harry Buckwitz.[16] The same year, the play was also performed in Hanover and Göteborg. The Russian revolutionary thinker Leon Bronstein, who called himself Trotsky (1879–1940) and whom Lenin (1870–1924) had chosen as his successor, opposed Stalin, who attained power after Lenin's death. Stalin banished and persecuted Trotsky and eventually had him killed in Mexican exile in 1940. Weiss wrote this play as an undogmatic contribution to the Lenin year, the hundredth birthday of the leader of the Russian Revolution. However, the socialist countries did not welcome Weiss's emphasis on the importance of Trotsky, whose memory had been extinguished from official textbooks in the Eastern bloc.

The introductory stage directions suggest that the sequence of fifteen scenes written in prose, which at times disregard chronological order, should take place in a swift and surprising manner (11).[17] As Rohrwasser concedes in his concise recent article on *Trotzki im Exil,* no plot outline can render the play's scenic labyrinth and its intricate and multilayered temporal structure, its sudden cuts and superimpositions.[18] The first scene begins with Trotsky sitting at a table and working on a manuscript, a pen in his hand. Throughout the play, Trotsky is repeatedly depicted in this working position, most notably in the final scene, right before he is killed by one of Stalin's agents.

While the first scene depicts the arrest of Trotsky and his family and friends by Stalin's police, the second scene, which takes place in the prison camp of Wercholensk in Siberia, revolves around a passionate debate among the political prisoners about the necessity of intellectual guidance for a revolution. Some prisoners, workers whom the play only introduces as "nameless" characters, express their deep mistrust of self-appointed intellectual leaders of the revolution:

> Unsre Planer [. . .] Wollen uns erklären, wie wir die Fabrik übernehmen sollen. Wissen nicht mal, wie man eine Maschine bedient. [. . .] Ihr bleibt Literaten. Liest ein Arbeiter [. . .] deine gelehrten Abhandlungen, Bronstein? (14–15)

Another critique is aimed at Trotsky's belief in the necessity of a strong party apparatus. Machajski warns him that the bureaucracy and hierarchy of a party will become a goal in itself and corrupt the revolutionary ideals by perpetuating the exploitation of the many by a self-appointed elite. Trotsky, however, dismisses Machajski's doubts as outdated and equals progress with scientific organizational work.[19] Passages like this, which call for open discussions of the best way to realize revolution, have contributed to the aggressive reaction to Weiss's play by the Eastern bloc countries. For a while, Weiss, who used to be heavily courted by the socialist regimes, became a persona non grata.

The third scene goes back in time to London in 1902. Trotsky visits Lenin in his temporary British exile to discuss strategies of toppling the Russian aristocracy. Lenin repeatedly presses his hands against his temples, indicating his health problems. Lenin takes an imaginary walk through London with Trotsky. They listen in while soldiers and workers talk about colonial wars. Differences between Lenin and Trotsky emerge in the fourth scene, which takes place in Brussels at a secret convention in 1903. The scene is introduced as an event that Lenin and Trotsky remember together and narrate to each other. The secret discussions emerge from their sharing of mutual memories of the meeting. They talk about not only their initially opposing strategic views on centralizing the party, but about excluding members who do not understand the necessity of strict discipline and hierarchical authority. Trotsky is initially opposed to the party split that Lenin favors. With a narrow majority of two votes, the Bolsheviks, who support the unquestioned authority of Lenin's leadership, now declare themselves the only legitimate communist Russian party. Lenin calls the Mensheviks useless and trapped in a petty bourgeois mentality.

Scene 5 depicts demonstrations and declamations by Trotsky and others in 1905 and ends with a brief trial and the sentencing of Trotsky. The sixth scene puts the focus on Trotsky's second term in a prison camp in 1928. Together with his wife Natalja Sedowa and his friends Parvus and Deutsch, he tries to make sense of the past events and attempts to find the strength to concentrate on future projects. But there is also room to think about literature. Commenting on a dogmatically Marxist interpretation of Dante's *Commedia*, Trotsky claims that this work is not reducible to a reflection of Florentine class interests:

> Ja, natürlich, Produkt eines gegebenen sozialen Milieus. Natürlich. Commedia, diktiert von bestimmten Klasseninteressen. [. . .] Historisches Dokument. Doch weil Auseinandersetzung mit seiner Zeit, Schilderung psychologischer Entwicklung, Gedankenverbindung mit uns herstellt. Sprengt die Zeitgrenzen. Ja. War zum Tod durchs Feuer verurteilt. Schrieb im Exil. Durfte nie mehr zurück. (36–37)

Characterizing Trotsky as an ardent admirer of Dante, Weiss once more interweaves the Italian poet into one of his plays. The difference and possible interaction between art and political praxis is negotiated in the seventh scene, which goes back in time to Zurich, where Lenin lived in exile around 1915. Some of Lenin's neighbors in Zurich included Hugo Ball and other founders of the dada movement. Ball calls for the useful enjoyment of an alliance of Lenin and Trotsky with his dada group:

> Ihr müßt euch verbünden mit uns, ihr Rationalisten, ihr Revolutionsingenieure. [. . .] Wir, die Emotionalen, die Unberechenbaren, und ihr, die Planer, die Konstrukteure. Keine Trennung. Sonst werden unsre Revolutionen im Sand versickern. Der neue Mensch muß ein Schöpfer sein. Die neue Kunst ist Leben. Atmen ist Kunst. Bewegung ist Kunst. (42)

Lenin, however, suspicious of the potentially depoliticizing effect and implications of any praise of irrationalism, suddenly shouts:

> Und weil die menschliche Intelligenz so winzig ist, eben weil sie so winzig ist, deshalb werde ichs nicht zulassen, daß sie diesen schwachen Schimmer noch auslöschen. (43)

While Trotsky favors a more open-minded aesthetic view than Lenin's, he also insists on the absence of any mystical or ecstatic elements. In Lenin's and in Trotsky's view, art is a legitimate political instrument, a tool that has to be used to change the world.[20] It is a woman, Lenin's fellow thinker Inessa Armand, who argues against communist censorship:

> Wer aber soll beurteilen, ob es revolutionäre Kunst ist? Wer bestimmt, was revolutionärer Kunst schadet, was ihr nützt? Wo sollen die Grenzen gesetzt werden? Wer bestimmt den Punkt, an dem die Einmischung beginnt? (44)

Lenin's answer remains vague and rhetorical.[21] Ending the sharp debate on principles and gently moving to a more personal level, Trotsky tries to persuade Lenin to abandon his asceticism and to enjoy music or at least fresh air. He shares the memory of his overwhelming first encounter with theater as part of his persuasive lobbying for more creative cultural enjoyment. This memory, first evoked in order to remind his comrade of the necessity of art as a mode of survival, also makes Trotsky silently reflect on the self-critical unspoken question about what has come out of sight in the years of class warfare:

> [. . .] wir dürfen nicht verkümmern. [. . .] als ich zum ersten Mal im Theater war, das war ungeheuerlich, das läßt sich gar nicht beschreiben. [. . .] Ich kanns nicht erzählen. Was hab ich gesehn? Was hab ich gesehn? (45–46)

Unimpressed by Trotsky's words, an embittered Lenin sticks to an enduring analytical state of mind. He rejects any offer of aesthetic relief by pointing out that in his view, beauty is an unbearable perversion as long as there is suffering:

> Was für wunderbare Sachen können Menschen sich ausdenken. Aber ich kanns nicht hören. [. . .] Sich so was Schönes ausdenken, während sie in der Hölle leben. Ich ertrag es nicht. (45)

This passionate dialogue between arguably irreconcilable positions, central to Weiss's play and to any critical self-understanding of modern art and political thought, never took place during the time when the dadaists and the Russian exiles were neighbors. Investigating the compatibility of unbound artistic expression and a concentrated focus on concrete political and economic change describes the precarious center of *Trotzki im Exil,* and of most of Weiss's writings.

The following last two scenes of the first act describe revolutionary actions in Russia. In a revealing passage in the ninth scene, which emphasizes their mutual respect and friendship, Lenin and Trotsky look back upon their many differences in terms of strategic viewpoints toward the realization of change. Trotsky emphasizes that their opposing views on revolutionary strategies have been fruitful challenges that were necessary for successful change:

> Haben einander vorangetrieben. Haben Gedanken voneinander übernommen. [. . .] Verschiedene Ansichten und Möglichkeiten mußten aneinanderstoßen und sich in der Praxis beweisen. Auch in Zukunft muß es Kontroversen, Widersprüche geben. Wären wir sonst Marxisten, Dialektiker? (54)

Lenin agrees that their polemical exchanges have always been based on mutual respect and friendship. However, Lenin, who is aware that he will not live much longer, issues a warning to Trotsky concerning the coming fight for power within the Communist Party:

> Wir sind einander gewachsen. Aber ich hab nur noch wenige Jahre. Studenweise bin sich schon weg, ausgelöscht. Die andern, sie werden dich nicht neben sich dulden, wenn ich nicht da bin. Deine Selbstsicherheit, deine Weltsicht, sie werden nur Hochmut, Eitelkeit drin sehn. Sie werden sich zusammentun und dich ausstoßen. (54–55)

The act ends by illustrating Lenin's premonition. Superimposed on a celebrated speech by Lenin in the decisive days of October 1917 is the arrest of Trotsky by Stalin's soldiers in 1929. Concrete times and places become fused components of nightmarish transitions.

The second act begins with a scene in which Trotsky, who compulsively uses a telescope, is in exile in Kronstadt, a Baltic island town near St. Petersburg and not far from the Finnish coast. In a discussion with his friend Blumkin and his son Lew Sedow, Trotsky rejects the idea of individual acts of terrorism as useless. In his view, only organized mass terror is acceptable.[22] At this point, Weiss inserts another chronological leap backwards. All of a sudden, the audience witnesses a discussion between Lenin, Trotsky, Schljapnikow, and Aleksandra Kollontai from 1921. Schljapnikow and Kollontai argue for a truly democratic government with the participation of workers and warn against the bureaucratic fossilization of power structures in the newly established state.

Lenin defends his rejection of these calls for a more lenient mode of administration by pointing at the still fragile state of the Soviet Union. While he welcomes internal debates, in his view, everyone who carries polemical skepticism outside of the party, does irremediable damage to the revolution. Therefore, Lenin argues, he was right in stripping Schljapnikow of his party membership. Nameless seamen and workers also demand more democratic rights. It is now Trotsky who orders the Red Army to punish the workers who want to be active participants in the new society (66–71). Weiss has no interest in depicting Trotsky and Lenin as innocent victims. This and other scenes highlight that both of them favored violence and disregarded individual human freedom and life when they thought that the revolution was in danger. However, the play makes it clear that the systematic perversion of Lenin's and Trotsky's revolutionary project is embodied by Stalin and his followers.

In scene 11, Lenin's death is juxtaposed with his frustration about the disproportionate role of bureaucracy and with his growing fear of Stalin's looming grab for power. Lenin is shown as sharing Trotsky's fundamental doctrine that the revolution has to be spread all over the world. Stalin will later denounce this view as counterrevolutionary internationalism. Pressing his temples with his hands again, Lenin's last reflections on the main structural dilemma of his political engineering project display angered resignation. Warning Trotsky about Stalin's greed for power, Lenin realizes that the centralized machinery of the Communist Party has turned against its inventors' ideas and ideals.[23]

The dialogue between Trotsky and Lenin all of a sudden becomes a posthumous conversation, switching to the "du" form. After a rhetorical propaganda speech by Stalin, who paints himself as Lenin's loyal heir, the scene ends with Trotsky's son Lew Sedow bringing his father the news of his daughter Sinaida's suicide in Berlin (75).

Scene 12, which takes place near Grenoble in 1935 but which, despite the chronological disorder, can also be put in the context of the student movements of the 1960s, contains a free-spirited and controversial dialogue about the future between students from all over the world and Trotsky. Asian, African American, Latin American, and European students discuss their respective strategic debates with Trotsky and offer a series of critical questions to him. A German student insists that a revolution that still keeps the mind under authoritative control is not only incomplete but betrays its own alleged purpose of liberation. Voicing Weiss's rejection of dogmatic party politics, the student also criticizes Trotsky's implementation of state violence towards fellow citizens and the lifeless constructs of art that have lost all surplus value of surprise and unpredictability:

> Ihr habt zwar die Klassen abgeschafft. Aber die Befreiung des Bewußtseins habt ihr verhindert. Sie, Genosse Trotzki, haben die Zwangsarbeit eingeleitet, die heute verwirklicht ist. Sie haben die Entmachtung der Gewerkschaften befürwortet, die heute Tatsache ist. Sie selbst wollten die völlige Staatskontrolle über das Proletariat. Sie haben auf die opponierenden Arbeiter einschießen lassen. [. . .] Anstatt revolutionärer Kunst, anstatt Kunst als Entdeckerfreude, Schreck vorm Unbekannten, Sentimentalität, hohler Idealismus. (81)

Trotsky's predictable counterargument warns against what he calls anarchist desires and cites the threat by other nations as the reason for a necessary authoritarianism of the state.

Scene 13 begins in another station of Trotsky's exiled life, this time in Norway. Trotsky is examined by a doctor, whose cynical comments indicate that he has connections to Stalin's secret service. From the stage background, a long scene from the Stalinist Moscow show trials emerges.

The final two scenes of the play, "Das Testament" (The Last Will) and "Die Hinrichtung" (The Execution), show the last days of Trotsky's Mexican exile. As is the case throughout the play, discussions with befriended intellectuals, artists, and activists form the center of the drama. The painter Diego Rivera and the writer and founder of surrealism, André Breton, visit Trotsky, who has just survived an assassination attempt. Breton condemns Stalin's show trials and the self-humiliating submissive stance of the defendants who publicly praised Stalin's dictatorship and denounced themselves as traitors. In Breton's view, not only Stalin and his judges and torturers, but also the compliant victims, the former elite of the revolution, have distorted the whole revolutionary project:

Es ist dies Schweigen, dieser Selbstbetrug, der den Marxismus zu einer Grabkammer macht. (102–3)

Trotsky responds that rational analyses were more important than ever before and that the show trials, while forming a devastating criminal act, only prove Stalin's corruption and greed for power, but do not tarnish the idea and the future of communism.[24] Using Breton as one of Trotsky's dialogue partners is not an invention by Weiss. The French writer, whose works Weiss admired, visited Trotsky in his Mexican exile, and they co-authored a manifesto of surrealism. Breton's novel *Nadja* had a major impact on Weiss's conceptions of the interplay between autobiography and the imagination, and he named his youngest daughter after Breton's protagonist. Breton also provided Weiss with poetic and programmatic emphases of the importance of Géricault's paintings and of Rimbaud's visionary calls for change, which maintain a central place in Weiss novel *Die Ästhetik des Widerstands.*[25]

In the final scene, the audience witnesses Trotsky's murder by the hands of a Stalinist agent. Trotsky, who is shown again in the position of concentrated reading and correcting, is killed with an ice axe, but the audience does not witness the murder. The stage becomes dark and silent before the axe hits Trotsky.

The drama *Hölderlin. Stück in zwei Akten* premiered in Stuttgart in 1971, under the direction of Peter Palitzsch. During the 1970s, the drama was performed in approximately thirty cities, mainly in Germany, but also in Sweden (1971), Hungary (1972), England (1973), and Yugoslavia (1973).[26] The poet and philosopher Friedrich Hölderlin (1770–1843), who spent the last thirty-six years of his life in a tower in Tübingen, is still the object not only of philological acumen, but also of biographical speculation. Weiss's play undertakes, among many other things, an intervention in the contested area of biographical and ideological interpretations of the poet and philosopher.[27] The debates about the exact nature of his mental illness became more controversial when the French scholar Pierre Bertaux suggested that Hölderlin simulated the illness. In his notebooks, Weiss, while supporting this main hypothesis, critiques what he sees as Bertaux's depoliticized reading of Hölderlin.[28]

The spelling of the text, which often employs irregular couplets, seems archaic because Weiss imitates orthographic conventions of Hölderlin's time. The prologue ends with the singer and commentator's announcement of an uncanny topographical coincidence. When the young Hölderlin studied theology in Tübingen, he was able to see, and probably passed daily, the tower that would become the retreat and location of his final four decades in mental inner exile. The Tübinger Stift (Württemberg's school of theology), Hölderlin's tower, and the mental institution where he was admitted are all just a few steps away from each other. All three buildings can be described as what the singer calls his prison. This statement will be echoed by the singer in the very last verse of the play, this time directed to the audience, leaving it open to how far the prison is extending through time and space, and how its perpetuation can be countered (113; 260).[29]

The first act begins with a scene at the Tübinger Stift in 1793. Hölderlin, Neuffer, Hegel, and other students, who, except for Hegel, are more or less enthusiastic about the French Revolution, discuss politics and philosophy while they decorate the school for the arrival of the ruler of Württemberg. Hegel warns against the use of violence and advocates patience and a belief in the gradual education of mankind, which in his eyes is too immature to act by itself. This rhetoric of justification of the current state of affairs and of restraint in the name of education will be echoed throughout the play by Fichte and Goethe, as well as by merchants and bankers. Hegel continues to lecture his roommates on the necessity of patient education and slow evolution (124).[30]

During his visit, the Duke of Württemberg realizes the rebellious atmosphere at the Stift. However, he displays a benevolent and relaxed mood when he indulges in sharing the latest good news from France, the murder of Marat. His self-congratulatory announcement is followed by the students' brief silence in shock, then by their screams and weeping (131).[31] This is one example of Weiss's intertextual references between his texts, since he can assume that the readers and audiences of the play are familiar with *Marat/Sade*. At the end of the scene, Hegel is standing aside. When one of the students, Hiller, is calling for a lifelong violent uprising, Hegel, having just taken a pinch of snuff, ends the scene with an ironic sneeze (131).[32]

The second scene is located in Waltershausen in 1794, where Hölderlin found his first job as a private teacher in the rank of a servant for an aristocratic family. Heinrich von Kalb, the father of the household, has spent time in America, where he was accompanying and fighting with George Washington and Lafayette. Fritz von Kalb, Hölderlin's student, not only undergoes the sexual problems of puberty, but is embarrassing his family even more with his persisting questions about the genocide of Native Americans and the enslavement of Africans in America. Heinrich von Kalb proudly instructs his son about his experiences with and the desirability of slavery. Quoting George Washington as a role model, he outlines his ideology of white supremacy and of the Eurocentric mission to cultivate humanity:

> Aug in Auge mit dem Praesidenten / Washington / vernahm ich seine Ansicht / daß Sclaverey zwar nicht / mit aufgeklärtem Geist überein-stimmt / dass es jedoch noch Generationen / langer Dressur bedarf / bis die Mohren fähig sind / sich sittsahm zu benehmen. (134)

Far from being impressed by these words, the eleven-year-old Fritz insists on demanding an answer to his questions about the reasons for the mass killings of Native Americans, since in his view they are the original owners of the country. The father, however, pushes his son aside and suspects that Hölderlin has indoctrinated him with such indecent, subversive, and thankless skepticism. Hölderlin's defense of Native American culture is brushed aside by Heinrich von Kalb as nonsense and mere "Poeterey" (136). Weiss ascribes an active political awareness to Fritz von Kalb, who goes on to juxtapose the violence that he suffers from his father and the violence that is inflicted on slaves and Native Americans. Fritz also observes that his mother, Charlotte von Kalb, experiences violent abuse and, suffering from her domestic constraints and from a cruel husband, is constantly weeping. Only the intonation of her weeping changes when the father leaves (139).[33]

Through the character of Wilhelmine Kirms, a governess and Char-lotte's employed companion, the play develops feminist contours. The only character in the play that does not censor her own expressions, she is unafraid to ridicule the male gender with sarcastic clarity:

> Ja grosse Zeichen von Gerechtigkeit / sezt in die Welt der Mann / und greift vergnügt Besiz / von Hauss und Geld und Leib der Frau [. . .] / Schwächlich schwächlich / ist dies ganze Geschlecht / mit sammt was ihnen / zwischen den Beinen hängt. (140–41)

While Charlotte is holding back her erotic desire for Hölderlin, ex-cept for one moment when she embraces him with desperate vigor, Wilhelmine does not restrain her wishes and explicitly criticizes what she views as Hölderlin's escape from the material world around him. She begins her attempt to liberate Hölderlin from self-reflexive introspection by familiarizing him with daily events in the lives of servants, such as the common practice of abortion for social reasons:

> [. . .] wenn die Magd / ihr Kind erwürgt / und unterm Dach im Stroh / der Knecht in seiner Ohnmacht / brüllt / da haben Sie die Welt / ganz plazend voll / und brauchen sich / nach Ihren Bildern / nicht weiter um zu sehn. (145)

Hölderlin does not know how to respond. Disconcerted and speechless, he covers his face with his hands. Switching to the intimate "du" form, Wilhelmine now offers her body to Hölderlin and makes it very clear that she allows herself the right to enjoy sensual pleasures without necessarily committing herself to a man. One century before the Russian writer Aleksandra Kollontai (1872–1952), Wilhelmine Kirms advocates free love. Yet her revolutionary views on sexuality leave Hölderlin perplexed, and he is afraid to accept her offer to make love without any commitment (145).

Language, the necessary material for his craft, becomes an object of suspicion for Hölderlin. He spends the night in Fritz's bedroom in order to prevent the boy from masturbating, again a biographical detail that Weiss did not invent. While Hölderlin engages in a desperate soliloquy about the corruptibility and eventual loss of language, Fritz watches fearfully (147–49).

The scene ends with a versified discussion between the singer and commentator and two workers. The workers respond to the singer's defense of Hölderlin's attempts to find the image of a new human being by pointing out that the common people's thoughts have almost all been extinguished, that they, as opposed to the intellectuals whose works usually ignore, but are sustained by, the workers' invisible labor, have no time for speculative self-complaints and speculations (149).[34] From the perspective of the workers, Hölderlin belongs to those who ignore the reality of physical labor and social injustice.

The third scene, a controversial conversation about art and politics between Schiller, Hölderlin, and Goethe, whose identity becomes clear to Hölderlin only after Goethe leaves, takes place in Jena in 1794. Hölderlin passionately argues for a new way of writing:

> In grosser Form will ich / das Gegensäzliche zusammenfassen / Riesige Blöke sind / für mich Gedichte / reichster und leuchtendster / Materie. (154)

Later, Weiss will call his novel *Die Ästhetik des Widerstands* a formation of blocks. Contouring their aesthetic and political differences, Hölderlin says to Schiller, his long admired role model:

> Ich weiss es graust Sie / wenn ich zu meiner Welt auch / deren ununterbrochne / Auflösung mit nehme / wenn ich vom Fliessenden und / vom Veränderlichen ausgeh / und Zeichen suche dafür / wie alle Schranken niederbrechen. (155)

It is not Schiller, to whom Hölderlin addresses these poetological concerns, who responds, but Goethe. Hölderlin does not recognize the famous poet. In his view, he is a mere stranger who interrupts an important debate. Weiss bases Goethe's words in this scene on original letters in which Goethe describes his encounter with and advice for Hölderlin to his friend Schiller. In seemingly benevolent but in fact condescending words, Goethe instructs him about the importance of a moderate state of mind and of a loving eye that confines itself to thankfulness and modesty, and that expresses itself in humble depictions of a carefully chosen "idyllisches Factum." An example for Weiss's philological research in preparation for this play lies in the fact that this passage is almost literally taken from two letters about Hölderlin that Goethe sent to Schiller in the summer of 1797 (156–57).[35]

When Schiller reiterates the dominant view of established intellectuals that patience is necessary and that slow educational changes are the precondition for change, the disappointed and desperate Hölderlin is addressed by the play's anonymous singer and commentator, who reminds him of the core conflict that every vision of change has to face, the gap between lofty theory and material praxis. While Goethe is leafing through a bundle of manuscripts, Schiller lectures on the education of human beings. Hölderlin contradicts him with his own list of priorities:

Nein / erst muss von Grund auf / alles umgeworfen werden / dass Neues / entstehen kann. (158)

Goethe and Hölderlin, who always talk at cross-purposes, or who rather recognize each other's purposes all too well, end their brief encounter in aggressive miscommunication. Hölderlin claims that not working toward fundamental political change is a sign of cowardice, but the celebrated writer does not deem this remark worthy of a response. Addressing only Schiller, Goethe diagnoses Hölderlin's impatience as deviant and as an illustration of the truism that blending aesthetic endeavors and political interests has to be avoided in order to focus on the purely human and on timeless values. When Goethe leaves, Hölderlin asks Schiller who the other visitor was who always interrupted their conversation. When Schiller mentions that it was Goethe, Hölderlin loses his ability to talk. Struck by the embarrassing surprise that the conservative pragmatist who annoyed him so much was in fact one of the cultural role models of his youth, the author of the poem *Prometheus* and other liberating texts, Hölderlin screams and breathes stertorously (159–60).

The fourth scene's prologue includes workers who voice their skepticism about all intellectual and theatrical rhetoric of social concern. A female worker insists that their sons should have access to universities instead of being exposed to hard physical labor and forced to remain illiterate (161).[36]

Weiss's stage directions imply an ironic criticism of Fichte, the most radical philosopher of his time, who wrote pamphlets in support of the French Revolution. The scene puts the emphasis on the fact that even he is afraid of the concrete consequences of his teachings and retreated to the same abstract humanistic ideology of patience and educational evolution that Goethe, Schiller, and Hegel have at their effortless disposal. When Fichte approaches the podium, the male and female workers leave (162).[37]

Weiss inserts passages of student fraternities' choruses that seem to foreshadow, and in fact use the same slogans as, the Nazis, highlighting the unfortunate reception history and the propagandistic misuses of some of Fichte's speeches against Napoleon (166; 169–71).[38] In the eighth scene of the second act, students burn books. While the historical Fichte resigned from his position of university president in Berlin because he was the only faculty member who wanted to punish fraternities that harassed a Jewish student, and while he never was a racist or a militarist, he was nevertheless turned into a forefather of fascism both by the fascists and by some modern scholars. Not unlike Nietzsche, who aimed his sharpest polemical attacks at Prussian militarism and anti-Semitism, Fichte's works have been, and still are, rather plucked for catchy half sentences than thoroughly read. In his postscript to *Hölderlin*, Weiss writes that it is suffocating to see how Fichte's progressive demands could be turned into their opposite and be misused by nationalists and fascists (420).[39]

The fifth and final scene of the first act takes place in Frankfurt, where Hölderlin and Hegel work as private teachers in the households of influential bankers and merchants who take walks and indulge in praising the blessings of the world market and the survival of the fittest. The stage directions suggest that through fast movements and constant repositionings, as well as by using music that repeatedly seems to recede and come closer again, the whole scene should be reminiscent of a danse macabre (172). A dance of death is also taking place in the form of a conversation between the merchants and bank owners who regret that there are no German colonies comparable to British and Dutch possessions overseas. They sugar their obsession for money with benevolent words of support for the arts and of gracious humanism and the necessity to educate and control peoples of other continents for their own good.

While Hölderlin is regularly humiliated by his employer and reminded that he is not much more than a servant, Hegel has managed to find a convenient arrangement and participates, as does Goethe, in the spirited discussions on trade and humanism. Weiss juxtaposes the elitist and hypocritical verbal exchanges of the owners of banks and of human beings on the one hand and brief and straightforward dialogues between workers who begin to wonder why they allow the aristocrats and mansion and park owners to be in charge while they easily outnumber them on the other (184).[40]

In his epistolary novel *Hyperion* (1792–98), Hölderlin includes one of the harshest criticisms of German indifference toward free thought and imagination that can be found in German literature. Weiss integrates some formulations from Hyperion's complaint and passages from Hölderlin's letters into this scene. When Goethe approaches "den Holterlein" and offers him aesthetic advice, Hölderlin replies:

> [. . .] es ist ein kleines Stük nur / von entlegner Helligkeit / meines eignen Landes / dessen Gegenwarth / in Finsternissen / sich verbirgt / In Griechenland war ich noch nicht / hier aber war ich allzu lang / und mein Anruf Griechenlands / ist Aufruf zur Zertrümmrung / des elendiglichen MachWercks / in dem wir uns zu jeder Stunde degradiren / [. . .] / Dies Land / es ist ein DungHauffen. (191)

Weiss's Goethe prefers not to respond and walks away, asking Hegel about a diagnosis of Hölderlin's psychopathology. Hegel's answer, the only passage in which he is not reduced to an opportunistic pragmatist, shows that he has not forgotten that the main intuitions of his philosophy derived from Hölderlin. However, Hegel's characterization of his former mentor has already transformed sympathetic understanding into a distanced prognosis of Hölderlin's inevitable self-destruction:

> Keiner / hat meinem Denken / so viel Anregung gegeben / wie Hölderlin / Manche seiner Visionen / hab ich mir in mein System / des Rationalen übertragen / Doch keiner auch / ist dem Zermürbenden so / ausgesezt wie er / Ein Wort beiläufig / ohne Absicht ausgesprochen / trift ihn ins Hertz / Die Welt wird ihn / bis auf den Grund / zerstören. (193)

The vulnerability of the poet and thinker who believes in change, and therefore experiences pain when the status quo gains strength and celebrates itself, has become the object of cold reflection. Weiss might refer here to the implicit pathological characterization of Hölderlin in Hegel's *Phänomenologie des Geistes,* published in 1807, when Hölderlin was already admitted to a mental institution. In his chapter "Das Gesetz des Herzens und der Wahnsinn des Eigendünkels" (The Law of the Heart and the Madness of Self-Conceit), Hegel attacks any emotionally motivated resistance to an existing political order as madness and defends hierarchical power structures as superior to its critics, since it has endured a certain time while some passionate opponents have perished. But the first act of the play does not end in intellectual sublimation of the existing order. Workers' choruses alternate with Hölderlin's friend, the poet Schmid, in emphasizing the material conditions and global forms of exploitation. Schmid extends his critique to the United States and its system of slavery (195).[41]

The second act of *Hölderlin* is set in 1799 in Homburg vor der Höhe, near Frankfurt, where Hölderlin's friend Isaak von Sinclair has found a job for Hölderlin as a librarian for a duke. Sinclair was a central figure for Hesse, and his name reappears as Weiss's chosen pseudonym for the long-delayed publication of his novel *Der Fremde* in 1980. Hölderlin is visited by old friends for whom he recites passages from his drama *Der Tod des Empedokles* (1798–99). Before the play begins, however, they engage in personal and political disputes. Arguing about Napoleon, Schmid's and Hölderlin's views stand in sharp contrast to those of Hegel. Schmid is characterized as a radical revolutionary who has become a volunteer soldier in the German fight against Napoleon, whom he despises as the traitor of the revolution (200).[42] Hegel, on the other hand, defends Napoleon as a heroic figure comparable to Caesar and Alexander, as a lucid and pragmatic politician whose deeds are justified because he is inhabited by the world spirit. Hölderlin interrupts Hegel impatiently and calls Napoleon a monster (201).[43] Schmid expresses his suspicion that Schelling and Hegel have turned into opportunistic conservatives who affirm the existing order of the state in order to achieve a tenured status at their universities. Hegel, far from taking offense to this insult, summarizes the pragmatic difference between him on the one hand and Schmid and Hölderlin on the other:

> Ich steh auf dem Boden / der Gegebenheiten / Du und Holder / ihr seyd immer im Begriff / euch weg zu werfen. (201)

Their political debate continues and includes a discussion of the characters in Hölderlin's drama *Der Tod des Empedokles,* in which the philosopher Empedocles is depicted as an aging spiritual leader who turns down the crown when the people of Agrigent offer it to him. Weiss's stage instructions ascribe the role of amplifying Hölderlin's own vision and voice to a chorus that remains invisible to the audience. During the play within the play, single members of the chorus step forward and give a voice to the characters of Hölderlin's drama.

While he is facing political intrigues that are orchestrated by Hermokrates, a power hungry high priest, and other opponents, Empedocles retreats to Mt. Aetna and jumps into the volcano. Schelling expresses a thorough interest and sympathy with Empedocles, while Hegel dismisses his behavior as a sign and result of inexcusable political incompetence. Admitting that the material upon which his play is based is not easily accessible for modern readers anymore, Hölderlin urges his friends to listen carefully in order to bridge the gap of alterity:

> Was ihm geschieht / ist unaussprechlich / streng und kalt / Die fremde Welt und / die Gestalten drinn / für die wir noch / Vergleichbares / nicht kennen / versuch ich / nah zu rüken / Höret gut zu / so lässt vielleicht / die grosse Trennung / von dem kühnen und / entlegnen Stoff / sich überwinden. (210–11)

It can be argued that Weiss's efforts to reintroduce Hölderlin to his audience parallels Hölderlin's attempts in this play to expose his potential audience and readership to the struggle of Empedocles. If Empedocles serves as a chiffre for the unattainability of spiritual and political change for Hölderlin, the figure of Hölderlin becomes one of Weiss's most incisive operational tools to mark the precariousness and the importance of an alliance of art and political praxis. In the postscript to his drama, Weiss highlights Hölderlin's consistent political stance and the fact that he never compromised his views. Weiss even considers the possibility that Hölderlin disintegrated less than his opportunistic and seemingly healthy visitors.[44] Horst Heilmann, one of the resistance fighters in Weiss's summum opus, the novel *Die Ästhetik des Widerstands,* is an avid reader of Hölderlin and Rimbaud, and lives in Berlin's Hölderlin Street.

Hegel and Schelling react to the *Empedocles* rehearsal with varying degrees of rejection. While Hegel comments that even an imperfect state is justified to defend itself against subversive outsiders such as Empedocles, Schelling employs a reconciliatory strategy and reads Hölderlin's play as an apotheosis of poetry. Poetry, Schelling argues, is the only remaining realm where human beings are able to revolutionize their personality (215).[45] Weiss puts the most concrete interpretive question into the mouth of the glazier Wagner, who asks how Empedocles and his small group of loyal followers can help the oppressed people when in fact without their help they would not be able to survive by themselves. Hölderlin tells Wagner that his skeptical question was right on target and that the point was to end the lethargic habit of waiting for charismatic leaders:

> Reisst euch / aus der Genügsamkeit / Erwartet nicht / dass euch zu helfen ist / wenn ihr euch selbst nicht helft / Beginnet eure eigne Zeit / und macht euch auf den Weg. (216)

Hölderlin defends his protagonist Empedocles by describing him as more alive and more lucid than the Agrigentians, a phrase that Weiss, in his notebooks, also uses to describe Hölderlin. The playwright within the play uses the antagonistic configuration of his Empedocles drama in order to criticize his former friends by counting Hegel and other seemingly omniscient and saturated spectators among the self-congratulatory opportunists who first idolize and then persecute any Empedocles. When Hegel criticizes the conceptualization and the character of Empedocles as too artificial, utopian, and incapable of calm and cunning self-reflection, Hölderlin counters the attack by identifying smart and distanced literary critics like Hegel as the source of Empedocles's suffering and of his alleged sickness (219–20).[46] The scene ends with the invisible chorus's insistence on the unfinished character of art and revolution:

> Deshalb erwägt / den Aufruf / der aus der Stille / von den Bergen kommt / und sezt ihm selbst / die Worte und / die Handlung. (225)

This gnomic apostrophe foreshadows Weiss's *Die Ästhetik des Widerstands,* in which the narrator and the protagonists discuss the Pergamon frieze and the disturbing fact that Heracles's face has been extinguished from it. Rather than mourning the loss of clearly delineated guidelines or facial features of a resistance leader, they agree to read it as an opportunity to fill that absence with their own thoughts and lives.

In the seventh scene of the second act, Hölderlin is imprisoned in Tübingen's mental institution, which today hosts the philosophy department of the Eberhard-Karls-Universität Tübingen. Immobilized by a straitjacket not unlike Jacques Roux in Weiss's *Marat/Sade* play, under medication, and deprived of his face and his sense of sight by a leather mask, he is interrogated about his political activities by Autenrieth, the director of the institution. Hölderlin hallucinates the appearance of former friends, first the revolutionary Buonarroti, then the love of his life, Susette Gontard, followed by his friend Isaak von Sinclair, Siegfried Schmid, and his mother. Weiss makes use of passages from authentic letters to and from Hölderlin for this scene. The sequence of dreamlike appearances amidst the interrogation ends with a singer who summarizes the scene and announces the transition to the following parts of the play, and who also directly addresses Hölderlin with a question that draws connections to contemporary victims of violence:

> [. . .] und die Eingekerckerten noch nicht befreyt / Möchten wissen ob deine Absage an die Revoluzion / blos Verstellung war oder Hohn / vor all deinen FolterKnechten und ÜberMännern / den SeelenDoctoren und politischen Kennern / Sag uns besteht für dich noch ein Hoffen / siehst du den Weg zur Erneurung noch offen / oder musstest du bei der Anstrengung scheitern / dir die Gränzen deines Denckens zu erweitern. (237)

Using the formulaic rhetoric of subservience that the historical Hölderlin employed throughout his decades in the tower, the protagonist replies slowly that a precise and exhaustive answer to this question will be provided in the distant future (238).

The final scene of the play echoes allusions to the Nazi dictatorship from the first act. Students burn books for political reasons, including Enlightenment texts by Diderot, Voltaire, and Rousseau, as well as by French revolutionaries such as Saint-Just, Robespierre, and Jacques Roux, who appears as the most radical activist and patient in Weiss's play *Marat/Sade*. This scene addresses the complex reception history of Hölderlin's myth and works in Germany. Hölderlin's central poetological term "Vaterland," which had nothing to do with Germany but denoted an imaginary Greek realm of breathable air and free and harmonious life, was abused not only by fascist ideologists but also by nationalists during the First World War, when it was turned into a code word to inspire young German soldiers to kill and to die more willingly. What the German military leaders did ignore was that Hölderlin's hymn *Germanien* (around 1801) belongs to a European tradition of pacifist literature. Splinters of Hölderlin's work, not unlike decontextualized parts of Nietzsche's writings, were violently extracted from their texts and splashed into militaristic propaganda stew.

Another embarrassing factor in German cultural history remains the fact that many German literary scholars, including Friedrich Beissner who presided over the still most influential Hölderlin edition, were active supporters of the Nazi system. Weiss critiques at once German cultural establishments from around 1800 and literary institutions and universities of his time when he has students act out declarations that conflate Hölderlin's work and their own nationalistic violence (242).[47] At first, Weiss's Hölderlin does not comprehend what the students say and what they are doing. Eventually, Hölderlin covers his face with his hands and sobs when he hears a student misusing his name by evoking him as the patron of the book burning (243–44).[48]

Hegel and Schelling visit Hölderlin in his Tübingen tower. This encounter is fictional. Hölderlin was a philosophical mentor for both Hegel and Schelling. However, they retreated from him as soon as he displayed his first symptoms of mental imbalance. The play is, however, congruent with biographical data in describing Hegel and Schelling as intellectuals who abandon the enthusiastic radicalism of their youth in order to embark upon successful academic careers. Both became established professors of philosophy and exchanged letters in which they distance themselves from Hölderlin, whom they refer to as incurably insane. Eventually, they not only discontinue their communication with him, but even cease to talk about him.

Basing his scene on biographical anecdotes that depict Hölderlin's subservient role-play with many visitors, Weiss portrays Hölderlin as employing an ironic stance toward his former friends who have become such successful intellectual celebrities. When Hegel tries to persuade him to recite passages from his lyrical work, Hölderlin cunningly replies:

> Lieber würd ich von Euro erstaunlichen / über alle Maassen erhobnen Majestäthen / erfahrn wies denn zugeht dort draussen / in der grossen von Ihnen durch und durch / erblikten verstandnen erläuterten und / gutgeheissnen Welt. (247)

Unwilling to notice Hölderlin's ironic undertone, a complacent Hegel begins to lecture with satisfaction about the seeming return of stability, recovering markets, and the seamless reintroduction of political and economic hierarchies. Hölderlin, in panic, retreats to the tower window and silently addresses the many oppressed ones, even alluding to the desirability of a violent uprising (248).[49]

With growing sarcasm, Hölderlin entices Hegel to continue his pseudo-rational praise of the growth of the Prussian nation (248).[50] Hegel enjoys the opportunity of literally having a captive audience and praises the growing strength of the "teutsche Nation." He enthusiastically outlines the role model function of the military and the advent of a much longed for purifying storm. Hölderlin reacts with roaring laughter and describes Hegel's rhapsodic praise as horror itself. When Hegel responds with the cynical statement that it is Germany's mission to regenerate the world, which foreshadows, and is reminiscent of, the popular Nazi slogan "am deutschen Wesen soll die Welt genesen," Hölderlin rushes to the window, tears it open, and laughs. He then recites anguished fragmentary verses that address an irreversibly approaching ferryboat of death, a growing impossibility to gain breath, and an inescapable omnipresence of lethal sounds, among which Hegel's words can be counted (249).[51]

When Schelling tries to subject Hölderlin to a more gentle and religious therapy by kneeling down before him and praying that he will pray, Hölderlin rushes to his piano, hammering it with his fists.

Finally, Weiss's Hölderlin is visited by a young journalist. The visitor summarizes their differences without condemning the poet's retreat from the outside world:

> Zwei Wege sind gangbar / zur Vorbereitung / grundlegender Veränderungen / Der eine Weg ist / die Analyse der konkreten / historischen Situation / Der andre Weg ist / die visionäre Formung / tiefster persönlicher Erfahrung. (254)

The journalist's name is Karl Marx. The encounter, invented by Weiss, serves to emphasize his belief in the complementary nature of exploratory writing and focused political projects. During the conversation with Marx, Hölderlin sometimes recedes into trancelike states and directs his words more often to himself than to his young visitor. However, Marx's comments stir up his forgotten political activist interests and bring Hölderlin close to a renewed awareness of himself and the world around him.

In the final scene of the play, an epilogue in the guise of a "tableau of an apotheosis," the protagonist Hölderlin becomes a distanced self-commentator who has already historicized himself. Hölderlin performs a summarizing endnote in which he postulates the necessity of a simultaneous emergence of imaginative thought and praxis. In Hölderlin's view, they have to form creative dialogues with each other rather than forming static oppositions:

> [. . .] nicht trennen will er aus dem Wircklichen den Thraum / es müssen Fantaisie und Handlung seyn im gleichen Raum / nur so wird das Poetische *universal* / bekämpfend alles was verbraucht und schaal / erloschen und versteinert uns bedrängt / und was mit Zwang und Drohung unsern Athemzug beengt. (260)

In his autobiographical journal *Rekonvaleszenz,* Weiss mentions that his uncle in Tübingen, to whom he was sent by his parents as a young boy for a summer of strict regulations and punishments, was probably a descendant of Ferdinand Autenrieth, the director of the mental institution who put Hölderlin in a straitjacket and a leather mask.[52] Weiss addresses the importance of his *Hölderlin* drama for a poetological and ethical discussion of writing by emphasizing that unlike his other works, this play is connected to his personal attempt to face surrounding con- tradictions and blockages.[53] Further thinking through the affinities be- tween himself and his colleague from around 1800, Weiss argues that Hölderlin perishes because he tries to connect his dream with reality outside. Accentuating his elective affinity to Hölderlin, Weiss writes that such a union is not possible yet, "jedenfalls nicht zu seinen Lebzeiten, und vielleicht zu meinen auch nicht."[54]

Der Prozeß. Stück in zwei Akten, Weiss's stage adaptation of Franz Kafka's novel *Der Proceß* (1925), premiered in two German cities on the same day in 1975. One production opened in Bremen, under the direc- tion of Helm Bindseil, and the other in Krefeld, directed by Joachim Fontheim.[55] Over the next two years, it was performed in a few other German cities as well as in Norway and Yugoslavia. In his introductory reflections on this play, Weiss points out that he was not interested in updating or transforming the original text's plot or style. He describes as his only goal to find scenic strategies in order to put Kafka's prose on stage. However, Weiss argues that his translation of Kafka's text into theatrical praxis requires that the protagonist is situated in his historical time and shown to be embedded in a web of social relations. Only then can personal idiosyncrasies as well as societal structures, "Verhaltenswei- sen, Vorkommnisse, Aktionen," be made visible on stage:

> Bei einer Übersetzung des Traums in die Sprache der äußeren Wirk- lichkeit (und für den Zuschauer entspricht die Bühne immer einer äu- ßeren Wirklichkeit) entstehen sofort Abhängigkeitsverhältnisse zur Zeitdimension. Die Bühne verlangt nach einer Logik. Auch in der äu- ßersten Absurdität noch ist jeder vollzogene Schritt auf einem vorange- gangenen Schritt basiert. [. . .] Etwas Vergangenes wird wiederbelebt und in seinem Ablauf demonstriert. Auf der Bühne wird festgestellt, wie K, der als Schriftfigur völlig auf sich selbst gestellt war, und sich selbst genügte, auf andere wirkt. (264–65)

This statement reflects the lexical ambiguity of the word "Prozess" which not only denotes a trial, but also a process. Weiss emphasizes the use of the stage as a laboratory that allows the spectators to witness artistic psychosocial experiments. In his introductory essay, Weiss devel- ops a Marxian reading of Kafka's text. According to Weiss's interpreta- tion, K, who inhabits a rather high corporate position and who makes use of patriarchal patterns of behavior towards women, perishes because he is incapable of breaking out of his class. Immobilized by his own his lack of political awareness, K remains stuck between the distorting mir- rors of an order whose stability he fails to question (267).[56]

Shortly before his death, Weiss revisits the Kafka project. Although Weiss dedicates *Der neue Prozeß. Stück in drei Akten* (1982) to Franz Kafka, this new theatrical version of Kafka's novel is not a close adaptation like Weiss's earlier Kafka drama.[57] This completely new play only borrows some topical elements and names from Kafka's prose. Weiss injects not only heavy doses of an anticapitalist impetus into the plot, but, as Kremer writes, he also adds the stubborn resistance of grotesque animality. *Der neue Prozeß* was Weiss's last play.[58] Weiss and his wife, Gunilla Palmstierna-Weiss, also directed the drama, which premiered in Stockholm in 1982. One year later, the first German performance was directed by Roberto Ciulli in Berlin. The first American version was put on stage at Duke University in 1998. Today, this drama reads like a lucid critique of globalization and multinational companies.

In his reflections on *Der neue Prozeß*, Weiss insists that Josef K and the other characters are his and his audiences' contemporaries. He dismisses any mystical or religious connotations, latent layers of attraction that might have been operative in Kafka's work. Weiss wants to focus on the internal contradictions of people who desperately attempt to adapt to or to liberate themselves from the rules of capitalist society.[59] Only two characters in the play, Leni and the subversive painter Titorelli, keep their personalities from being split. Weiss's commentary to his last play highlights that K is to be shown as an exemplarily scrupulous man who is at once ridiculed, humiliated, and officially elevated to the highest rank by his corporation in order to provide them with an image of ethical concern and with a compassionate face. K realizes too late that the company has turned his civil presence and humanistic ideals into their alibi.[60]

In the beginning scene of the first act, K is surprised by a grotesque nocturnal visit. Three men from his company, Franz and Willem, two workers who will later make swift careers and who will eventually literally watch him die like a dog in the final scene of the play, as well as the engineer Kaminer, let themselves into his room in the middle of the night to examine the disturbing noise that he has complained about. K's room is full of books, newspaper articles, and pictures of Don Quixote and Dante, and of witch burnings, reproductions of paintings by Bosch, Brueghel, Rousseau, and Picasso, and sculptures that are modeled after Degas and Gauguin. Insisting that their measuring device does not indicate any acoustic disturbances, the visitors do not believe K's claim that he can still hear a noise (341–42). The door to his landlady's apartment and to K's series of embarrassing humiliations opens at the end of this scene. The nocturnal visitors and the nephew of K's landlady, a military officer who eagerly awaits the next war, indulge in a loud conversation over breakfast in the second scene.

In the third scene, Frau Grubach, his landlady, helps K to get dressed, obviously a daily routine. She tries to comfort him about the rude behavior of the disturbing guests and of her nephew, who all ridiculed K, claiming that he was out of touch with life's necessities and a nuisance since he was whining about small details such as the noise in his apartment that they interpret as a product of his overly sensitive imagination. K eventually reveals the core of his discontent to Frau Grubach, his unsuccessful search for comprehensive explanations and for a clear understanding of everything, his longing for a free society in which nothing and nobody is misunderstood (345).[61]

At times, seemingly negligible stage directions turn out to foreshadow later events. For example, when his landlady is binding his tie, K exposes his neck, and at the beginning of scene 4, everything that used to be identifiable in the room is fading (346–47).[62] In the fourth scene, K reiterates his need for a comprehensive knowledge of his surroundings. He confides to Rabensteiner, a career minded colleague who reminds him of the necessity of possessing expertise in the real estate market and global capital transactions, that a only a concrete and overarching order is the object of his desire:

> Grade das Gesicherte ist es, das mich unsicher macht. Grade das Feste, Geordnete läßt mir alles fragwürdig erscheinen. Nicht, daß ich die Ordnung nicht wollte. Ich will die Ordnung! Aber eine andre Ordnung. Wie soll ich Ihnen das erklären — ich will eine größere Ordnung, eine Ordnung, in der alles übereinstimmt. (349)

K makes unsuccessful attempts to court his colleague and next door neighbor, Fräulein Bürstner, who herself is entrapped in the hierarchical structures of their company, but masks her humiliation with an aggressive attitude. She seemingly enjoys the fact that K is even more miserable. There is, however, a brief moment in the ninth scene when the two of them have a true exchange of thoughts about art, which K identifies as his tool to temporarily forget his helplessness because it points at something inherently different from what surrounds him in daily life. Fräulein Bürstner counters K's utopian identifications by reminding him of art's closeness to death (360–61).

Having been relieved of his previous function, which included the handling of complaints, a task that he has pursued with fairness and sympathy and, in the eyes of the company, in an all too lenient way, K is promoted to a rather nebulous position. His new job is to provide the firm with an image of ethical correctness and compassion. With Leni, his new secretary who becomes a true friend and who does not follow her original order to report on K to the company, K visits several illegal political meetings. When K is wondering why so many people are attending the meetings, Leni responds that the lack of organizational predictability forms the main point of attraction (377).[63] But the spark of spontaneous resistance does not glimmer for a long time in the play. One of K's new responsibilities consists of conceptualizing a plan to provide the company with aesthetic ornaments. As Kaminer puts it in words that display a cunning satisfaction, "Kunst ist Teil unsrer Politik" (380).

Scene 19, toward the end of the second act, provides contours of a state of mind that might enable one to disentangle oneself from the web of globalized greed and opportunism, which the play depicts as almost inescapable. In his reflections on his art and craft, the painter Titorelli refuses all nostalgic escapism and insists that being an artist means to do violence to life. According to Titorelli, art should not deliver any harmonious components for the sake of achieving soothing edification. When K and Leni tentatively ask him whether he creates clarity or beauty, Titorelli replies that purity is an illusion of consumers of art. In his eyes, his paintings embody dirt, blood, and feces (383).[64] Titorelli has also given up the myth of the inspired solitary artist. He frequently invites people from the street to participate in the production of his paintings, the messier the process of cooperation, he points out, the better. His vulnerability, which manifests itself in repeated emotional breakdowns, and his emphasized disillusionment about his craft and the world of which it is a part have led the painter Titorelli to a mental state of emptiness that allows him to survive in a rebellious niche. He has created a minimal habitat of creative resistance for himself in which nothing is predictable (384).[65] Titorelli is the only character in the play that dares to voice his opposition to corporate globalizers. When an American ambassador, who displays an elaborate interest in ethics and in the arts, enthusiastically thanks him for delivering humanistic paintings to office buildings, Titorellis's laconic and dismissive response is unequivocal. He insists that his paintings are not for them but rather aimed against them (395).[66] Throughout the rest of the play, Weiss parodizes rhetorical strategies of a powerful elite, which presents itself as immensely concerned about peace and human progress but cynically uses these terms as code words for war and the ruthless destruction of human values.

At the end of both *Prozeß* plays, K is stabbed. He dies "wie ein Hund." While in Kafka's novel, K himself uses these final words to comment on his life and death as a continued shameful embarrassment, Weiss's dramas of the trial and process of K's not-lived life end with Willem, one of his killers, using the very same words while watching him die (336; 407).[67] Weiss's *Prozeß* dramas leave out that in Kafka's novel the protagonist concedes, seconds before his death, that counterarguments had been forgotten and that the logic of obedience and suffocation, as unshakeable as they might appear, does not resist a human being who wants to live.[68]

As the discussions of these plays show, Weiss was far from being a deconstructionist. He can be read as a modernist who still seeks lucidity and a recognizable nexus of mind and society. *Der neue Prozess,* his final play, puts the processes and procedures of obedience on trial and insists on the necessity to be rewritten by creatively receptive readers and audiences.

Notes

[1] All following excerpts and quotations from this play refer to the following edition: *Die Verfolgung und Ermordung Jean Paul Marats dargestellt durch die Schauspielgruppe des Hospizes zu Charenton unter Anleitung des Herrn de Sade. Drama in zwei Akten.* In Peter Weiss, *Werke in sechs Bänden. Vierter Band,* edited by Suhrkamp Verlag in cooperation with Gunilla Palmstierna-Weiss (Frankfurt a.M.: Suhrkamp, 1991), 155–255.

[2] See *La Stampa,* July 22, 1993, 24; July 13, 1997, 26.

[3] For a survey of the reception history of the play, see Christine Frisch,*"Geniestreich," "Lehrstück," "Revolutionsgestammel": Zur Rezeption des Dramas "Marat/Sade" von Peter Weiss in der Literaturwissenschaft und auf den Bühnen der Bundesrepublik Deutschland, der Deutschen Demokratischen Republik und Schwedens* (Stockholm: Almqvist & Wiksell International, 1992).

[4] "Interniert von wegen politischer Radikalität / [. . .] / Leider hat die Zensur sehr viel / gestrichen von seinen Aussagen im Spiel / denn sie gingen in ihrem Ton zu weit / für die Ordnungsbewahrer in unserer Zeit."

[5] *"Sie steht ständig unter der Obhut von zwei Schwestern, die sie stützen, kämmen und ihr die Kleider ordnen. Ihre Bewegungen sind die einer Somnambulen."*

[6] "Wer beherrscht die Markthallen / Wer hält die Speicher verschlossen / Wer hat die Reichtümer aus den Schlössern ergattert / Wer sitzt auf den Ländereien / die an uns verteilt werden sollten." Coulmier reacts to the unexpected radical turn, 168: "Herr de Sade / [. . .] / Ich muß doch um etwas Besänftigung bitten / [. . .] / und wir sollten uns bemühen / die längst überwundenen Mißstände / in einem etwas verklärten Schimmer zu sehen." The stage directions offer the dirty and realistic reverse side of Coulmier's humanistic call for serenity, 168: *"Die Patienten werden von den Pflegern zurückgedrängt. Ein paar Schwestern stellen sich vor den Patienten auf und singen eine Litanei zur Beruhigung."*

[7] "Jeder Tod auch der grausamste / ertrinkt in der völligen Gleichgültigkeit der Natur / [. . .] / die Natur würde schweigend zusehn / rotteten wir unsere ganze

Rasse aus / Ich hasse die Natur / ich will sie überwinden / ich will sie mit ihren eigenen Waffen schlagen / in ihren eigenen Fallen fangen / [. . .] / Dieses reglose Zusehn dieses Gesicht aus Eis / Daß nichts sie erschüttern kann."

[8] Sade summarizes his diagnosis and prognosis of society and nature in these lines, which seem to sum up the twentieth century and its continuation, see 179: "[. . .] nur ein anonymes entwertetes Sterben / in das wir ganze Völker schicken könnten / in kalter Berechnung / bis es einmal soweit ist / alles Leben / aufzuheben." Marat, however, while not questioning Sade's observation, insists on the urgent importance of an inventive and decisive intervention, see 180: "In der großen Gleichgültigkeit / erfinde ich einen Sinn / Anstatt reglos zuzusehn [like nature's face of ice, according to Sade, see the preceding footnote] / greife ich ein / und ernenne gewisse Dinge für falsch / und arbeite daran sie zu verändern und zu verbessern / [. . .] / und alles mit neuen Augen zu sehn."

[9] "Falsch Sade falsch / mit der Ruhlosigkeit der Gedanken / läßt sich keine Mauer durchbrechen / Mit der Schreibfeder kannst du keine Ordnungen umwerfen / Wie wir uns auch abmühen das Neue zu fassen / es entsteht doch erst / zwischen ungeschickten Handlungen."

[10] See 193–95: "[. . .] ob radikal oder gemäßigt / alle wollen sie Blut lecken / [. . .] wir nennens / Gerechtigkeit wenn wir verurteilen und köpfen / [. . .] / Marat / siehst du den Irrsinn dieser Vaterlandsliebe / ich sage dir / ich habe diesen Heroismus längst / aufgegeben / ich pfeife auf diese Nation / so wie ich auf alle andern Nationen pfeife / [. . .] / Ich pfeife auf alle guten Absichten."

[11] "Deine mönchische Kleidung ist nach meinem Sinn / denn das ist jetzt das beste / immer bereit zu sein / sich im Sack zu verkriechen / aufzutauchen in günstigen Momenten / dann schnell wieder weg wenns sein muß / Deine Kutte Jacques Roux / ist ein gutes Mimikri."

[12] See 204–5: "Ich tat alles um sie freizusprechen oder entkommen zu lassen / Ich sah daß ich nicht fähig war zum Mord / [. . .] / als die Karren mit ihrer Ladung regelmäßig zum Richtplatz fuhren / und das Beil fiel und hochgezurrt wurde und wieder fiel / [. . .] / da war dieser Vergeltung schon jeder Sinn genommen / es war eine mechanische Vergeltung / [. . .] / ausgeführt in einer stumpfen Unmenschlichkeit / in einer eigentümlichen Technokratie."

[13] "Marat / diese Gefängnisse des Innern / sind schlimmer als die tiefsten steinernen Verliese / und solange sie nicht geöffnet werden / bleibt all euer Aufruhr / nur eine Gefängnisrevolte / die niedergeschlagen wird / von bestochenen Mitgefangenen."

[14] "Es war unsre Absicht in den Dialogen / Antithesen auszuproben / [. . .] / Jedoch finde ich wie ichs auch dreh und wende / in unserm Drama zu keinem Ende / [. . .] / So sehn Sie mich in der gegenwärtigen Lage / immer noch vor einer offenen Frage."

[15] See for example Weiss's statement in a letter to the magazine *Neue Kritik* from December 1965, quoted in Martin Rector, "Die Verfolgung und Ermordung Jean Paul Marats dargestellt durch die Schauspielgruppe des Hospizes zu Charenton unter Anleitung des Herrn de Sade," in *Peter Weiss' Dramen: Neue Interpretationen*, edited by Martin Rector and Christoph Weiss (Opladen and Wiesbaden: Westdeutscher Verlag, 1999), 57–88. Here: 82: "Natürlich ist es auch dialektisch wichtig, daß im

Marat-Stück die beiden Hauptfiguren Marat und Sade gleichstark einander gegen-
überstehen." Weiss de-emphasizes the play's turbulent dramatic effects in an inter-
view with Volker Canaris from 1971, in *Peter Weiss im Gespräch,* edited by Rainer
Gerlach and Matthias Richter (Frankfurt a.m.: Suhrkamp, 1986), 187: "Ich kann mir
Aufführungen des 'Marat' vorstellen, wie sie bisher noch nicht verwirklicht wurden.
Zum Beispiel als sehr verhaltenes Kammerspiel. Das 'Theatralische' im Marat hat sich
oft als schädliche Eigenschaft gezeigt." On Weiss multiple drafts of *Marat/Sade,* see
Arnd Beise and Ingo Breuer, "Vier, fünf oder mindestens zehn Fassungen? Entste-
hungsphasen des Marat/Sade von Peter Weiss," in *Peter Weiss Jahrbuch* 1 (1992):
86–115. Also compare Herbert Wender, "Entwicklungsstufen und Fassungen in der
Textgeschichte des Marat/Sade: Anmerkungen zum Beitrag von Beise und Breuer
in PWJ 1 (1992)," in *Peter Weiss Jahrbuch* 3 (1994): 153–65.

[16] All following excerpts and quotations from this play refer to the following edition:
Trotzki im Exil. Stück in zwei Akten. In Peter Weiss, *Werke in sechs Bänden. Sechster
Band,* edited by Suhrkamp Verlag in cooperation with Gunilla Palmstierna-Weiss
(Frankfurt a.M.: Suhrkamp, 1991), 7–107.

[17] "*Die Auftritte schnell, überraschend.*"

[18] Michael Rohrwasser, "*Trotzki im Exil,*" in *Peter Weiss' Dramen: Neue Interpretationen,* edited by Martin Rector and Christoph Weiss (Opladen and Wiesbaden:
Westdeutscher Verlag, 1999), 193–209. Here: 193; 197: "Aufbau und Zeitstruktur
des Dramas sind vielschichtiger, als es chronologisch vereindeutigte Inhaltsangaben
[. . .] vemuten lassen. [. . .] ein Gang ins Labyrinth der Szenen notwendig [. . .]
'Schnitten,' die abrupt eine andere Situation konfigurieren oder von langsamen
'Überblendungen,' die in der Regel mit den Schaltpolen Feldbett und Schreibtisch
vonstatten gehen."

[19] 16: Machajski argues: "Eine Partei, wie ihr sie euch vorstellt, wird nur wieder zu
einem neuen Mittel der Herrschaft. Ausbeutung des Proletariats durch eine neue
Elite von Beamten, Technikern, Wissenschaftlern. Ihr sprecht zwar vom Absterben
des Staats. Aber das werdet ihr vergessen, wenn ihr erst mal euern Machtapparat
habt. Wir wenden uns von Anfang an gegen den Staat, gegen die Institutionen,
gegen die Bürokratie." Trotsky's impatient response: "Sprache des vorigen Jahrhun-
derts, Machajski. Fortschritt liegt in der Macht der Forscher, Rechner, Organisato-
ren."

[20] 43: "Die Kunst muß dazu beitragen, die Welt zu verändern." Lenin goes a step
further by insisting that art has to be a tool of the party and that there is no absolute
freedom of artistic expression, see ibid.: "Es gibt keine absolute Freiheit für die
Kunst. Kunst muß parteilich sein."

[21] Lenin's unsatisfactory answer, ibid.: "Das Proletariat setzt die Normen."

[22] 64–67.: "Terror. Dieser Begriff hat viele von uns verwirrt. Wir wiesen den indivi-
duellen Terror ab. [. . .] Der einzige Terror, den wir je anerkannten, war der Mas-
senterror."

[23] See 74: "Wir wollten den Arbeiterstaat. Wir haben versucht, diesen Staat lebendig,
demokratisch zu machen. Wir konnten ihn nicht errichten ohne die zentralisierte
Partei. Und jetzt hat sich die Maschine gegen uns gekehrt. [. . .] Stalin, er muß aus
seinem Amt entfernt werden. Vielzuviel Macht in seinen Händen. Wartet nur drauf,

daß ich verschwinde. Um die Partei ganz an sich zu reißen. [. . .] Sie, Davidowitsch, sind der Fähigste. Aber Sie sind so voll von Ideen, daß Sie zu Extremen neigen. [. . .] Ja, Sie haben selbst Material geliefert zu dem monolithischen Staat, der jetzt aufwächst."

[24] See 101 and 103: "Breton. Wenn die Vorgänge nicht mehr faßbar scheinen, gerade dann muß unsre Vernunft einsetzen. Wir haben nur diese einzige Waffe. [. . .] Die Sowjetunion wird versteinern, wenn nicht Klarheit geschaffen wird über diese Zeit. Was geschehen ist, beweist nicht die Falschheit des Sozialismus, sondern die Gebrechlichkeit, die Unerfahrenheit in unsern revolutionären Handlungen. Es war uns nicht gelungen, menschliche Schwäche, menschliche Feigheit, menschliche Niedertracht zu vertilgen."

[25] See André Breton, *Oeuvres complètes* III (Paris: Gallimard, 1999), 8–15, and *Oeuvres complètes* II (Paris: Gallimard, 1992), 459: "'Transformer le monde,' a dit Marx; 'changer la vie,' a dit Rimbaud: ces deux mots d'ordre pour nous n'en font qu'un." Rimbaud's role in Peter Weiss's works is outlined by Monique Boussart, "Zur Rolle Rimbauds in Peter Weiss' Werk: Vom Alter ego zur mythischen Figur," in *Peter Weiss: Neue Fragen an alte Texte,* edited by Irene Heidelberger-Leonard (Opladen: Westdeutscher Verlag, 1994), 127–39.

[26] All following excerpts and quotations from this play refer to the following edition: *Hölderlin. Stück in zwei Akten.* In Peter Weiss, *Werke in sechs Bänden. Sechster Band,* edited by Suhrkamp Verlag in cooperation with Gunilla Palmstierna-Weiss (Frankfurt a.M.: Suhrkamp, 1991), 109–260.

[27] See Pierre Bertaux, *Hölderlin. Essai de biographie intérieure* (Paris: Hachette, 1936). Pierre Bertaux, *Hölderlin und die Französische Revolution* (Frankfurt a.M.: Suhrkamp, 1970). For a recent study of Hölderlin's poetic production in the tower see Bart Philipsen, *Die List der Einfalt. NachLese zu Hölderlins spätester Dichtung* (Munich: Fink, 1995).

[28] *Notizbücher 1971–1980* (Frankfurt a.M.: Suhrkamp, 1981), 797–804. See Pierre Bertaux's works, *Hölderlin. Essai de biographie intérieure* (Paris: Hachette, 1936) and *Hölderlin und die Französische Revolution* (Frankfurt a.M.: Suhrkamp, 1970).

[29] "[. . .] da lag der Thurm schon da / ganz nah am Nekar drauf er runtersah / durchs nidre Fenster seiner Cammer sonderbar / lag dort sein Kercker und er nahm ihn wahr. [. . .] stand dort am Nekar immerdar / sein Kercker nimmst ihn heut noch wahr."

[30] "Gewalth enthält das Element der Rache / der Blindheit und er Angst / Was umgestürzt wird und zerfällt / macht nur die Oberfläche nicht / das innre Wesen dieser Welt aus / der Grund des Seyns / ist die Idee / Wenn die Idee / Besiz ergriffen hat / von ihrer ganzen Zeit / dann ist die Zeit reif // zur Erneurung / Dazu führt nur / andauernde / geduldige / Erziehung."

[31] "Der abscheulichste und Bluth Trieffendste / aller Jacobiner / der rothe Marat / ist von einer aristocratischen Heldin / zu Todte gestochen worden. *Einige Sekunden Stille. Dann Schreie, Weinen.*"

[32] "*Hegel hat eine Prise Schnupftabak genommen. Er niest.*"

[33] "Wenn der Vatter weg ist / weint die Mama / ganz anders immer als / wenn er bei ihr drinnen / ist im Zimmer."

[34] "[...] von uns da wurde nicht viel überbracht / haben nur ein paar kleine Lieder hinterlassen / zu singen in den Höfen und Gassen / Während sie in ihrem Welt Schmertz warn / mussten wir ihnen die Ernte einfahrn / und ihnen ihre Stuben und Möbel baun / dass sie ungestört könnten nach innen schaun."

[35] "Vorerst bedarf es / eines gemässigten Naturells / dann eines Auges das / die Gegenstände rein sieht / eines Gemüths sodann das liebt / was es vor Augen hat und / schliesslich eines Triebs der Hand / das Gesehne wieder hin zu geben / so sollten Sie sich denn / ein einfaches idyllisches / Factum wählen / und dieses mit Bescheidenheit / uns zeichnen / Wir möchten sehn / wies Ihnen mit / der Menschen Mahlerey gelänge / auf die doch alles ankömmt." Weiss follows almost exactly the words that Goethe uses in his letters to Schiller from June 28 and August 23, 1797, see Friedrich Hölderlin, *Sämtliche Werke und Briefe. Band III*, edited by Jochen Schmidt (Frankfurt a.M.: Deutscher Klassiker Verlag, 1992), 631, 633: "Vielleicht täte er am besten, wenn er einmal ein ganz einfaches idyllisches Factum wählte und es darstellte, so könnte man eher sehen wie es ihm mit der Menschenmalerei gelänge, worauf doch am Ende alles ankommt. [...] Gestern ist auch Hölterlein bei mir gewesen, er sieht etwas gedrückt und kränklich aus, aber er ist wirklich liebenswürdig und mit Bescheidenheit, ja mit Ängstlichkeit offen. [...] Ich habe ihm besonders geraten kleine Gedichte zu machen und sich zu jedem einen menschlich interessanten Gegenstand zu wählen."

[36] "Da sollten auch unsre Söhne bei stehn / wo auf den Acker und inn Steinbruch gehn / die dürfen nicht das Lesen lern und Schreiben / weil sie solln in Unwissenheit bleiben."

[37] "*Fichte ersteigt das Podium. Die Arbeiter und Arbeiterinnen ab.*"

[38] "Erwache Teutschland Teutschland erwache / [...] dem Feinde [...] was dem Feinde gebührt / [...] / Und wir wolln uns von fremdländischen Racen / nicht länger zerreissen und unterwerfen lassen / raus schmeissen die levantinischen ./ und lateinischen Buben / die decadenten Franzosen und / vor allem die Juden / endlich erblühen lassen und genesen / was verborgen liegt im teutschen Wesen / [...] / Teutschlands grosse Stunde wird kommen / [...] / dass uns morgen gehöre die ganze Welt."

[39] "Beklemmend ist es sodann, zu sehn, wie seine wohlgemeinten Forderungen sich von nachfolgenden nationalistischen Gesinnungsarten verdrehen und bis in das faschistische Unheil hinein verwenden lassen."

[40] "Eins versteh ich nicht / sind doch viel mehr von unsereinem / als von denen da im Park / Was müssen wir von denen uns / denn plaken lassen."

[41] "Versaut und verrottet dies ganze Europa / und das nördliche America auch / Spannen ihre Neze rings um die Erde / Schäze an sich zu reissen und Sclaven."

[42] "Weils gegen den grössten / Verräther der Revoluzion geht / [...] hat er nichts anderes im Sinn / als ganz Europa / aufzufressen."

[43] "Ein Ungeheuer ist er."

[44] *Werke* 6, 414: "Hölderlin, als einziger, hebt sich von dieser Schwäche ab, nichts kann ihn dazu zwingen, sein Gedankenbild zu verleugnen [...] So ist vielleicht er, in seinem Turm, der von allen am wenigsten Gebrochene."

[45] "Wir sprechen von Dichtung / Hier sind wir erlöst / vom unseelgen Zwang / zum gemeinsamen Handeln / und wircken instinctiv / ins Unendliche / Nur in der Kunst / sag ich / vermögen wir unsre / Persöhnlichkeit total / zu revoltiren."

[46] "Er ist weder todtesschwach / noch ein Verzweifelter / lebendiger ist er als mancher / [. . .] / Klarer sind ihm die Sinne / als allen euch untern / in Agrigent / [. . .] Ihr seyd die Verblendeten / Versteht ihr nicht / dass dieses Fiebern diese Athemnoth / eure Seuche ist [. . .]"

[47] "Nur der reine teutsche / Geist soll bestehn / In deinem Nahmen Hölderlin / übergeben wir / das ArthFremde / dem Feuer."

[48] "Für die LobPreisung Hölderlins / Gegen die tollen Hunde / die mit communistischer / Revoluzion / die Welt zerstören wolln / Wir übergeben dem Feuer / Buonarroti."

[49] "[. . .] o aus dem Dunckeln kommt / und werft den Tisch / an den ihr nie geladen / o werft ihn um / und um."

[50] "Weiter / erzählt weiter / was sonst noch Trefliches / in der cultivirten Welt / sich ereignet."

[51] "*Hölderlin eilt zum Fenster, reißt es auf, lehnt sich hinaus, wild lachend.* 'Er naht er naht / der FährKahn naht / o der Othem vergeht dir / hörst nur noch des Todtes Thöne.'"

[52] *Werke* 2, 420: "Daß mein Onkel, Gerichtsrat Autenrieth, der gleichen Familie entstammte, die auch in Hölderlins Leben eine Rolle gespielt hatte [. . .] daß ein Christian Friedrich Autenrieth mit Hölderlin am Theologischen Stift studiert, und ein Profesor Ferdinand Autenrieth das Klinikum geleitet hatte, in das Hölderlin eingeliefert und in Zwangsjacke und eine vom Professor konstruierte lederne Gesichtsmaske gesteckt worden war. Die 'strenge Observanz,' die der Medizin-Professor über den erkrankten Dichter verhängte, kam auch mir nun unter dem Regiment seines Nachfahren zu, wodurch sich meine Schwäche, meine Benommenheit und periodische Verwirrung vertiefte."

[53] *Werke* 2, 507: "Ich bewerte dieses Stück, mehr als irgendeine andre meiner bisherigen Arbeiten, als Unterlage für meinen eigenen Versuch, die Widerstände, Widersprüche und Verbautheiten ringsum in mein Blickfeld zu rücken und mit ihnen fertig zu werden."

[54] *Werke* 2, 442: "Er geht [. . .] zugrunde [. . .] weil er versucht seinen Traum mit der äußeren Realität zu verbinden, er geht zugrunde, weil eine solche Einheit noch nicht möglich ist, jedenfalls nicht zu seinen Lebzeiten, und vielleicht zu meinen auch nicht."

[55] All following excerpts and quotations from this play refer to the following edition: *Der Prozeß. Stück in zwei Akten.* In Peter Weiss, *Werke in sechs Bänden. Sechster Band,* edited by Suhrkamp Verlag in cooperation with Gunilla Palmstierna-Weiss (Frankfurt a.M.: Suhrkamp, 1991), 261–336.

[56] "Er verharrt zwischen den Zerrspiegeln seiner Ordnung, die er für unabänderlich hält. An dieser seiner eigenen Schwäche zerbricht er."

[57] All following excerpts and quotations from this play refer to the following edition: *Der neue Prozeß. Stück in drei Akten.* In Peter Weiss, *Werke in sechs Bänden. Sechster*

Band, edited by Suhrkamp Verlag in cooperation with Gunilla Palmstierna-Weiss (Frankfurt a.M.: Suhrkamp, 1991), 337–407.

[58] Detlef Kremer, "*Der Prozeß / Der neue Prozeß,*" in *Peter Weiss' Dramen: Neue Interpretationen,* edited by Martin Rector and Christoph Weiss (Opladen and Wiesbaden: Westdeutscher Verlag, 1999), 235–64. Here: 260: "Vor allem aber hat die Widerständigkeit grotesker Kreatürlichkeit [. . .]Gewicht erhalten [. . .]"

[59] *Werke* 6, 425: "[. . .] ohne mystische oder religiöse Obertöne. [. . .] Menschen geschildert, die, unter dem Druck der Zeit, gebrochen sind und in heftige innere Widersprüche geraten. Sie versuchen verzweifelt, sich den Regeln der kapitalistischen Gesellschaft anzupassen, oder sich von deren Zwängen zu befreien."

[60] *Werke* 6, 425: "Alle, mit Ausnahme von Leni und Titorelli, sind von sich selbst entfremdet worden. [. . .] Josef K [. . .] allmählich angegriffen von Zweifeln. Doch ehe er erkennt, in welchem Maß er sich selbst betrogen hat, findet auch er sich ausgeschaltet. Mit seinen Idealen, seinem Streben nach Verbesserungen, seinen Einsichten in die großen, überall stattfindenden Ungerechtigkeiten und Ausbeutungen, ist er von seinen Arbeitgebern ausgenutzt worden: sie haben seinen Humanismus zu ihrem Alibi gemacht."

[61] "Liebe Frau Grubach — wie soll ich es sagen — ich will alles verstehn — ich erkläre es mir — alles müßte sich doch erklären lassen — das ist es — es dürfte eigentlich gar keine Mißverständnisse geben."

[62] *"K hält den Hals hin, läßt sich die Krawatte umbinden [. . .] Alles, was im Zimmer noch kenntlich war, erlischt."*

[63] "Das ist es gerade — daß nichts festgelegt ist — da zieht die meisten an."

[64] "'Schmutz ist es für mich. Abschaum, Ausgeburt des Leidens. Blutet alles. Eingeweide sinds. Kot ist es.' K 'Wie kann es wie Reinheit wirken?' Titorelli 'Weil Sie es so sehn wollen.'"

[65] "Hier ist es leer. Absolut leer. Nichts läßt sich voraussehen."

[66] "Nicht für Sie — g e g e n Sie —"

[67] Compare Franz Kafka, *Der Proceß. Roman,* edited by Hans-Gerd Koch (Frankfurt a.M.: Fischer, 1999), 241: "'Wie ein Hund!' sagte er, es war, als sollte die Scham ihn überleben."

[68] Franz Kafka, *Der Proceß. Roman,* edited by Hans-Gerd Koch (Frankfurt a.M.: Fischer, 1999), 241: "Gab es Einwände, die man vergessen hatte? Gewiß gab es solche. Die Logik ist zwar unerschütterlich, aber einem Menschen der leben will, widersteht sie nicht."

4: Scenarios of Stagnation: Early Prose

WEISS'S EARLY PROSE IS WORTH studying as a transitory but necessary experimental phase of his writing. Without the excessive explorations of narrative deadlocks and exercises in disturbing repetitive-
ness that marks his early prose, Weiss, who conceded the slow maturation process of his art, would probably not have been able to produce his
more complex and inexhaustibly rich later works. The fact that much of
his early prose was rejected by publishers and only became accessible
after Weiss had become famous might indicate the unfinished character
of the early prose texts that often read like self-absorbed psychoanalytic
vignettes and dream journals. However, the apparent shortcomings of
most of Weiss's early prose can also be read as conscious failures and
attacks on conventional aesthetic techniques. A microscopic view replaces
any desire for recognizable coherence. His aesthetic experiments and his
obsession with gloomy introspective scenarios, inherited from Kafka and
the French writers Camus, Sartre, and Robbe-Grillet, will remain an
important undercurrent of Weiss's later work. In rudimentary form, one
could even argue that already in his early prose, Weiss tries to blend
blurry journeys into the unconscious with observations of the social
world and its forms of violence. Hardly any twentieth-century writer
refuses to seek refuge in easy closure to the extent that Weiss does. It is
hard simply to enjoy Weiss's works in one reading because his writings
for the most part lack any offer of reconciliatory relief. Working through
Weiss's texts, however, the reader might experience another form of
immense pleasure. Questions about the possibilities of writing and perceiving the world regain fresh contours by the dialogues that Weiss's
works inspire. The reader might ask how we can write, what modes of
expression are open to us, how we can be political without becoming
sterile and predictable, and how we can explore emotions without do-
mesticating them through rigid interpretive schemes. Because his
thought process is constantly shifting between the poles of unconscious
desires and ethical commitment, Weiss's works offer continuous thought
in motion. Weiss's early prose often leaves the reader disturbed and
frustrated. It does not offer much relief from a dominant, spiraling,
almost autistic tension. However, even the almost autistic introspections

of his early prose, like all of Weiss's works, makes the reader curious about the not-yet-written and the unending process of writing and understanding. In this regard, Weiss turns his reader into an imaginative writer.

During the 1930s, Weiss wrote a number of unpublished novellas and fictional diaries in the style of Hermann Hesse's works.[1] His literary career began with a prose poem sequence in Swedish, *Från ö till ö* (From Island to Island), which was written in 1944 and published in 1947.[2] The lyrical narrative voice understands the process of writing and the search for geo-symbolic interpretations as an existential response to being wounded from, and by, birth (10).[3] The volume's concluding segment emphasizes a corresponding desire for a return into the maternal womb. A labyrinth is characterized as a protective shelter that harbors the threat of lethal petrification (52).[4] The topos of fear, death, and petrification resurfaces in the ekphrastic descriptions of the Pergamon frieze in Weiss's main work, *Die Ästhetik des Widerstands.*[5]

Weiss's next prose poem or lyricized prose fragment collection in Swedish, *De Besegrade* (The Defeated), written in 1947 and published in 1948, emerged from the articles that he wrote for a Swedish newspaper. The text represents dreamlike explorations of postwar Berlin in the immediate postwar years. A plurality of narrative poetic voices approaches Berlin with a parachute, and observations of the destroyed city and its people alternate, or merge with, dream sequences and childhood memories that include a dead little sister.[6] The voice of a prison or concentration camp survivor, or the voice of a murdered prisoner, affirms an inner invulnerability. It is immediately followed by another voice that concedes that it provides a locus for evil, destruction, and decay (70–71).[7]

With many German postwar writers, especially those who formed the "Gruppe 47," with whom he later had a somewhat ambiguous relationship, Weiss shares a distrust of harmonizing vocabularies and assumes the role of a language critic:

> Ich glaube nicht an die großen schönen Worte und den guten Willen, ich sehe nur Verlogenheit, Haß und Zerstörung. Ich werde erstickt, doch ich lebe. Ich lebe der innersten Räume wegen, die es in meinen Träumen gibt. (97)

Integrated into the text are concrete observations of surviving children who have witnessed the death of family members and the rape of their mothers and who replay the traumatizing scenes with their dolls. The children are explicitly presented as the defeated ones (111–14).[8] *De Besegrade* is neither a journalistic nor a poetic work, and the text runs the risk of conflating genres unsuccessfully rather than creatively transgressing literary conventions.[9]

Weiss's Swedish prose from the 1940s seems to be trapped on an aesthetic dead-end street. While some passages confront the reader with evocative intensity, they do not deliver much more than variations on Kafka's mode of depicting inescapable violence. In his Swedish story "Ur anteckningar" (1948, Journal Notes), Weiss processes his experiences as a lumberjack. The first person narrator imagines the trees to be female human bodies who are raped and cut and whose skin is peeled off by an anonymous perpetrator.[10] In his Swedish prose piece "Den Anonyme" (1949, The Anonymous Man), a first person narrator describes a crucial reading experience that helps him to stoically await his execution.[11]

Der Vogelfreie (1948, The Outcast), the first novel that Weiss wrote in German, was rejected by several German publishers in 1948 including Peter Suhrkamp.[12] Weiss translated it into Swedish under the title *Dokument I* and published 350 copies privately in 1949. Weiss used this novel as a film script for his experimental movie *Hägringen* (1959, The Mirage). The original German version was not published until 1980, under the new title *Der Fremde* (The Stranger), which is reminiscent of Albert Camus's novel *L'Étranger*.

The homeless and vulnerable protagonist finds himself encapsulated in anonymity and only slowly gains a sense of identity and orientation. More and more, his painful efforts to understand his environment and to map out inner and outer landscapes help him to overcome his exiled isolation in an unwelcoming city where he is met with aggressive suspicion. The novel's beginning and final paragraphs, both free of any punctuation marks, can be read as psychoanalytically inspired variations on the famous first lines of Dante's *Divina Commedia*, "Nel mezzo del cammin di nostra vita / Mi ritrovai in una selva 'scura" (In the middle of the path of our life / I found myself in a dark forest):

> auf dem federnden glattgewalzten Weg nähere ich mich der breiten Dunkelheit, die von den Seiten her anwächst und mir ihre Mitte entgegenhebt. (147)

The narrator interprets his central lack of home as an advantage when he says that being a nameless Nothing precludes the enjoyment of a personal identity, but allows him to perceive the city more precisely, not unlike a seismograph (189).[13] His acute perceptions, however, soon convince him that his city exile is nothing but a fictitious and phantasmagoric product of an imagination in fear and pain (209).[14]

In a restless passage that consists of a spiraling list of surreal instruments, the protagonist describes his exposure to an overwhelming multiplicity of acoustic sensations (163).[15] His explorations lead the outcast to the conviction that he has powerful bodily omniscience at his disposal. He declares that neither temporal nor spatial boundaries limit his perceptiveness. The narrative voice declares that it witnesses the sexual act whose result it is. The details of this dreamlike vision include a basement and the awareness that outside on the streets people were killed. A bleeding face stares into the window while the unborn narrator observes how he is conceived (182–83).[16]

In the cityscape of his exile, the novel's "I" experiences a creative epiphany. Dancing becomes his mode of expression, which allows him to fuse erotic impulses with an unfulfilled desire for universal dialogue (180–81).[17] But the solitary dance, whether imagined or practiced, does not meet any response. The desire for a fulfilling dialogical life is expressed in the utopia of a society where human beings begin to recognize each other and engage in genuine communicative exchanges. The narrator's conceptions of a world free of aggression and misunderstandings remain in the subjunctive, indicating their hypothetical status. Compensatory fantasies reveal the narrator's temporary helplessness:

> Was würde geschehen, wenn man sich aus dieser Existenz herausbräche
> [. . .] Da würde man singen auf eine niegekannte Weise, würde tanzen
> [. . .] Man würde völlig neue Worte sagen, man würde merken, daß
> man ja noch nie miteinander gesprochen hat, noch nie einen Gedanken
> ein Gefühl ausgedrückt hat [. . .]. (188)

While it is unquestionable that any political commitment is absent from *Der Fremde*, it would be wrong to rigorously separate the novel from Weiss's later works. The outcast feels absorbed by impressions and driven to reinterpret them (161; 169; 201).[18] His programmatic self-descriptions, which emphasize the need to lose oneself in explorations of the unconscious but at the same time adhere to an at least rudimentary belief in rational control, read like a passage from Heilmann's last letter in *Die Ästhetik des Widerstands*. The narrative voice of *Der Fremde* is integrated into *Die Ästhetik des Widerstands*. However, in his final epic work, Weiss balances the immersion in unconscious impulses and in autistic isolation, in which *Der Fremde* remains entrapped, with an emphasis on rational thought and meaningful communication. Throughout Weiss's literary works and reflections on writing, the insistence on the simultaneous presence of painfully immobile obstacles on the one hand and fragile and vaporous utopian thought on the other forms an organizing principle that demands interpretive flexibility as well as slow and patient readings (214).[19]

Echoing the vagueness of the introductory scene of the experience of a female Titan's hand that is neither threatening nor sheltering, *Der Fremde* ends in a hovering state of ambiguity:

> Die Hand der Gigantin liegt über mir, sie ist nicht drohend und nicht beschützend [. . .] Dann nur noch Steinmassen, ohne Licht ohne Form [. . .] und die schwarzen Hohlwege fließen um mich aus, ohne Versprechungen ohne Abweisungen. (147; 219)

Der Fremde revolves around the outcast's emphatic desire for closeness and for being recognized (170).[20] This longing to know and to experience a complete release of erotic energy, and liberation from conventional and perceptive restraints and expectations, is revisited in one of the central yet often overlooked passages in Weiss's works, an early morning notebook entry from 1978 that tries to recapture and translate a dream into words.[21] What can be read as a continuation of the stream of desired or remembered experiences in *Der Fremde*, the protagonist's depiction of a consciousness completely free of fear, links the drive to understand with the longing for complete and unforced love relationships.

The Swedish original text of Weiss's novel *Situationen*, written in 1956, still only exists in manuscript form, since all Swedish publishers who were contacted by Weiss in early 1957 rejected the work. Only in 2000, a German translation by Wiebke Ankersen has been published. The first person narrator describes his life and his discussions with a group of friends, a small circle of seemingly cynical and detached but in fact melancholic and desperate artists and intellectuals. The novel is rich in passages that contain a substantial self-critique of the intellectual in the postwar Western world.[22] When the narrator, like the narrator in Weiss's novel *Fluchtpunkt* (1962), watches a documentary film about the Shoah, he concedes his lack of resilience and of any heroic impulse and uses a reference to Dante in a self-critical way (90).[23]

Weiss's next novella, which was written in Swedish like the earlier works *Från ö till ö* and *De Besegrade,* is titled *Duellen.* The text was written in 1951 and privately published in 1953.[24] Unlike most of Weiss's prose works, *Duellen* is written from a third person perspective. The male protagonist is obsessed by a woman named Lea. His imagination has turned her into an aesthetic object. Slowly, he realizes that a liberating separation is necessary for him in order to survive. The final passage of the text is rich in references to Rilke's "Erste Duineser Elegie"

(1912) and to his poems "Der Schwan" (1905/06) and "Leda" (1907/08).[25]

Der Schatten des Körpers des Kutschers (The Shadow of the Coachman's Body), an experimental prose text that Weiss scholars, for lack of a better term, usually call a "micro-novel," was written in 1952 but not published until 1960, when it marked Weiss's literary debut on the German book market. The text records in minute detail observations on a farm and depicts a world that, as Pasinato writes, is not localized but that could take place everywhere.[26] The narrative's collage-like style of scopic drives and visual tensions and deferments corresponds to texts that emerged from the French "Nouveau Roman" group. Like the French writer and director Alain Robbe-Grillet's novels, for example *Le Voyeur* (1955), which installs a series of immobile and parallel gazes, *Der Schatten des Körpers des Kutschers* employs a camera gaze and suggests a filmic style of slow motion and close-up scenarios.[27]

The nameless protagonist and narrator, two functions that often coalesce in Weiss's prose, gives a minute report of his visual observations. Throughout the first third of the text, he writes in the present tense, suggesting an immediate and unprocessed notation of sense data. The farm is inhabited by several adults, who appear to be unrelated, to each other, and by a small family with two children. The mostly nameless characters that are the object of the narrator's exploratory and voyeuristic gaze include a farm laborer, a military officer, a sick doctor, "Herr Schnee" (Mr. Snow), who collects stones, a maid, and a coachman. From the vantage point of an outhouse, the observer, who, like the narrator of *Der Fremde*, functions as a seismograph, begins to record his surroundings with his pencil, turning seeing into his primary concern (30).[28]

The title refers to the end of the narrative, when the observational eye, which is also witnessing domestic aggression, for example the corporal punishment of a child, becomes a voyeur of silhouettes and describes how he sees the shadows of a coachman and a maid engage in sexual intercourse (26–29). Alone in his bed, the narrating observer regularly conducts ophthalmic self-experiments. He puts salt into his eyes, hoping to approach uncharted visual territory and to attain more precise visions (15–16; 34–35). While the family remains in a living room next door, the group of strangers join together for dinner (17–21). The narrator documents their monotonous habits and the subsequent "pattern of the concatenation of the movements and sounds" in anthropological detail throughout the evening (21–22).[29] In addition to registering his visual impressions, the protagonist and narrator is also a witness of distorted sound fragments, such as "Wassersucht" (edema), "Wasser sucht" (looking for water), or "was er sucht" (what he is looking for) (42).

The text's final sentence, in which the narrator concedes that his inability to rationalize his trains of thought have led him to insomnia, lacks a period, leaving the reading experience without any closure even on an orthographical level.

The unusual double genitive in the title *Der Schatten des Körpers des Kutschers* suggests an enhanced distance between observer and visual object.[30] The characters remain shadows of objects without any psychologically rich personalities. Their inner worlds remain inaccessible to the narrator, who does not even try to seek any recourse to a coherent logic. The myopic focus of the narrator provides daily life chores with abysmal absurdity. The lack of emotions in an aseptically observed and minutely depicted world leaves the reader without any orientation. The narrator refuses to tell a story along recognizable plot lines. His estranged gaze renders a meticulous picture not of living and individual faces, but rather of surface patterns and the reconfiguration of visually recycled phenomena. As Soboczynski writes, the narrative is void of any closure and operates with arbitrary beginnings and open endings.[31] Language, the outside world, and its perception form a collage that is not held together by any moralistic message. As the writer Ror Wolf observes, *Der Schatten des Körpers des Kutschers* is engaged, and engages the reader, in a self-perpetuating flow of geometrical patterns and rotating movements of textual world segments.[32] The text displays the vanishing of coherent communication. It exemplifies the deadlock of mimetic or realistic writing by taking it to an absurd extreme.

Weiss's experimental novella *Das Gespräch der drei Gehenden* (1963, The Conversation of the Three Walkers) interweaves a nonlinear series of reminiscences and microscopic topographical descriptions. Although the title announces a conversation, the text can be more aptly characterized as a casual intertwining and shifting configuration of monologues that, like their speakers, are only loosely connected with each other and do not display any teleological desire for direction or narrative closure.[33] It is never clear who is speaking, perceiving, and remembering, and this apparent blurring of identity boundaries operates as an organizing and destabilizing textual principle. The protagonists and narrators are three exchangeable and unidentifiable men whose names are Abel, Babel, and Cabel. The three men, who appear to be undistinguishable, have met each other by coincidence on a bridge and in a park (297).[34] They tell each other about memories and current observations and reflections, but it is neither clear who is speaking nor of what their respective identities consist. They walk restlessly and utter words, in separate yet continuing paragraphs, whose speaker is never identified. The juxtaposition of compulsive walking and the impossibility of coherent communication in *Das Gespräch der drei Gehenden* is further developed by the Austrian writer Thomas Bernhard in his novel *Gehen* (1971).[35]

Connective topical tissue is provided by reoccurring locations and themes, for example pregnant women, ending relationships, and a ferryman. Scenes of domestic abuse and violence culminate in references to warfare and allusions to the Shoah (337–38). At times, a speaker recasts his previous fragmentary utterances, trying unsuccessfully to recollect his memories in a more precise manner (335).[36] *Das Gespräch der drei Gehenden* ironically undermines any stabilizing fortifications, or what the German text calls "Befestigungen." The missing period at the end of the final sentence emphasizes the conscious lack of narrative cohesion. Despite the title, a conversation never takes place. The text is organized around an irreconcilable contradiction between concrete and detailed descriptions on the one hand and a lack of comprehensible coherence on the other. Abel, Babel, and Cabel, whose names after all not only suggest onomatopoetic monotony but can also be associated with murder (Abel), an overwhelming intersection and loss of language (Babel), and the technological commodification of dialogue (Cabel), frustrate the reader's conventional expectations.

Despair and madness are the main ingredients that Weiss's early prose reiterates in an exhaustive manner. In his later novels, Weiss moved beyond the stagnant circularity of the narrative deadlocks discussed in this chapter. In the form of thematic undercurrents and as explicit topics of discussion, psychological complexity and mental imbalance remain important thematic filaments in Weiss's more successful plays and novels.

Notes

[1] See for example "Die kleine Geschichte von 5 Seeräubern und einem Mädchen," unpublished manuscript, 46 pages, with illustrations, Peter Weiss Archive, Academy of the Arts, Berlin, 76/86/6011, written 1934; "Günter an Beatrice. Bearbeitet und herausgegeben von Peter U. Fehér," unpublished manuscript, 116 pages, with illustrations, written 1934, Peter Weiss Archive, Academy of the Arts, Berlin, 76/86/6014; "Fluch und Gnade oder Wolfgang Hungers kleine Chronik," unpublished manuscript, 17 pages, Peter Weiss Archive, Academy of the Arts, Berlin, 76/86/6072, written 1936; "Ulule Schömgözewö, ein Fragment," unpublished manuscript, 18 pages, Peter Weiss Archive, Academy of the Arts, Berlin, 76/86/6068, written 1930s; "Vom versunkenen Leben," unpublished manuscript, 15 pages, Peter Weiss Archive, Academy of the Arts, Berlin, 76/86/6070, written

1930s; "Chloë. Aus Caspar Walthers hinterlassenen Aufzeichnungen," unpublished manuscript, 60 pages, Peter Weiss Archive, Academy of the Arts, Berlin, 76/86/6027, written 1937; "Die Gezeiten. Eine Erzählung aus unseren Tagen," unpublished manuscript, 127 pages, with illustrations, Peter Weiss Archive, Academy of the Arts, Berlin, 76/86/6010, written 1938.

[2] Excerpts and quotations from this text refer to the following German translation: *Von Insel zu Insel.* In Peter Weiss, *Werke in sechs Bänden. Erster Band,* edited by Suhrkamp Verlag in cooperation with Gunilla Palmstierna-Weiss (Frankfurt a.M.: Suhrkamp, 1991), 7–52.

[3] "Es kostete mich mein ganzes Leben, mich von der Geburt zu erholen. Ohne Wurzeln riß man mich aus dieser Erde, die ich seitdem beharrlich suche und niemals fand. Im Anfang war alles ein einziger Schrei, ein einziger Schmerz, ein einziger Verlust, eine einzige klaffende Wunde. [. . .] später heilte sie so gut, daß man sie kaum sah; aber sie blutete inwendig, sie blutete nach innen. Alles was ich tat in diesem leben: nach Symbolen suchen für diese Erde, die meine Wurzeln hatte."

[4] "Das große Labyrinth nimmt dich auf, die unendliche nächtliche Grotte, durchflutet von ihren schwarzen Wasserläufen [. . .] Sprachlos gehst du [. . .] bis du hilflos tastend dem Abgrund folgst und hinabstürzt und zu Stein wirst unter Steinen."

[5] *Die Ästhetik des Widerstands. Erster Band* (Frankfurt a.M.: Suhrkamp, 1975), 7: "Rings um uns hoben sich die Leiber aus dem Stein, zusammengedrängt [. . .]"

[6] Excerpts and quotations from this text refer to the following German translation: *Die Besiegten.* In Peter Weiss, *Werke in sechs Bänden. Erster Band,* edited by Suhrkamp Verlag in cooperation with Gunilla Palmstierna-Weiss (Frankfurt a.M.: Suhrkamp, 1991), 53–121. Here: 77; 67: "Nackt liege ich in der Sonne, spüre den heißen Sand unter mir, und friedlich liegen neben mir meine tote kleine Schwester und die Köpfe meiner Brüder. [. . .] Meine tote Schwester lebt ein magisches Leben. Sie wird niemals älter."

[7] "Und in mir spüre ich das Unverwundbare. [. . .] das Böse in dir [. . .] die Zerstörung sich in dir entwickelt [. . .] der ganze Verfall ringsum dein eigener Verfall [. . .]"

[8] "Besiegt sind die Kinder. [. . .] Vor dir lag die entstellte Leiche deiner Schwester [. . .] Wenn ihr all eure Angst aus euch herausspielen könntet! [. . .] Und du, die du Vergewaltigung spielst mit deiner Puppe. Du hast die fremden Soldaten gesehensich über deine Mutter stürzen. Wirst du jemals Versöhnung empfinden? [. . .] verirrte, hilflose Kinder! [. . .] Sie sind Besiegte."

[9] Beise criticizes the narrative voice in *De Besegrade* as narcissistic and arrogant. He rejects the work because, in his view, the narrator, whom Beise holds to be identical with Weiss, is too self-absorbed to describe the victims of war from an unassuming perspective. See Arnd Beise, *Peter Weiss* (Stuttgart: Reclam, 2002), 178–79.

[10] "Ur anteckningar." In *Utsikt* 7/1948. German: "Aus Aufzeichnungen." Translated by Annie Bourgignon and Marcus Hertneck. In Annie Bourgignon, *Der Schriftsteller Peter Weiss und Schweden* (St. Ingbert: Röhrig, 1997), 285–88. Here: 286.

[11] "Den anonyme," in *Utsikt* 5/1949. German: "Der Anonyme." Translated by Annie Bourgignon and Marcus Hertneck. In Annie Bourgignon, *Der Schriftsteller Peter Weiss und Schweden* (St. Ingbert: Röhrig, 1997), 289–90. Another important

Swedish text by Weiss is his unpublished and undated novella "En glasdörr," Peter Weiss Archive, Academy of the Arts, Berlin, 76/86/6029.

[12] Excerpts and quotations from this text refer to the following edition: *Der Fremde. Erzählung.* In Peter Weiss, *Werke in sechs Bänden. Erster Band,* edited by Suhrkamp Verlag in cooperation with Gunilla Palmstierna-Weiss (Frankfurt a.M.: Suhrkamp, 1991), 145–219.

[13] "Ein Nichts. Namenlos. Eine Art Seismograph."

[14] "[. . .] die Phantasmagorie der Stadt, diese Ausgeburt der eigenen Furcht und Pein."

[15] "Und die Pauken und die Kessel und die Hörner und die Posaunen und das Blech und die sausenden Gummikreisel und die mit Hochspannung geladenen Saiten der Harfen und das knarrende quietschende Holz und Leder und die schluchzenden von Dampf getriebenen Pfeifen [. . .]"

[16] "[. . .] ich bin ein einziges Auge in einziges Ohr! [. . .] Ich wohne meiner eigenen Zeugunge bei, sehe den Mann und die Frau [. . .] in einem Keller, während draußen Schüsse krachen und ein blutüberströmtes Gesicht ins Feuer blickt und stöhnt: Ich bin getroffen!"

[17] "Wie aber soll ich mich verständlich machen — ich kam ja hierher nach einer Verbannung [. . .] Ich komme hierher, als der, der ich bin, und will mich als solcher zeigen. Ich will das Unmögliche und hier singen und tanzen. [. . .] Ich tanze quer durch die Menge und spreche mit allem, alles spricht zu mir. Alles stellt mir Fragen, jeder Mensch jedes Tier jeder Karren jeder Stein, und meine Antwort ist der Tanz."

[18] "Hellwach aber nehme ich die Situation meiner Existenz wahr. Hellwach, ohne Rückendeckung und ohne geschlagene Brücken, ohne Armee, ohne Feldzeichen kämpfe ich. [. . .] Kommt hier nicht alles darauf an, daß man erklärt, immer wieder erklärt, jedes Wort jeden Gedanken erklärt? [. . .] Ich bin meine Offenheit. Ich selbst: die Stärke einer Empfindung. Ich selbst: die Wachheit meiner Sinne. Ich suche nichts. Nehme nur entgegen, vertiefe die Zeichen, finde andre Zeichen klingend darunter [. . .]"

[19] "[. . .] beides ist gegenwärtig: das Harte Schmerzliche Unausweichliche und das Zerstäubende das Wandelbare."

[20] "[. . .] ein altes, nie befreites Verlangen nach Nähe und Erkanntwerden [. . .]"

[21] *Notizbücher 1971–1980. Band 2* (Frankfurt a.M.: Suhrkamp, 1981), 743–746: "Ich war dort gewesen [. . .] dieses Glück [. . .] war körperlich, es hing zusammen mit Lauten, mit einer besondren Stimme, die ich hervorzubringen vermochte, ich konnte singen [. . .] es mußte mir beigebracht werden [. . .] eine der Frauen [. . .] sie unterwies mich, ganz nackt, ich hielt sie, berührte ihre Brust, ihr Geschlecht [. . .] ich hatte die Kunst des Glücks noch nicht gelernt, die Frau mußte mich diese Kunst erst lehren [. . .] ich würde verstehn, verstehn lernen [. . .] diese Gesichter, so voller Erfahrung und Liebe, manchmal voll Verzückung — sie nahmen sich meiner an, aber gleichzeitig galt es nicht mir, sie lehrten mich eine Kunst, aber ich persönlich ging sie nichts an [. . .] ich habe gesungen, auf diese Art, die mich selber bestürzte [. . .] o diese Gesichter, so stark und eindringlich, und gleichzeitig so gleichgültig mir gegenüber, sie würden mir alles geben, und es war mit keinen Versprechungen, Verpflichtungen verbunden [. . .] ich hätte dort bleiben können, wenn ich in jenem

Augenblick den Verstand verloren hätte, hätte für immer dort bleiben können, wenn ich wahnsinnig geworden wäre — o wäre ich es!" Far from merely representing an autobiographical anecdote about an occasional dream, this journal passage concisely describes the personal core and utopian sexual horizon of Weiss's literary projects, the need to find words in order to survive and to overcome suffocating conventions and societal hierarchies.

²² All following quotations and excerpts from this text refer to the following German translation: *Die Situation. Roman,* translated by Wiebke Ankersen (Frankfurt a.M.: Suhrkamp, 2000). Here: 250: "Wir sind zu keinen Resultaten vorgedrungen, wir haben uns nur durch Bilder und Worte bewegt, und morgen wird derselbe Prozeß wiederholt, morgen [. . .] haben manche Worte, manche Bilder eine größere Dichte in uns gewonnen, vielleicht, vielleicht nicht, vielleicht gilt es nur, alles noch einmal durchzugehen, noch viele Male [. . .]"

²³ "Bei mir gab es keinen Heroismus, ich hätte nie an einer Widerstandsbewegung teilnehmen, eine aggressive Handlung ausführen können [. . .] ich weinte [. . .] und doch habe ich die brennende Stadt genießen können. Bilde ich mir ein, daß ich ein Dante bin, unverletzbar, ausgesandt, das menschliche Leiden zu erforschen?" Compare *Fluchtpunkt,* in *Werke* 2, 246.

²⁴ Excerpts and quotations from this text refer to the following edition: *Das Duell.* In Peter Weiss, *Werke in sechs Bänden. Erster Band,* edited by Suhrkamp Verlag in cooperation with Gunilla Palmstierna-Weiss (Frankfurt a.M.: Suhrkamp, 1991), 221–87.

²⁵ Compare Rainer Maria Rilke, *Sämtliche Werke. Erster Band: Gedichte. Erster Teil,* edited by Ernst Zinn (Frankfurt a.M.: Insel, 1987), 685; 510; 558: "Denn das Schöne ist nichts / als des Schrecklichen Anfang [. . .] während er unendlich still und sicher / immer mündiger und königlicher / und gelassener zu ziehn geruht. [. . .] Und die Aufgetane / erkannte schon den Kommenden im Schwane / [. . .] er bat um Eins, // das sie, verwirrt in ihrem Widerstand, / nicht mehr verbergen konnte. [. . .] / und wurde wirklich Schwan in ihrem Schooß." The widespread disdain of Rilke's allegedly apolitical stance still prevents scholars from noticing parallels between Rilke's and Weiss's literary projects, for example the central reference to Rilke's elegies in the last sentence of *Die Ästhetik des Widerstands,* whose "schwingende Bewegung" does not have to be read as solely pointing at a Herculean gymnastics of violent rebellion. Connotations to the evocation of poetry and music as a tool of survival at the end of Rilke's "First Duino Elegy" should not be ignored, see Rilke, *Gedichte. Erster Teil,* 688: "[. . .] das Leere in jene / Schwingung geriet, die uns jetzt hinreißt und tröstet und hilft." Weiss's prose rhythm, not to mention the diction of his plays, often transgresses genre boundaries, and intertextual correlations with lyrical texts need to be explored further.

²⁶ Antonio Pasinato, *Invito alla lettura di Peter Weiss* (Milano: Mursia, 1980), 46: "[. . .] in quel tratto di mondo non localizzato, ma ovunque localizzabile [. . .]" All following quotations and excerpts from this text refer to the following edition: *Der Schatten des Körpers des Kutschers.* In Peter Weiss, *Werke in sechs Bänden. Zweiter Band,* edited by Suhrkamp Verlag in cooperation with Gunilla Palmstierna-Weiss (Frankfurt a.M.: Suhrkamp, 1991), 7–56.

²⁷ Alain Robbe-Grillet, *Le Voyeur* (Paris: Éditions de Minuit, 1955), 9: "Une série de regards immobiles et parallèles [. . .]" Robbe-Grillet's latest novel, *La Réprise* (The

Recapturing, 2001), joins Weiss in exploring aspects of the history of Berlin and can be read as an ironic afterword to Weiss's last novel, *The Aesthetics of Resistance*. The affinities between Weiss's text and Robbe-Grillet's early novels have been noted by several scholars, see for example José Maria Carandell, *Peter Weiss: Poesia y verdad* (Madrid: Taurus, 1968), 63: "[. . .] la misma idea del espacio, un tratamiento seme-jante de los cuerpos (cosas y personas) [. . .]" Carandell writes that Weiss's paradoxi-cal experiment of a collage-like choreography of the static goes far beyond Robbe-Grillet's notations of visual sensations, see ibid.: "Las mismas cosas reales son tratadas con técnica coreográfica ec cuanto, después de ser descritas en situación estática [. . .] empleando con gran eficacia la técnica del collage literario."

[28] "Mit dem Bleistift die Geschehnisse vor meinen Augen nachzeichnend, um damit dem Gesehenen eien Kontur zu geben, und das Gesehene zu verdeutlichen, also das Sehen zu einer Beschäftigung machend [. . .]"

[29] "Aus der Einförmigkeit der gemeinsamen Mahlzeit [. . .] entwickelt sich [. . .] eine Vielfalt von Geschehnissen. Die Unregelmäßigkeit der Verteilung der Gäste im Raum schafft schon zu Anfang ein schwer überblickbares Muster in der Verkettung der Bewegungen und Laute."

[30] In her recent poem "triptychon," Katharina Höcker inverts the title, adding more connotative richness to it: "[. . .] schaffe den / schatten des kutschers des / körpers satz zu satz tiefer / ins werk [. . .]" See Katharina Höcker, *nacht für nichts. dichtun-gen* (Lüneburg: zu Klampen, 2001), 26.

[31] See Adam Soboczynski, "Von Schatten oder Schwarz auf Weiß: Überlegungen zu *Der Schatten des Körpers des Kutschers* von Peter Weiss," in *Peter Weiss Jahrbuch* 8 (1999): 68–88. Here: 71: "Der Text bildet keine abgeschlossene Geschichte, sie fängt willkürlich an und könnte fortgeführt werden [. . .]"

[32] Ror Wolf, "Die Poesie der kleinsten Stücke," in *Über Peter Weiss*, edited by Volker Canaris (Frankfurt a.M.: Suhrkamp, 1970), 25–27. Here: 25: "[. . .] einer Motorik [. . .] einem Gefüge sich bedingender, sich provozierender Stücke. [. . .] eine Poesie, in der die Teile nicht nur wichtiger sind als das Ganze, sondern in der Tat das Ganze überhaupt nicht vorkommt [. . .]" See also Helmut J. Schneider, "Der Verlorene Sohn und die Sprache: Zu *Der Schatten des Körpers des Kutschers*," in *Über Peter Weiss*, edited by Volker Canaris (Frankfurt a.M.: Suhrkamp, 1970), 28–50. Here: 35: "Linien, Wege, Bewegungen strukturieren diesen Text"; Christine Ivanovic, "Die Sprache der Bilder: Versuch einer Revision von Peter Weiss' *Der Schatten des Körpers des Kutschers*," in *Peter Weiss Jahrbuch* 8 (1999): 34–67. Here: 57: "[. . .] eben nicht die Wirklichkeit als bloße Realität zu antizipieren, sondern gerade das Auseinander-klaffen von Wirklichkeit, Wahrnehmung und (möglichem) sprachlichem Ausdruck aufzudecken."

[33] See, for example, Antonio Pasinato, *Invito alla lettura di Peter Weiss* (Milano: Mursia, 1980), 57: "Non di 'colloquio' quindi si tratta, ma di monologhi di tre persone incontratesi casualmente e raggruppatesi senza finalità precise." Expanding on Pasinato's concise characterization of the text, I argue that the narrative segments or fragments encounter, regroup, and possibly abandon each other just like Abel, Babel, and Cabel do. All following quotations and excerpts from this text refer to the following edition: *Das Gespräch der drei Gehenden*. In Peter Weiss, *Werke in sechs*

Bänden. Zweiter Band, edited by Suhrkamp Verlag in cooperation with Gunilla Palmstierna-Weiss (Frankfurt a.M.: Suhrkamp, 1991), 295–344.

[34] "Es waren Männer die nur gingen gingen gingen. Sie waren groß, sie waren bärtig, sie trugen Ledermützen und lange Regenmäntel, sie nannten sich Abel, Babel und Cabel, und während sie gingen sprachen sie miteinander."

[35] Thomas Bernhard, *Gehen* (Frankfurt a.M.: Suhrkamp, 1971).

[36] "Was ich über das ehemalige Haus des Fährmanns sagte, war falsch. Ich bin nie in dem Haus gewesen, ich stand nur am Zaun [. . .]"

5: Autobiography and Fiction: *Abschied von den Eltern, Fluchtpunkt,* and *Rekonvaleszenz*

THE GERMAN AUTHOR and literary scholar W. G. Sebald, whose novels explore the work of mourning and remembrance, refers to his reading experience with Weiss's *Abschied von den Eltern* (1961, Leave-taking) and *Fluchtpunkt* (1962, Vanishing Point) as the beginning of his own efforts to think through the recent history of German violence.[1] Weiss's notebooks and semiautobiographical novels are permeated by self-critical remarks about the precariousness of turning one's life into a text. Shortly after the subsequent deaths of his mother and father in 1958 and 1959, Weiss wrote two major works of autobiographical fiction. The narrator of *Abschied von den Eltern* examines his complicated relationship to his parents.[2] At the beginning and at the end of the text, the narrator expresses his intense regret about his prolonged lack of communication with his parents:

> Die Trauer, die mich überkam, galt nicht ihnen, denn sie kannte ich kaum, die Trauer galt dem Versäumten, das meine Kindheit und Jugend mit gähnender Leere umgeben hatte. Die Trauer galt der Erkenntnis eines gänzlich mißglückten Versuchs von Zusammenleben, in dem die Mitglieder einer Familie ein paar Jahrzehnte lang beieinander ausgeharrt hatten. Die Trauer galt dem Zuspät [. . .] Aus dieser Zeit würgt sich ein Schrei aus mir heraus, warum haben wir diese Tage und Jahre vertan, lebendige Menschen unterm gleichen Dach, ohne einander ansprechen und hören zu können. (59; 139)

The terrifying childhood experience of hearing his mother calling his name out loud merges with the narrator's fear of and desire for closeness to the maternal body (64–65). He remembers his mother as aggressive and violent, especially towards her maid Auguste, who at times obediently punishes herself in order to appease the mother. Auguste is characterized as being always gentle. Unlike the mother, she spends a great amount of time with the child, providing continuity and reliability, while the mother often disappears (65–66). The narrator remembers the physical pain and the humiliation that were inflicted on him by a neighbor child and by a teacher (71–74).

The only possible trace of a liberated and joyfully uninhibited child-hood occurs during a visit of a befriended family. Fritz, the father of the family, encourages the children to run around naked. Years later, Fritz helps to ease the tension when the narrator, who has just given up his plans to run away from home, has to confess that he will not be pro-moted to the next grade. The narrator remembers his momentary insight as a child that an alternative to a childhood marked by feelings of insecu-rity, guilt, and fear was possible (84).[3]

The narrator's puberty is filled with humiliating experiences and acts of violence, punishment, scenes of restraint, and the suffocating routine of an artificially idyllic family life (107). Having been forced by his par-ents to join the boy scouts, he is exposed to, and later actively partici-pates in, homoerotic experiments and the popular game of singling out a physically weaker boy whose life is threatened:

> Alle Zerstörungslust und Herrschsucht in uns durfte sich entfalten. [. . .] Ich war mit dabei, als man einen Schwachen zum Ofen schleppte und ihn zwang, das heiße Eisen zu küssen, ich war dabei, als man einen Gefangenen auf einem Floß in ein überschwemmtes Grundstück hin-ausstieß und ihn mit Lehmklumpen bewarf [. . .] (86)

Similar episodes reappear in Weiss's novel *Fluchtpunkt*. The narrator of *Abschied von den Eltern* concludes that, far from signaling an ethical achievement, the fact that he personally did not commit any war crimes might be a mere result of contingent circumstances.

An avid reader who fills his room with his own drawings, the teen-ager feels an explosive force inside of him and is frustrated that his par-ents ignore his creative beginnings. As a form of protest and in order to explore his sexual appetite, he repeatedly visits his sister Margit during the night. Naked, they touch each other's bodies. However, the text emphasizes the gentleness and mutual consent between brother and sister and suggests that they stop short of making love (95–96).[4] Elfriede, a housemaid, is another voluntary object of the young man's modest sexual advances (96).[5] The terror of hearing his name called out loud returns and this time marks the beginning of the narrator's most trau-matic personal experience. His beloved sister dies in a car accident in front of the family house (99–102).

In London, where the family finds a temporary exile, the protagonist makes a new friend at a café. In the course of the brief but intense friend-ship with Jacques, a young and poor artist, the protagonist partly suc-ceeds in shaking off the sterile routine that used to enfold him. In vivid dialogues with Jacques, his artistic projects take on new life, and he rediscovers the joy of sharing unconventional thoughts and inventing a nexus of sounds and forms with a like-minded person (118–19).[6]

After thirteen days that are filled with mutually inspiring conversations that culminate in the spontaneous organization of an unsuccessful but nevertheless exhilarating exhibition, Jacques suddenly decides to leave London, and their friendship comes to an early end.

Introducing another important autobiographical event, the narrator receives a letter from "Haller," that is Hesse, his favorite author. Although being excited about receiving a letter from his admired author and enthusiastically experiencing the fact that somebody recognizes him as a full person for the first time, the letter's reconciliatory wisdom disappoints the young artist (125).[7]

Having moved to Prague in order to study at the art academy, the protagonist experiences episodes of impotence. His fear of the female body and of intimate closeness to a woman is triggered by the fact that every woman with whom he begins to share intimate closeness all of a sudden reminds him of his dead sister. Suffering from loneliness, he even thinks of taking his own life. What prevents him from committing suicide is his concrete hope for an end of his personal isolation and his belief that a loving unity with a woman will not always remain an unrealizable wish. The narrator convinces himself that is possible to overcome loneliness and to experience genuine love (132).[8] Eventually, the young man has an effortlessly fulfilling sexual experience that is completely free of any fear or inhibition. In retrospect, he emphasizes that a temporary suspension of any need to control or to fight himself or his partner contributed to this singular experience of peaceful fulfillment (135).[9]

However, these moments of release and temporary harmony still do not lead to the protagonist's emancipation from his parents. Material reasons force him to move back into their home temporarily and to work in his father's factory where he produces textile patterns. He feels encapsulated by the factory and experiences the building as a body that encloses him (139).[10] While the factory is described with allusions to a biological body whose threatening order attains maternal connotations, the narrator's mother destroys most of his paintings because she feels threatened by their lack of order and stability (136).[11]

Even though he still has not succeeded in separating himself from the constraining world of his parents, the protagonist reserves time for his creative expressions and paints every night, working to unearth what the German original text calls "verborgene Äußerungen eines Unbekannten, Verleugneten," leaving open whether the secret manifestations originate in an unknown and repressed realm or derive from an unknown and repudiated man, or both (139–40).[12] Secretly, the protagonist saves enough money to leave his parents abruptly. After a disturbing dream about the encounter with a double that accentuates the self-perpetuating internalized terror of his youth, he breaks with his family. Fully aware that the painful process of finding his own place in the world is always endangered by relapses into weakness and disheartenment, the narrator takes his maturation process to a new level when his restlessness forces him to leave his parents, "auf der Suche nach einem eigenen Leben" (141).[13]

Fluchtpunkt, an autobiographical novel narrated from the perspective of an exiled young man, can be read as a sequel to *Abschied von den Eltern* but is a text that stands on its own.[14] The novel begins with the first person narrator's arrival in Stockholm on November 8, 1940, when he is twenty-four years old (145).[15] The title contains not only a reference to a painting technique, but also suggests psychological and political readings, since "Flucht" denotes "escape."

Unlike his friend Max Bernsdorf, who physically and emotionally suffers from his Swedish exile because he is still rooted in his home region and eagerly waiting for the day when he can return to Germany, the narrator, a young painter and writer, admits that he feels indifferent to any questions of nationality or ethnicity.[16] Defying any conventional concept of home, he describes himself as stranger who feels more attached to Gauguin's Tahiti or Van Gogh's Arles than to his biological family or native country (145–47; 165).[17]

When the first person narrator thinks about a specific childhood event, he begins to question the stability of his ethical principles. He vividly remembers how a game with other boys turned into an exercise in singling out somebody, attacking him, forcing him to jump on a raft, and endangering his life. This memory leads him to admit that under certain circumstances he might as well have become a Nazi:

> Ich hätte auch auf der andern Seite stehen können [. . .] Ich hatte einmal an einem Pogrom teilgenommen. Ich sah den Freund, über den wir hergefallen waren, vor mir. [. . .] Aus Dankbarkeit, daß man mich verschonte [. . .] diesmal einen anderen gewählt hatte, ergriff ich die Partei der Stärkeren und überbot sie an Grausamkeit. [. . .] Deutlich sah ich nur, daß ich auf der Seite der Verfolger und Henker stehen konnte. Ich hatte das Zeug in mir, an einer Exekution teilzunehmen. (149–50)

Not accepting any schematic and faceless dichotomy between German soldiers and their victims, the narrator is puzzled by the fact that he is still alive while his best friend from childhood died in Denmark in a

German uniform (147–48).[18] The narrator's remembrance of the school friend Uli, whose early death is also mourned in Weiss's journal *Rekonvaleszenz* (1970/71), precludes a conveniently generalizing, mythic dichotomy of good versus inhuman (407).[19] Unlike Thomas Mann and more akin to Brecht, Weiss never propagated a postulate of a collective and inherent German guilt. Instead, he wrote his play *Die Ermittlung* against the purposeful forgetfulness of German postwar leaders. The narrator of *Fluchtpunkt* is disillusioned by inhuman economical continuities and deplores the global cynicism of oppressive regimes and markets by which even Bach could be misused and distorted (148).[20]

Dialogical encounters with his artist friends and their work are indispensable for the narrator. Through his insistence on the concrete reality of the material environment, his friend and mentor Max Bernsdorf helps the narrator gain inner stability in his new exile (152).[21]

The character of the painter Anatol is based on Weiss's friend and painter colleague Endre Nemes (1909–1985). Anatol's and the narrator's different painting styles and perceptions of art and of the world reflect the contrasts between their personal relations to their Jewish heritage. Anatol's works evoke vivid images of warfare and physical details of a violent death in the narrator (167–68). While the narrator does not identify with his father's Jewish background, Anatol focuses on his heritage and is unwilling to ignore the emerging terror and persecution:

> Bleich und besessen starrte er hinaus in die Fluchtrichtung, mit seinem Blick das Chaos erforschend. Er war Ahasverus. Er gehörte einer Rasse an. Er war solidarisch mit den Verfolgten. Meine Bilder lagen unter dicken Glasglocken, in einem Vakuum. In Anatols Bildern lag eine Gewalt, sie rissen die Welt auf. Meine Bilder verdeckten und verschwiegen (167).[22]

The narrator's maturation process is also sustained by his friendship with Hoderer. This character is based on the social psychologist Max Hodann (1894–1946), who had a strong impact on Weiss during his early years in Swedish exile. Hodann also plays a major role in Weiss's novel *Die Ästhetik des Widerstands*. The narrator of *Fluchtpunkt* is fascinated by Hoderer's open mind and by his passion for social justice. Even, and especially, when the middle-aged man's words are interrupted by an asthma attack, the narrator is unable to draw his eyes away from Hoderer. Feeling as though he himself needs help, the narrator finds nourishment in Hoderer's gaze, which he perceives as being full of compassion and experience. This emotional realization leads him to question his uncommitted apathetic existence. He calls his former life an endless and formless monologue (172).[23] After Hoderer's suicide, the narrator dreams about an encounter with him. Hoderer remains silent, and the narrator's questions concerning the Nazi crimes, moral responsibility, and political activism remain unanswered. The narrator's apostrophic desperation turns into resilient anger when he addresses the dead Hoderer in an imaginary attempt to have a dialogue:

> Was willst du denn, rief ich. Soll ich verzweifeln, daß ich nicht ermordet worden bin. Soll ich mich töten, wie du. [. . .] Was soll ich denn tun, fragte ich. Aber er antwortete mir nicht mehr. Für wen soll ich denn Partei ergreifen. Keine Antwort. (247)

Like the narrator and protagonist in Weiss's Swedish novel *Situationen* (1956), the narrative eye and voice of *Fluchtpunkt* becomes aware of the Shoah while watching a documentary movie whose indelible pictures lead to memories of friends who had become victims of the Shoah and also to a painful confrontation with personal moral imperfection (246).[24] At the end of the novel, the narrator evokes the memory of his friend and fellow painter Peter Kien in a desperate apostrophe that shifts into a laconic and bitter report:

> Fliehe, Peter Kien, bleibe nicht hier. Fliehe, verstecke dich, du mit deinem hilflos offenstehenden Gesicht, mit deinem fassungslos starrenden Blick hinter den dicken Prismen deiner Brille, fliehe, ehe es zu spät ist. Doch Peter Kien blieb zurück. Peter Kien wurde ermordet und verbrannt. Ich entkam. (133)

The novel takes a stand against a mystifying demonization of the Nazi regime. Weiss's narrator is convinced that military leaders and their followers, far from possessing any demonic or mythic qualities, are average minds wearing uniforms (246).[25] Mourning for his friends Uli and Peter Kien, he refuses to buy into any convenient ideological explanation for the German crimes.

A nocturnal encounter with Else, a woman whom he had just met the same day, exemplifies the narrator's search for sexual fulfillment, a topos that is also of importance in *Abschied von den Eltern*. Not knowing anything about each other's lives, the two spend the night together in an atmosphere that is free of any fears or expectations. They gently explore each other's physical closeness, and the narrator overcomes his former fear of impotence and alienation (173).[26]

However, the narrator rejects Else's offer that he stay with her. In an attempt to persuade his young friend that he has to end his personal isolation, Bernsdorf sharply criticizes the narrator's belief that compassion, devotion, and passion could only come into being if thoughts, ways of life, level of education, and goals were compatible.[27] One year after their sexual encounter, he visits Else again with the vague hope that she might welcome him as the father of their child. His blurry expectations are not fulfilled. Else does not have a child but a new lover, and they are in the middle of their dinner (196–97). In the spring of 1942, a new girlfriend, Edna, is pregnant, but they decide to have an abortion and visit a Hungarian emigrant doctor (200–202). Later, when Edna is pregnant again, they decide that they want the child.

Exactly six years after his arrival in Stockholm, the narrator sees a theater performance in western Sweden where he has opened an exhibition of his paintings. There, he views an actress whose theater performance mesmerizes him. The sentence that introduces the name of his new love, Cora, echoes the laconic exactness and documentary style of the novel's first sentence (145; 281).[28] Like his previous relationships, the shared love with Cora does not last long. The only moment of at least a glimpse of an unforced understanding and recognition, which is not distorted by mutual idealizations and projected images, occurs more than a decade later when the narrator visits Cora after one of her guest performances in Stockholm. They spend a night together without any illusions or pressure. The narrator realizes that Cora has aged. During this night, and probably because both the narrator and Cora know that it will be their last encounter and that they will not expect any new commitments, what used to be an addictive obsession with Cora turns into genuine love and compassion (285).[29]

Convinced that in the existing societal order fulfilling dialogical encounters will always be brief exceptions, the narrator refuses to be constrained by any conventions, traditions, and institutions. Immune and opposed to any form of patriotic heroism, he champions the courage to invent an individualistic, antiheroic way of life and to consider his isolation from any city or language a strength (168).[30] However, momentary euphoric celebrations of an unbound existence give way to periods of hopelessness and depression. Terrified by the omnipresent violence throughout Europe and taking rumors of concentration camps seriously, the narrator questions the relevance of art. He undergoes a phase of fundamental skepticism about the continued validity and justifiability of artistic expression (179).[31] Since he is not only plagued by political developments, but also by unresolved family conflicts, he seeks psychoanalytic treatment. Having read about the suicide of the Swedish writer Karin Boye, whose inner conflicts are also discussed by the protagonists in Weiss's novel *Die Ästhetik des Widerstands,* he chooses Baahl, a doctor with whom Boye had lived. While acknowledging his analyst's genuine friendliness, the young patient distrusts Baahl's habitus of a natural healer, his peaceful balance and gentle wisdom. Their generational distance leads him to suspect that the doctor silently sides with the world of his parents and their ideals of economic success and a stable order. What the narrator calls his own wilderness and terror is, as he concedes in frustration and disappointment, not addressed at all throughout the therapeutic treatment. Despite his eventual termination of the sessions with Baahl, the narrator experiences the sessions at least partly as a helpful series of experiments. He begins to embrace language because it can serve as a tangible tool for a rational clarification of identity (179).[32] What makes the psychoanalytic sessions even more complicated is a linguistic difference. The narrator has to translate the memories and sounds of his German childhood into Swedish (180).[33] The narrator links his experience with psychoanalysis in a foreign language to his struggle and search for a language that can become his creative medium. Both his native German language and Swedish, the language of his current environment, at times seem to be unattainable for an effortless and subtle use. He eventually decides that German will help him most to recapture the hidden source of what he endeavors to explore and express, the reality of his early past (190).[34]

The protagonist temporarily earns his living through hard manual labor, working as a farmhand and a lumberjack in Swedish forests before he joins his father's factory as a graphic designer (202–16). Not only through the experience of exhausting physical work in northern Sweden, where he reaches the limits of his capability to endure extreme temperatures and the constant danger of accidents, but also in the course of a medical problem, the narrator is reminded of the physicality and fragility of his life. He gains a closer awareness of his bodily organs when he experiences acute pain. A kidney stone has to be surgically removed. This medical episode also leads to a more relentless emergence of childhood memories of sexual explorations and embarrassments (239–45).

Writing is not only described as an art or a therapy, but also as a potentially autistic endeavor. Weiss exemplifies this possibility with the character of a scientist who becomes obsessed with trying to contain the world in one comprehensive book. The mathematician Hieronymus abandoned a successful career in order to compose a monstrous and incoherent text collage that is supposed to reflect the whole epoch of destruction. Physically exhausted and approaching insanity, Hieronymous is brought to a mental institution (247–54).

Apart from Hesse, Hamsun, Novalis, and the letters of Van Gogh, now Henry Miller's novel *Tropic of Cancer* (1961), which was banned in the United States for many years due to its frank depictions and negotiations of sexuality, gains central importance for the narrator, who reads it as a liberating antidote to a reality that parallels Kafka's texts. In Miller's straightforward prose, the narrator finds uninhibited affirmation of concrete life and fundamental physical desire (269–70).[35]

During a conversation with Fanny, Anatol's lover and a writer, it becomes clear to the narrator that her poetological views and writing practices stand in stark contrast to his motivations for composing texts. For Fanny, writing is nothing but an enjoyable game, and she denies any connection between her texts and her life. Refusing to adopt any auctorial agenda, Fanny sees no need to transport social concerns or to examine her soul through writing (269–70).[36] Fanny rejects writing as self-examination. In her view, burdening literature with psychological intentions is driven by what she dismisses as the rigid moral of self-correction. When the narrator disagrees by pointing out that he favors a continuous creative process over arrangements of completed works of art, Fanny draws a parallel between his championing of the provisional status of creativity and his incapability to love a whole person and to establish a stable relationship (270–71).[37]

The narrator displays a strong skepticism toward language and is convinced that writing always comes too late and produces a mere surrogate for lost realities (286).[38] However, life without the enriching confluence of diverse literary traditions is unthinkable to him. His ceaseless receptivity prevents the narrator from excluding any of the works, writing styles, and thought strategies that he previously admired. His openness for flexible reinterpretations allow for an ongoing eclectic reception of literary works (289–90).

The last passage of *Fluchtpunkt* describes the narrator's sudden trip to France. In Paris, he experiences a momentary loss of identity and linguistic belonging. But this crisis leads to a new awareness of his freedom and of the possible contours of concrete creative projects. Realizing that with and in the Swedish language, he is neither able to reach his inner worlds nor to address and approach the world outside, the narrator decides to start from the beginning and to reconnect with his native German tongue. The realization of his absolute freedom loses its terrifying aspect when he gains confidence in his ability to give a name to everything. This productive change of perspective, and the decision to embrace the language again that comes to him naturally, without assuming any national identity or pretense, provides the protagonist with an immense psychological release. By redefining and claiming his language as a useful and transportable tool rather than an imprisoning system of obligations, he is finally able to voice his needs and to believe in the possibility of experiencing a dialogue of effortless understanding (293–94).[39] The narrator emerges from a long phase of isolation. He recovers from a long series of communicative failures. Finally, he realizes that genuine dialogues are possible and that the isolation that had shaped his previous life can be overcome. The exiled young artist holds on to a new and reassuring horizon of creative opportunities. The vanishing point of survival becomes a promising point of departure for him (294).

The novel is rich in poetological reflections that question the very possibility of writing life in the form of a coherent, let alone teleological, plot. Deploring irreversible architectonic changes in Stockholm, his home for the two preceding decades, the narrator reflects on the paradoxes and the hypocrisy of writing an autobiography. Any remembered segment of his past, the narrator argues, is not verifiable anymore because the only witness who could refute him, his former self, has disintegrated. Writing about one's own past, he argues, suppresses everything that was blurry and undefined and therefore fabricates a merely simulated clarity (159).[40] In his notebooks, Weiss criticizes himself for having omitted a central autobiographical episode that would have altered the impression that the protagonist of *Fluchtpunkt* is capable of achieving a clearer self-understanding. In retrospect, the author regrets that the novel took an artificial turn into the temporal and ethical logic of a "Bildungsroman," assuming a wrong tendency toward an alleged stabilization of the protagonist's personality:

> Denn mehr als eine Aussage über meine Wahnvorstellungen und Verirrungen, was es eigentlich hätte sein sollen, wurde das Buch zu einer Beweisführung meiner vermeintlichen Ausdauer und Stärke und der Folgerichtigkeit meiner Handlungen. [. . .] Es ist das Bild meiner Beherrschtheit, das ich angreifen muß.[41]

Constantly subjecting his own works to a thorough critique and seeing writing as a permanent learning process about conflicting cooperative possibilities of ethics and aesthetics characterize many of Weiss's reflections. Emphasizing the precariousness of any autobiographical undertaking is Weiss's way to continue it.

Rekonvaleszenz (1970/71, Convalescence), the journal that Weiss wrote after he suffered a heart attack in the summer of 1970, is organized around the central desire for uninhibited and honest self-reflection. Weiss expresses the urgent need to write completely unrestrained by internalized censorship and to allow for dissolutions of cognitive prejudices: "Widerstandslos schreiben."[42] In *Rekonvaleszenz*, Weiss explores the contrastive tension between political awareness and openness toward the unconscious. The precarious twofold project consists of maintaining a clearly pronounced and committed political position and at the same time trying to relearn how to listen to dreams and the imagination (348).[43] Weiss reconstructs his dreams and remembers them as a realm that allows for a wide spectrum of emotional responses that are usually seen as incompatible with political commitments (349).[44]

In many passages, Weiss reiterates his political convictions, especially his hatred of American military engagements and economic pursuits and his protest against the lack of freedom under various socialist regimes. But *Rekonvaleszenz* is especially instructive when reflections about thinking and writing display a complex interplay of creative impulses and his self-critical faculties.

While Weiss also remembers nightmares of violent attacks, of being singled out and tortured to death, his dream reports repeatedly introduce a blissful alternative world of effortless communication without any fear or inhibition, a world where trustful and spontaneous affection is shared with strangers (350; 537).[45]

The convalescent writer reminds himself of the urgent need to elucidate and examine not only a growingly destructive political world but to juxtapose it with insights into the corporeal aspects of human fragility (352).[46] Journal entries from early September contain a passage whose style stands in stark difference to the rest of the text. In a series of anaphoric parallelisms of celebratory exclamations that all begin with an emphatic affirmation, this extended prosaic hymn negotiates the same dialectic that the rest of the diary, and Weiss's work as a fragmentary whole, set out to reformulate and work through again and again, without ever resolving or explaining away its inherent tension:

> [. . .] es lebe das kurze, brüchige, haltlose Dasein [. . .] es lebe das Hinuntersteigen in die Regionen der Zwecklosigkeit [. . .] Es lebe das Unwirkliche, dem ich so oft meine Gegnerschaft angesagt habe [. . .] es lebe das Nachgeben an alles was mich herabziehn will ins Unkenntliche. [. . .] Es lebe das Wirkliche [. . .] es lebe die Aufgabe, mit all unsern Toten in uns [. . .] zwischen den Lebenden dahin zu balancieren [. . .] es lebe das wilde Ansinnen, alles ringsum in leuchtender Greifbarkeit entstehen zu lassen. (405–8)

Echoing the skeptical attitude of his novel's narrative voices towards autobiographical endeavors, Weiss, in an entry from October 23, 1970, negotiates the usefulness of autobiographical texts and questions the possibility of writing about oneself without subjecting the written word to internalized censorship. Weiss asks whether and how it is possible for a writer to be open and honest to himself. In his view, the exhibitionism of autobiographical writing is only justifiable if it contributes to our understanding of reality (459).[47] In this context, Weiss programmatically calls for courageously uninhibited texts that defy conventional expectations:

> [. . .] es fehlt das Geschriebene, in dem nichts verborgen werden soll, in dem es kein schlechtes Gewissen gibt [. . .] keine Furcht davor, daß es von jemandem mißverstanden werden [. . .] könnte [. . .] in dem alles nur der Erweiterung des Fassungsvermögens gilt, in dem mit keinem andern Maßstab, keinem andern Wert gerechnet wird, als mit der Wahrheit, die in dir selbst lebt. (462)

The political counterpart and reverse side of this statement, which thinks together ethical concerns and aesthetic imagination, is the conviction that accepting propaganda is an act of complicity (540).[48] Weiss defines the task of an author as a defense and ceaseless exploration of perceptive and conceptual openness:

> Und diese Funktion ist ein Aufnehmen von Eindrücken, deren Verarbeitung nach persönlichen Perspektiven, die Einbeziehung aller Widersprüche, Schwankungen und Revidierungen, das ständige Erweitern des Blickfelds, das Abweisen des Definitiven. (513)

Turning his personal difficulty to end texts, the lack of closure, into a programmatic oscillation between the part and the whole, a figure of thought that Weiss inherits from German Romanticism and idealism, he claims that even thematically and stylistically anarchic texts can be embedded in a coherent cultural network. Far from promoting playful fragmentation as a goal in itself, Weiss insists on the comprehensive continuity of his works. He even suggests that while they are always revisable, his writings represent a totality (517).[49] The interplay of fragments and their shifting nexus also informs Weiss's creative reception of cultural traditions and his approach to world literature. He aligns himself with Goethe's belief in world literature beyond national confinements (522).[50]

Through its series of critical self-examinations, *Rekonvaleszenz* not only argues for creative perceptiveness. The journal successfully exemplifies the balancing act of imaginative thinking and rational praxis in the midst of physical and ideological limitations and destructiveness.

Notes

[1] Winfried Georg Sebald in *Süddeutsche Zeitung,* December 22, 2001, 16. The interview was conducted by Uwe Pralle, four months before Sebald's death in a car accident: "Für mich begann die reflektiertere Auseinandersetzung mit der deutschen Vergangenheit mit der Lektüre von Peter Weiss. [. . .] besonders *Abschied von den Eltern* und *Fluchtpunkt* [. . .]"

[2] Throughout the chapter, quotations and excerpts from this text refer to the following edition: *Abschied von den Eltern. Erzählung.* In Peter Weiss, *Werke in sechs Bänden. Zweiter Band,* edited by Suhrkamp Verlag in cooperation with Gunilla Palmstierna-Weiss (Frankfurt a.M.: Suhrkamp, 1991), 57–141.

[3] "Diese beiden Begegnungen mit Fritz W waren die Glanzstunden meiner Kindheit, sie zeigten mir, wie anders mein Leben, unter anderen Bedingungen, hätte verlaufen können, und sie zeigten mir den Schatz von unverbrauchter Freude, der in mir war, und der immer noch in mir liegt, unter Geschwüren und Verfilzungen."

[4] "Ich fühlte die Sprengkraft, die in mir lag, und ich wußte, daß ich mein Leben dem Ausdruck dieser Sprengkraft widmen mußte, zuhause aber sah man meine Versuche als Verwirrungen an, mit denen man nicht ernsthaft zu rechnen brauchte. Herausfordernd verließ ich nachts mein Zimmer, nackt, in einer namenlosen Erregung. [. . .] schlich mich, nackt, in das Zimmer in dem Margit, meine Schwester, lag. [. . .] lautlos betasteten wir einander [. . .] und dann legten wir uns aneinander, rückten uns eng aneinander, und mein Glied wurde steif und drängte sich an die warme Spalte ihres Schoßes, und so lagen wir [. . .]"

[5] In a later scene, Elfriede tries to initiate sexual intimacy, but the young man escapes into his room, see 113.

[6] "[. . .] sprach ich von meinen Bildern, die während der letzten Monate ganz in mir erloschen waren, und während ich von ihnen sprach, belebten sie sich wieder, und nahmen Farbe an, und ich merkte, daß auch meine Stimme verschwunden gewesen war, und daß ich mit meinen Worten das Sprechen wieder lernte. Indem ich meine Bilder vor Jacques aufsteigen ließ, wurde ich daran erinnert, daß ich ein anderes Leben besaß [. . .] und dieses andere Leben, mein eigenes Leben, nahm eine solche Leuchtkraft an, daß mir der Atem stocken wollte. [. . .] Überall fanden wir Formen, Töne, Zusammenhänge." The sudden disappearance of Jacques is also mentioned in Weiss's autobiographical journal *Rekonvaleszenz* (1970/71), see *Werke* 2, 407.

[7] "Jemand hatte meinen Namen auf einen Brief geschrieben, jemand glaubte an meine Existenz [. . .] Die Stimme war allzu entlegen für mich in ihrer Reife. [. . .] Die Worte waren mir zu sanft, zu versöhnlich." This passage refers to Hermann Hesse's letter to Weiss from January 21, 1937, which is edited in Raimund Hoffmann, *Peter Weiss: Malerei. Zeichnungen. Collagen* (Berlin: Henschel, 1984), 163.

[8] "Und dann erlebe ich vielleicht eines Tages, daß es gar keine Einsamkeit gibt [. . .]"

[9] "[. . .] und es war kein Kampf und keine Anstrengung, es war spielend leicht, das Leben spielte mit uns und ich lehnte mich nicht mehr dagegen auf."

[10] "Zwei Jahre verbrachte ich in der Fabrik. Ich führte meine Arbeit in der Dunkelkammer der Druckabteilung [. . .] in einer kleinen, verschlosseneen Kammer aus, tief im Leib der dumpf dröhnenden Fabrik."

[11] "Mit dieser Vernichtung hatte sie sich von der Drohung befreit, die diese Bilder auf die Geordnetheit und Behütetheit ihres Heims ausgeübt hatten."

[12] "Und doch enthielt diese Zeit, die mir völlig erloschen schien, Äußerungen eines geheimen Lebens. In den Nächten in meinem Zimmer, an den Sonntagen, entstanden Bilder, Zeichnungen, Gedichte, verborgene Äußerungen eines Unbekannten, Verleugneten."

[13] "Und die Unruhe, die jetzt begonnen hatte, ließ sich nicht mehr eindämmen, nach Wochen und Monaten langsamer innerer Veränderungen, nach Rückfällen in Schwäche und Mutlosigkeit, nahm ich Abschied von den Eltern. [. . .] Ich war auf dem Weg, auf der Suche nach einem eigenen Leben."

[14] All following quotations and excerpts from *Fluchtpunkt. Roman* refer to the following edition: Peter Weiss, *Werke in sechs Bänden. Zweiter Band,* edited by Suhrkamp Verlag in cooperation with Gunilla Palmstierna-Weiss (Frankfurt a.M.: Suhrkamp, 1991), 143–294.

[15] "Am 8. November 1940 kam ich in Stockholm an."

[16] The character of Max Bernsdorf is based on Weiss's friend Max Barth (1896–1970).

[17] "Die Emigration war eine einzige Zeit des Wartens für ihn. Er wartete auf den Tag der Rückkehr. Es gab für ihn noch eine Landschaft, mit der er verwurzelt war. [. . .] Es gab keine verlorene Heimat für mich und keinen Gedanken an eine Rückkehr, denn ich hatte nie einem Land angehört. [. . .] Ich war verwandt mit Gauguin auf Tahiti, mit van Gogh in Arles, mit Myschkin in Sankt Petersburg [. . .] Die plötzliche Ernennung zum Ausländer und Halbjuden [. . .] beeindruckte mich nicht, da mir die Fragen der Nationalität und rassischen Zugehörigkeit gleichgültig waren. [. . .] Von sozialen Argumenten wußte ich nichts. [. . .] Ich leugnete vor Max meine Zugehörigkeit zu einer Familie, so wie ich meine Zugehörigkeit zu einer Nation und Rasse leugnete. Nur in einer Freundschaft, in einer Liebesbeziehung wollte ich Verwandtschaftliches erblicken, oder in der Begegnung mit Kunstwerken."

[18] "Uli, mein Schulfreund, war Weltbürger wie ich. Wir waren Entdeckungsreisende zusammen, in den Bibliotheken, den Museen, den Konzertsälen. Als ich mit meiner Familie nach England auswanderte [. . .] Uli, und meine anderen Schulfreunde, blieben zurück. Uli ertrank bei der Okkupation Dänemarks. Seine Leiche wurde an den Strand geschwemmt."

[19] "[. . .] es lebe Uli, mein Jugendfreund aus dem Berlin vor dem Tausendjährigen Reich, der so voll war von Phantasien, Ideen, unerhörten Möglichkeiten, und der, steckend in der Uniform der mit dem Hakenkreuz geschmückten Mörder, als aufgeschwollene Leiche an der dänischen Küste lag [. . .]"

[20] "[. . .] selbst Bach konnte entstellt werden."

[21] "Schon in Prag hatte ich im Zusammensein mit Max erfahren, daß die Beklemmung und Unsicherheit vergehen konnte, daß jedes Ding seine Form, seine Farbe, sein Gewicht und seinen Namen hatte. In seiner Gegenwart war die Welt einfach und selbstverständlich, voller Menschen, Tiere und Bauwerke."

[22] Compare the emphasis on corporeality and terror in "Anatol's" paintings in Weiss's notes about his visit with Endre Nemes from 1978, in *Notizbücher 1971–1980.*

Zweiter Band (Frankfurt a.M.: Suhrkamp, 1981), 751–55. Here: 754: "Doch es hat sich nicht viel geändert, die Nerven werden immer noch bloßgelegt, die Folterungen zerren an der Haut, in dem Drama, in dem wir alle agieren, geht es immer noch um Leben und Tod. So zeigt dieser Maler, wie die Mächte ringsum uns bis in die Sehnen und Muskeln gehn, bis in die Organe, bis ans Skelett."

[23] "Während die anderen seine Schwäche übersahen, konnte ich ihn nicht mit meinen Augen loslassen, und sein Blick traf mich, ein Blick voller Anteilnahme und Erfahrung, und es war, als sei ich es, der Hilfe benötigte. In einer solchen Situation ließ sich mein Abseitsstehn nicht verteidigen. [. . .] in meinem unendlichen, formlosen Selbstgespräch."

[24] "[. . .] gehörte ich nicht eher zu den Mördern und Henkern. Hatte ich diese Welt nicht geduldet, hatte ich mich nicht abgewandt von Peter Kien und Lucie Weisberger, und sie aufgegeben und vergessen. [. . .] vor diesen endgültigen Bildern. [. . .] mit diesen unauslöschlichen Bildern vor Augen." Compare Weiss's Swedish novel *Situationen* (1956), translated into German by Wiebke Ankersen (Frankfurt a.M.: Suhrkamp, 2000), 90.

[25] "Und dann sahen wir sie, die Wächter dieser Welt, sie trugen keine Hörner, keine Schwänze, sie trugen Uniformen [. . .]"

[26] "Mit Berührungen konnten wir einander von unserer Nähe überzeugen. [. . .] wir brauchten nicht miteinander zu sprechen [. . .] Unsere Bewegungen waren langsam, ohne Gier. Alle Gedanken und Erwägungen waren verbannt," in his unpublished fragment "L. sass neben dem Kachelofen," written in 1951, Weiss explores a more explicit mode of describing sexuality. Peter Weiss Archive, Academy of the Arts, Berlin, 76/86/6061.

[27] "Denn beim zweiten Mal genügte der Körper nicht mehr, und Mitgefühl, Hingabe und Leidenschaft konnten erst entstehen, wenn die Gedanken, die Lebensweise, die Absichten des anderen lockten. Max wollte in dieser Äußerung ein Zeichen von Verachtung sehen. Er sprach mir die Möglichkeit zur Liebe ab, wenn ich von meiner Partnerin ein Verständndis für die Kunst der Fuge, oder die Fähigkeit, Joyce zu lesen, forderte."

[28] "Am 8. November 1940 kam ich in Stockholm an. [. . .] Am 8. November 1946, meinem dreißigsten Geburtstag, traf ich Cora."

[29] "[. . .] und zum ersten Mal sah ich sie freistehend, nicht umfangen von meiner Einbildung [. . .] Wir waren ungebunden, ich wollte nichts erreichen, und sie brauchte sich nicht zu verteidigen, und weil ich [. . .] sie so sah, wie sie in dieser Nacht war, ohne Glorie, geschunden, geschwächt, und doch noch kindlich, so konnte sie von ihrem Dasein sprechen [. . .] Unser Zusammensein war entdämonisiert, entdramatisiert. [. . .] Wir waren uns bewußt, daß wir dieses Vertrauen nur ein einziges Mal, in der Ausnahme dieser Nacht, erleben konnten, und daß die völlige Anspruchslosigkeit ihre Bedingung war."

[30] "Nur für meine Flucht, meine Feigheit, wollte ich eintreten, keinem Volk, keinem Ideal, keiner Stadt, keiner Sprache angehören, und nur in meiner Losgelöstheit eine Stärke sehen."

[31] "Das Bewußtsein der Zerstörung war übermächtig geworden. [. . .] Gerüchte von Massenerschießungen und Konzentrationslagern drangen über die Grenzen [. . .]"

Wogen von Selbstmorden [. . .]. Wie konnte es noch möglich sein, in dieser Bedrängung zu arbeiten. War nicht jedes Wort, das auf ein Papier geschrieben, jede Farbe, die auf eine Leinwand gesetzt wurde, eine Vermessenheit angesichts des Leidens, für das es keine Begrenzung mehr gab."

[32] "[. . .] ich wollte nur ein sorgfältiges Auseinanderlegen und Vergleichen, wollte Zusammenhänge erkennen, wollte wissen, was mit mir geschehen war. Indem meine Worte sich an einen anderen richteten, waren sie einer ständigen Prüfung unterzogen, es war ein Monolog, der mich wachsam machte, und der mir vieles, in langsamen Umkreisungen und Untergrabungen, verdeutlichte."

[33] "Ich erprobte hier in Baahls Zimmer zum ersten Mal die neue Sprache, die Sprache dieses Landes, in Zusammenhang mit eigenen Gefühlen und Impulsen. Die Erfahrungen, die in einem anderen Lebenskreis entstanden waren und mit den Lauten und Eigenarten der Kindheitssprache verbunden waren, verloren das Ursprüngliche und Blutige, die Einfälle konnten nicht frei strömen, sondern wurden kontrolliert, bearbeitet, übersetzt, und wenn sie ausgesprochen wurden, waren sie schon weit von ihrem Ursprung entfernt."

[34] "[. . .] wenn ich alles, was ich ausdrücken wollte, greifbar zurückversetzte in die Wirklichkeit, aus der es einmal in mich eingedrungen war."

[35] "So mußte ein Buch sein. [. . .] in einem fruchtbaren Chaos begann das freie Leben. Alles war greifbar und möglich [. . .] Indem alles Versteckte freigelegt worden war, und nichts anders anerkannt wurde als die eigene Stimme, nichts anderem Folge geleistet wurde als den eigenen Wünschen, erschien ein neuer Urmensch [. . .]"

[36] "Sie schrieb nicht, um [. . .] innere Zusammenhänge herzustellen und sich selbst besser zu verstehen, sondern nur um die Spannung und Freude zu verspüren, die bei dem langsamen Lebendigwerden ihrer Figuren entstand. [. . .] ihr einziger Wunsch war, das Spiel, das sie sich gestellt hatte, zu Ende zu spielen."

[37] "Das Spiel mit frei erfundenen Figuren erschien mir wie eine Konstruktion, eien Notlösung. [. . .] Wir wollen genau dasselbe, sagte Fanny, nur sitze ich beim Schreiben an einem sicheren Brett, während du dir den Boden unter den Füßen wegreißt. Du erfährst mit deinem Versuch genau so wenig über dich selbst, wie ich mit meinem. [. . .] Ich habe es längst aufgegeben, mich selbst zu verbessern, denn auf die Moral des Verbesserns läuft doch die ganze Selbstprüfung hinaus. [. . .] Ich antwortete, daß ich in meiner Arbeit nicht eine freistehende Mechanik sehen könne [. . .] ich könne mir keine abgesonderten Kunstwerke denken, nur [. . .] eine fortlaufende Veränderung und Umwertung, und deshalb gäbe es nur ein Journalführen für mich, ein Aufzeichnen von Notizen, Skizzen, Bildstadien [. . .] doch nie diese Bremsklötze eines Romans, eines durchgeführten Bildes. Du liebst nicht, sagte sie plötzlich. Du müßtest eine Frau finden, die du lieben könntest. Einen bestehenden Menschen. Dann könntest du dir auch ein bestehendes Buch, ein bestehendes Bild denken."

[38] "Immer liegt ein Zuspät im Aufzeichnen, ein Ersatz für etwas Verlorenes."

[39] "Die Freiheit war absolut, ich konnte mich darin verlieren und ich konnte mich darin wiederfinden [. . .] und ich konnte wieder beginnen zu sprechen. Und die Sprache, die sich jetzt einstellte, war die Sprache, die ich am Anfang meines Lebens gelernt hatte, die natürliche Sprache, die mein Werkzeug war, die nur noch mir selbst

gehörte, und mit dem Land, in dem ich aufgewachsen war, nichts mehr zu tun hatte. Diese Sprache war gegenwärtig, wann immer ich wollte und wo immer ich mich befand. [. . .] Ich konnte sprechen, konnte sagen, was ich sagen wollte, und vielleicht hörte mir jemand zu, vielleicht würden andere zu mir sprechen und ich würde sie verstehen."

[40] "Tausendfach verändert sind unsere Gedanken, Empfindungen, Erwägungen, versuchsweise werden sie hingeschrieben, zwanzig Jahre später, nicht mehr überprüfbar, denn der einzige Zeuge, der mich widerlegen könnte, mein damaliges Ich, ist verwittert, in mich aufgegangen. Mit dem Schreiben schaffe ich mir ein zweites, eingebildetes Leben, in dem alles, was verschwommen und unbestimmt war, Deutlichkeit vorspiegelt."

[41] *Notizbücher 1960–1971* (Frankfurt a.m.: Suhrkamp, 1982), 96–97.

[42] All following quotations and excerpts from *Rekonvaleszenz* refer to the following edition: Peter Weiss, *Werke in sechs Bänden. Zweiter Band,* edited by Suhrkamp Verlag in cooperation with Gunilla Palmstierna-Weiss (Frankfurt a.m.: Suhrkamp, 1991), 345–546. Here: 460.

[43] "[. . .] und auf eine andre Stimme zu hören, die sich bemerkbar machen wollte."

[44] "[. . .] ein Nachtleben [. . .] das [. . .] intensive Begegnungen zuließ und Emotionen, die zu Tränen oder zu wildem Gelächter führten."

[45] "Ich geriet neben andre [. . .] und da war diese Vertrautheit, diese Intimität [. . .] Zuneigung ohne Umwege, Zärtlichkeit ohne Fragen [. . .]."

[46] "[. . .] aus Einblicken in das Dickicht der eigenen Nerven und Organe, in diesen ungeheuer verletzbaren Lebensklumpen, vollgeladen mit Eindrücken, Impulsen, Reflexen, Verwitterungen und Fäulnissen. [. . .] ja, etwas muß unbedingt klargestellt, unbedingt ermittelt werden, und dieser Wunsch war es, der mir die Tränen in die Augen trieb."

[47] "Wie weit aber ist dem Schreibenden Offenheit, Ehrlichkeit gegenüber sich selbst, möglich. [. . .] Untrennbar von der Schilderung des Intimsten deines Eigenlebens ist der Gedanke, daß du dich in dieser Situation einem fremden Beobachter aussetzt, und darauf muß die Frage folgen, ob ein solcher Exhibitionismus gerechtfertigt sei, ob er beitragen könne zur Erweiterung unseres Wirklichkeitsbildes [. . .]"

[48] "Jede Lüge, die wir hinnehmen, ist unsre eigene Lüge."

[49] "[. . .] daß alles was ich schreibe, Teil einer größeren Kontinuität ist, daß ein bestimmter, hervorgehobener Ideenkreis nur das Fragment einer Totalität ausmacht. [. . .] Das Dilemma, daß es an sich kein Finale gibt, und daß ich mich bereits im Übergang zu einer neuen Variation befinde, kenne ich von fast allen Stücken und Prosaarbeiten her."

[50] "Ich bin Traditionalist, weil ich nicht das Entscheidende in einem einzelnen Werk sehe, sondern weil das eigentlich Vitale für mich in dem verflochtenen Muster liegt, in dem alles aufeinander einwirkt und sich gegenseitig zu neuen Inhalten und Formen anregt."

6: Poetics and Politics: Essays, Open Letters, and Fragments

THROUGHOUT HIS LITERARY CAREER, Peter Weiss developed his views on art, politics, and the role of the writer. He published his aesthetic reflections and programmatic interventions in the form of essays, notebooks, open letters, and speeches. They were usually first published in newspapers, small independent theater booklets, or anthologies, and most of them have been collected in his volumes *Rapporte* (1968) and *Rapporte 2* (1971). Weiss's programmatic outlines and analyses of a wide range of works of art are inextricably linked to the composition of his plays and novels. The uneasy relationship between art and politics is discussed in many of his literary works. In his final novel *Die Ästhetik des Widerstands,* the genre boundary between essay and fiction collapses almost completely.

In his essay "Avantgarde Film," written in 1955, the year in which he also wrote a book in Swedish, *Avantgardefilm* (1956), Weiss discusses the mutual amplification and eventual convergence of documentary and surrealist tendencies in Luis Buñuel's films, for example *Un Chien Andalou* (1929). *L'Age d'Or* (1930), also by Buñuel, is a film that, according to Weiss's notebooks, taught him to relearn the language of seeing. Weiss also celebrates Buñuel's film *Terre sans Pain* (1932) as a documentary depiction of poverty in rural Spain that could not be emulated by any surrealist vision.[1]

While the visual arts play a crucial role in his literary works, all creative media are of importance to Weiss. In his poetic essay "Der große Traum des Briefträgers Cheval" (1960, The Great Dream of Cheval the Mailman), Weiss offers a dense description of a French mailman's private monumental architectonic project. Ferdinand Cheval (1836–1924) spent the last forty-one years of his life in Southern France, realizing his dream to build a phantasmagoric monument, which makes free, associative, and eclectic use of architectonic styles throughout the world and its fictions. The essay on architecture turns into a dream protocol. Weiss reads Cheval's garden and its buildings as organic manifestations of his own psyche and imagines himself to be both contained within a dream and able to decipher this dream's language.[2] In celebrating the ability to understand objects without any impulse to take them into cognitive or material possession, the essay suggests strong affinities between epistemic and erotic desires. Weiss writes that observing and thinking should become processes that step outside possessive control habits. In the context of art, he argues, identities should not be perceived as static entities. In his poetic essay on Cheval, Weiss presents art as an experiment that treats personal identity as a palimpsest in motion. The perfection of art, Weiss maintains, is based on the extent to which it represents how names and identities temporarily permeate and extinguish one another.[3] Cheval's architectonic project is interpreted by Weiss as a free-floating association of dream thoughts. In this essay, Weiss gives an example of creative reception that expresses his desire for self-transformation through artistic experience.[4] An allusion to Cheval's project can also be found in Weiss's last play *Der neue Prozeß*.[5]

In 1962, Weiss participated in a celebration of August Strindberg's work in Berlin with a speech titled "Gegen die Gesetze der Normalität" (Against the Laws of Normalcy). Having translated Strindberg into German, Weiss celebrates him as one of his predecessors whose literary oeuvre successfully refuses to be compatible with any one-dimensional ideology. For Weiss, Strindberg stands out as a writer who, unafraid to endure internal conflicts, even embraced them and turned them into productive material for his work. According to Weiss, Strindberg abstained from seeking easy solutions and from taking refuge in harmonizing masks. Weiss's praise of the courage to display internal contradictions reads like a comment on his own writings. In Weiss's view, Strindberg would not have succeeded in creating new modes of creative expression without painfully turning himself into an object of literary vivisections.[6] Characterizing Strindberg's self-endangering creative curiosity, Weiss implicitly reflects on his own uncompromising life. Weiss uses his speech on Strindberg to reflect on his own project of committed ethical engagement that forms a liberating alliance with unrestrained aesthetic explorations. As he does with Hölderlin, Weiss tries to rehabilitate Strindberg by inverting conventional labels. Refuting any diagnoses of Strindberg's alleged psychological disorders, Weiss suggests that not Strindberg but society was insane. Weiss ends his speech by emphasizing that in his view, Strindberg remained unbroken and succeeded in keeping all of his senses wide open.[7]

In his essay on mourning the Shoah, "Meine Ortschaft" (1965, My Place), written after a visit in Auschwitz-Birkenau in 1964, Weiss describes an extreme form of silence that he experienced when he saw the buildings and the displayed items in the museum. The essay ends with the uncannily ambiguous sentence "es ist noch nicht zuende." This laconic statement reveals a disturbing double meaning.[8] "It" denotes both the narrator's life and work and the threat and reality of systematic killings that have not ceased. The simultaneous continuation of violence and of life and hope forms a contrastive motivation for the writer not to end his work.

Weiss uses Dante as a central point of reference and departure for his own projects and sees his own work as a continuation of the *Commedia*. In "Gespräch über Dante" (1965), Weiss emphasizes Dante's juxtaposition of concrete political critique and the subjective realm of dreams, a precarious confluence and permanently endangered balancing act that constitutes Weiss's whole work.[9] In his poetological poem "Vorübung zum dreiteiligen Drama divina commedia" (1965), Weiss imagines how Dante might rewrite his epos upon a return to the twentieth century. Dante is celebrated as a poet who has diminished the realm of the allegedly unspeakable by translating terror into solid words and by calling criminals by their names. Weiss defines Dante's task as finding language and making it live amidst the terror of absolute emptiness.[10] However, the poem is not without any skeptical criticism of Dante and refuses to buy into the Italian poet's idealization and beatification of Beatrice. Dante's eulogies of the woman he was afraid to approach, Weiss's text argues, are marked by a fear of intimate closeness but could nevertheless inspire authors to experiment with new methods of erotic writing.[11]

"Laokoon oder Über die Grenzen der Sprache" (1965, Laocoon, or on the Boundaries of Language), Weiss's acceptance speech of the City of Hamburg's Lessing Award, is full of autobiographical reflections concerning the existential role of language in childhood and exile. Weiss, however, creates a neutral distance by employing a third person perspective, indicating that more is at stake than a reflection on his personal experience with the German language amidst historical and contemporary atrocities. In this speech, Weiss negotiates poetological challenges that the German Enlightenment thinker, philologist, and playwright Gotthold Ephraim Lessing addresses in his influential essay *Laokoon oder Über die Grenzen der Mahlerey und Poesie* (1766). Weiss continues Lessing's discussion of significant generic differences between painting and writing and the degree to which these different modes of creative praxis can capture mythological as well as factual violence. Both Lessing's and Weiss's essay titles refer to the statue of the painful death of Laocoon and his sons. Laocoon was a Trojan priest who warned his fellow citizens that the wooden horse was not a Greek gift, but a lethal trick. According to Virgil's *Aeneid*, the goddess Athena punished Laocoon by sending two huge snakes that strangled him and his sons. In his novel *Die Ästhetik des Widerstands,* Weiss practices the difficult art of describing the ways in which works of art, from the Pergamon frieze to Picasso, represent violence, as the statue of Laocoon and his sons does. Weiss's Laocoon speech, however, does not interpret an ancient myth. Instead, it discusses physical nature and the psychological impact of language acquisition. Weiss outlines his view of the impact that language has on a child's gradual self-realization. Language, Weiss argues, can be understood both as a manifestation of isolation and as a medium to overcome it.

Emphasizing the temporality of our uses of language, Weiss defines speaking, writing, and reading as productive conflicts and mutual dialogical revisions of utterances and responses that refuse to be stabilized into any static order:

> Das Sprechen, Schreiben und Lesen bewegt sich in der Zeit. Satz stößt auf Gegensatz [. . .] Behauptetes wird widerrufen [. . .] Der Schreibende und Lesende befinden sich in Bewegung, sind ständig offen für Veränderungen.[12]

Far from establishing an irreconcilable contradiction, Weiss's contrastive descriptions of writing processes complement each other. At times, Weiss writes, an author's complete openness can allow the words to come into being effortlessly. However, the writer's responsibility for maintaining a precarious balance between representing traumatic memories and making them accessible to rational exploration turns the production of literature into painfully slow labor. According to Weiss, writing and thinking do not function in linear ways and do not lead to an easy access to unquestionable truths. Weiss suggests that we pluralize insights without accepting any claim to ideological ownership. He postulates an ideal writer who always resists preformulated patterns and who does not calculate the outcome of his projects in advance. For Weiss, writing is an unpredictable project of researching oneself and the world. Setbacks and despair are constitutive components of the search for textual coherence. In Weiss's poetics, writing is a form of physical and mental survival. The slow process of clarifying understanding through writing, Weiss insists, emerges from doubts and contradictions.[13]

In his controversial programmatic text "10 Arbeitspunkte eines Autors in der geteilten Welt" (1965, 10 Practical Guidelines for an Author during the Cold War), Weiss claims that he adopts the guidelines of socialism. He attacks the lack of political commitment as presumptuous and denounces the alleged autonomy of art. However, he calls for a free and undogmatic exchange of opinions in that same passage, something overlooked by many critics.[14] His notebooks complicate any discussion of Weiss's political allegiance even more:

> Was ich sagen will, ist nicht einheitlich. Ich habe keine Vorstellung von einem Standpunkt.[15]

Enraged by the Vietnam War, Weiss visited Vietnam during the bombings and published an astounding number of articles in which he attacked the American government's military politics and the complacency of the West, including "Vietnam!" (1966), "Brief an H. M. Enzensberger" (1966), "Che Guevara!" (1968), and "Die Luftangriffe der USA am 21.11. 1970 auf die Demokratische Republik Viet Nam" (1970). However, Weiss never limited his criticism to capitalist countries. Whenever he noticed that administrations of the Eastern bloc prevented intellectuals from voicing their opinions, Weiss did not hesitate to protest openly. For example in an open letter to the Czech Writers' Organization in 1967, he strongly objected to the attempt to silence the Czech playwright Pavel Kohout, and in a 1970 open letter to a Russian publicist, he sharply criticized the systematic obliteration of the memory of Trotsky. Not only in articles and open letters, but also in personal discussions with East German leaders, Weiss undertook numerous efforts to call for more tolerance and less censorship in the countries of the Eastern bloc. In a notebook entry from 1971, Weiss draws a parallel but also distinguishes between the silencing of independent minds in capitalist and socialist countries:

> Es handelt sich um 2 verschiedne Arten von Repression. Die eine ist bedingt von Profitüberlegungen, die andre von dogmatischer Ideologie [. . .][16]

In his influential poetological essay "Das Material und die Modelle. Notizen zum dokumentarischen Theater" (1968), Weiss programmatically argues for an inextricable link between documentation and poetry:

> Das dokumentarische Theater enthält sich jeder Erfindung, es übernimmt authentisches Material und gibt dies, im Inhalt unverändert, in der Form bearbeitet, von der Bühne aus wieder. Im Unterschied zum ungeordneten Charakter des Nachrichtenmaterials, das täglich von allen Seiten auf uns eindringt, wird auf der Bühne eine Auswahl gezeigt [. . .] Diese kritische Auswahl, und das Prinzip, nach dem die Ausschnitte der Realität montiert werden, ergeben die Qualität der dokumentarischen Dramatik.[17]

In Weiss's view, the creative quality of a documentary play consists of what rhetorical theory traditionally calls *dispositio,* the concise positioning of carefully selected material. Weiss's documentary dramas share this feature with his collage works, and the discussion of structural aesthetic correlations between Weiss's literary texts and collages is still a desideratum that future research on Weiss needs to approach.

In his programmatic reflections on documentary drama, Weiss distances himself from a theater that, in his view, ignores or obfuscates concrete political realities. In works of theater such as Samuel Beckett's plays, Weiss believes that the attacks on existing hierarchies and structures of violence remain locked within disinterested and meaningless circles. Like Brecht, Weiss wants the audience to think for themselves. He attacks the existentialist emphasis on the world's alleged absurdity and insists that art can help to explain reality:

> Deshalb wendet sich das dokumentarische Theater gegen die Dramatik, die ihre eigene Verzweiflung und Wut zum Hauptthema hat und festhält an der Konzeption einer ausweglosen und absurden Welt. Das dokumentarische Theater tritt ein für die Alternative, daß die Wirklichkeit, so undurchschaubar sie sich auch macht, in jeder Einzelheit erklärt werden kann.[18]

In his literary fragment "Bericht über Einrichtungen und Gebräuche in den Siedlungen der Grauhäute" (1953, Report on the Institutions and Customs in the Grey Skins' Towns), Weiss employs the satirical topos of a traveler from a different culture who visits a technologically advanced city. The visitor describes buildings, objects, and modes of behavior without being in possession of their inherent logic or context, thus opening the possibility for the conclusion that modern Western society embodies a conglomerate of absurdities. As Hiekisch points out, this fragment on the incompatibility of perspectives continues the depiction of writing as a process of estranged observation that plays a central role in Weiss's narrative *Der Schatten des Körpers des Kutschers*.[19]

Weiss's literary fragments that were not published during his lifetime include the prose piece "Gespräch in einem Raum" (1960), which describes a conversation between several men during which Jörn, one of the protagonists, remembers his mother's violence towards him. The dialogue is characterized by tolerance, patience, and the protagonists' complete acceptance of each other. This fulfilling experience of a successful dialogical exchange of thoughts, emotions, and memories does not find a continuation in Weiss's untitled prose fragment, which begins with the words "Wäre ich schon in der Mitte meines Lebenswegs hier angelangt" (1969, Had I arrived here already in the middle of my life's path).[20] This text, which operates with explicit references to Dante's

Divina Commedia, negotiates the institutionalized terror of hypocritical intellectual exchanges that are marketed as cultural media events. While real names are not mentioned, the fragment, a report of a nightmare, alludes to aggressive confrontations in the context of the German literary market. The manuscript ends by describing how the narrator, who tries to gain a safe passage across the river of death, is beaten away from the Acheron ferry by Charon. Not even the Greek underworld offers an exile to the dreaming narrative eye.[21]

Thousands of Weiss's notebook pages, numerous letters, literary texts, and theoretical reflections are stored in the Peter Weiss Archive of the Academy of the Arts in Berlin. Unfortunately, they are still unpublished. For scholars who visit the archive, the notebooks are available on microfilm, and a wide range of original manuscripts can be read there. Each new issue of the *Peter Weiss Jahrbuch* usually includes a first edition of a new textual fragment.

Notes

[1] "Avantgarde Film," in *Rapporte* (Frankfurt a.M.: Suhrkamp, 1968), 7–35. Here: 20–28. See also *Notizbücher 1971–1980. 1. Band* (Frankfurt a.M.: Suhrkamp, 1982), 418: "[. . .] phantastisch, was für eine Sprache, ich lernte das Sehen wie eine neue Sprache." *Rapporte,* 27: "In seinen beiden ersten Filmen machte Bunuel [sic] die Sprache des Traums zu einer Sprache der Wirklichkeit. Die verborgenen, verdrängten Kräfte schilderte er im harten, kalten Tageslicht, wie Journalfilmbilder. In seinem nächsten Film geht er ganz von der äußeren Wirklichkeit aus, und was er dort [. . .] zeigt, übertrifft jede surrealistische Vision."

[2] "Der große Traum des Briefträgers Cheval," in *Rapporte* 2 (Frankfurt a.M.: Suhrkamp, 1971), 36–50. Here: 37: "Dies hier ist meine eigene, innerste Welt. [. . .] Ich bin im Innern eines Traums. Verstehe die Sprache dieses Traums. Verstehe die Formen, die Symbole, die Hieroglyphen dieses Traums. Jede kleinste Einzelheit hat ihren Sinn. In jeder kleinsten Einzelheit drückt sich das Einmalige dieses Lebens aus. Wurzeln und Fasern, Verwurzelung mit Ursprung, Geburt."

[3] *Rapporte* 2, 39: "Diese Wirrnis von ineinander hineingreifenden, einander unlesbar machenden, einander auslöschenden Namen gibt dem Material seine Vollendung."

[4] *Rapporte* 2, 49: "Ich verändere und erweitere mich an dieser Begegnung [. . .]"

[5] *Werke* 6, 375–76.

[6] "Gegen die Gesetze der Normalität," in *Rapporte* (Frankfurt a.M.: Suhrkamp, 1968), 72–82. Here: 76; 82: "Doch gerade hier, in seiner Ambivalenz, in seiner Fähigkeit, das Erreichte zu widerrufen, liegen die Spannungen in seiner Arbeit. Er wagt es, den inneren Widerstreit auszusprechen, er wagt es, sich in seinen Gegensätzen zu zeigen. [. . .] Er machte sich selbst zum Gegenstand der Untersuchung, der Vivisektion. Er stellte sich dar auf seinem Vordringen im völlig Weglosen und öffnete Möglichkeiten für neue Ausdrucksformen."

[7] *Rapporte*, 82: "In einer Welt, die krank, vergrämt und verfahren war, stand er selbst lebendig, gesund, mit weit offenen Sinnen."

[8] "Meine Ortschaft," in: *Rapporte* (Frankfurt a.m.: Suhrkamp, 1968), 113–25. Here: 125: "Eine Weile herrscht die äußerste Stille. Dann weiß er, es ist noch nicht zuende."

[9] "Gespräch über Dante," in *Rapporte* (Frankfurt a.M.: Suhrkamp, 1968), 142–69. Here: 155: "[...] kommt die Rede ständig aus dem Subjektiven, Traumhaften, doch das Material, das sie aufbrodeln läßt, spiegelt die äußere Wirklichkeit. Jede erscheinende Person und Ortschaft wird bei ihrem authentischen Namen genannt, gegenwärtig sind die Zeitgenossen und die Figuren der Geschichte [...]" For Dante's role throughout Weiss's attempt to capture the horrors of the twentieth century on stage, see Christoph Weiss, *Auschwitz in der geteilten Welt: Peter Weiss und die "Ermittlung" im Kalten Krieg* (St. Ingbert: Röhrig, 2000).

[10] "Vorübung zum dreiteiligen Drama divina commedia," in *Rapporte* (Frankfurt a.M.: Suhrkamp, 1968), 125–41. Here: 135; 138: "[...] gelang es Dante / Worte zu finden für einen Stoff, der allen gehörte, doch ungreifbar schien, / und was sich bisher der Sprache entzogen hatte, war jetzt / vernehmbar. [...] er besitzt nichts als die Wirklichkeit / von Worten, die jetzt noch aussprechbar sind, und es ist seine Aufgabe, / diese Worte zu finden, und sie leben zu lassen, in der absoluten Leere."

[11] *Rapporte*, 141.

[12] "Laokoon oder Über die Grenzen der Sprache," in: *Rapporte* (Frankfurt a.M.: Suhrkamp, 1968), 170–87. Here: 179.

[13] *Rapporte*, 173; 187: "In den offenen Stunden entstehen die Worte von selbst. [...] jedes Wort, mit dem er eine Wahrheit gewinnt, ist aus Zweifeln und Widersprüchen hervorgegangen."

[14] *Rapporte 2*, 23: "[...] Bindungslosigkeit der Kunst eine Vermessenheit [...] ein freier undogmatischer Meinungsaustausch [...]"

[15] *Notizbücher 1960–1971. 1. Band* (Frankfurt a.M.: Suhrkamp, 1982), 56.

[16] *Notizbücher 1971–1980. 1. Band* (Frankfurt a.M.: Suhrkamp, 1981), 9.

[17] *Werke 5*, 465.

[18] *Werke 5*, 472.

[19] See Sepp Hiekisch, "Zwischen surrealistischem Protest und kritischem Engagement: Zu Peter Weiss' früher Prosa," in *Text + Kritik 37* (1982): 22–38. Here: 31: "Der Text ist ein Versuch, die Konzeption des 'Kutschers' zu radikalisieren."

[20] "'Wäre ich schon in der Mitte meines Lebenswegs hier angelangt . . .' Aus einem Prosafragment." *Peter Weiss Jahrbuch 1* (1992): 9–20. Here: 17: "Die Empfindung des Reichtums vor dem Ausgesprochenen setzte sich nicht nur aus den vernommenen Worten zusammen, sondern aus unserem Gehör für Untertöne, für Andeutungen, aus den Verarbeitungen unserer Fantasie, aus der völligen Offenheit für einander, aus unserm restlosen gegenseitigen Acceptieren. Wir erhielten Form voreinander, waren uns stark unseres Lebens bewusst."

[21] "'Wäre ich schon in der Mitte meines Lebenswegs hier angelangt . . .' Aus einem Prosafragment." *Peter Weiss Jahrbuch 1* (1992): 9–20.

7: Perception as Resistance: *Die Ästhetik des Widerstands*

WEISS'S MAIN CONTRIBUTION to world literature, the three-volume novel *Die Ästhetik des Widerstands* (The Aesthetics of Resistance), which was published between 1975 and 1981, resists clear genre classification.[1] The narrative's prosaic descriptions of artwork change into disturbingly dense and evocative poetic representations of corporeal pain and endangerment. The historically based novel documents the lives and deaths of German resistance fighters against the Nazi regime.[2] Despite its documentary character, the text remains a work of fiction, operating with an abundance of intertextual allusions and mythological undercurrents. The protagonists patiently expose themselves to the works of Dante, Kafka, Géricault, and many others. In letters and vivid discussions that they consider to be an integral part of their fight against the Nazi regime, they constantly revise their understanding of specific works of art. Weiss's novel stands in a rich literary tradition. Not only does it explicitly thematize Dante's and Kafka's works, but it also continues the project of blending philosophy and literature that the modernist novelists James Joyce, Marcel Proust, and Robert Musil had so brilliantly explored.[3]

Die Ästhetik des Widerstands, whose characters are all based on real people, forces the reader to think through the complex connections between memory, art, and survival. The text celebrates the courage and mourns the executions of members of the resistance group "Rote Kapelle" (Red Orchestra, or Red Chapel) that fought against the Hitler regime.[4] Told by a nameless first person narrator who joins the resistance group, the novel operates with sudden temporal and geographic shifts and cuts. The locations described include Berlin, Stockholm, Paris, and Spain. At times, paintings, texts, and monuments take on a life of their own. The narrator and his friends lose any reflexive distance and immerse into the poem or painting that they try to understand. *Die Ästhetik des Widerstands* partly invents and partly documents the protagonists' thought exchanges about political action as well as discussions of dreams and rich interpretive explorations of works of art. The text suggests that resistance fighters have enhanced their perceptive abilities and gained orientation despite ubiquitous ideological distortions and physical threats both from the Nazis and the Stalinists. Far from luring them onto an escapist route, their ongoing encounters with works of art help the protagonists to recognize ideological manipulations from all sides.

Not only the book title's terminology, but also its genitival construction contains a multifaceted ambiguity and provides room for competing or overlapping interpretations. The concept of "Ästhetik" does not only denote the theory of beauty in art and nature, but also a critique of sense perception, of cognitive processing, and the human imagination. The possible meanings of "Widerstand" range from a political fight to psychological obstacles and inhibitions. Marxian and psychoanalytic interpretive configurations converge with each other.[5] A tentative and necessarily clumsy translation of the title, which paraphrases its central terms "Ästhetik" and "Widerstand," might read as follows: "The perception of the precarious beauty of fighting back while facing blockages and impasses."

The novel includes numerous passages in which an unrestrained passion to understand art and their violent world is shared by friends who think through paintings and books as well as strategies to fight a fascist terror regime. *Die Ästhetik des Widerstands* is itself an illustration of the fact that historical analysis and aesthetic experiments are capable of mutual inspiration and support. Understanding art and its connections to history almost becomes the novel's "protagonist." *Die Ästhetik des Widerstands* invites the reader to realize that he or she is not a distant consumer but part of the text's attempt to be open for new ways of perception.

In his notebooks, which were published in 1981 and 1982, Weiss maintains that aesthetic questions can never be disentangled from political questions and that the two are in fact identical.[6] *Die Ästhetik des Widerstands* refrains from separating polis from psyche and transgresses any alleged boundaries between political and introspective aspects of human lives. Weiss's opus magnum suggests that poetic deregulation and sober political awareness do not have to exclude each other. The novel refrains from aseptically isolating the realm of dreams and the imagination from the daily task of precise planning. For Weiss's protagonists, art and politics are inseparable human activities. The novel consists of dense narrative blocks that integrate aesthetic and political concerns.

In his temporary Swedish exile, the narrator works in a factory whose name, "Separatorwerke," could also be used as an apt name for many one-sided commentaries on Weiss's novel. *Die Ästhetik des Widerstands* requires readers neither to reduce it to an unpolitical dream protocol that celebrates violence nor to a tractate on the sustainability of communist hopes. It is important not to privilege one aspect or character in Weiss's dramas and novels while discrediting or playing down the significance of its complementary opposition. In Weiss's plays, antagonists with seemingly opposing views, for example Marat and Sade, Breton and Trotzki, or Marx and Hölderlin, are inextricably linked, and the audience or the reader can put together her own selection of arguments. The same conceptual openness that characterizes Weiss's best plays also permeates his final documentary novel. It is crucial not to discipline the tensions that are condensed by *Die Ästhetik des Widerstands,* and not to explain away the conflicts that its protagonists such as Heilmann, the social psychologist Hodann, the independent publisher Münzenberg, and the narrator expose themselves to.

For the protagonists, interpreting works of art is not a luxury but an open process of political awareness. Only in alliance with explorations of art and the unconscious does the fight against fascism take on its reflexive strength, which is necessary to understand oppression and to acquire the ability to overcome it. Discussions of paintings and other works of art, far from being a mere ornamental essayistic framework of the novel, maintain a place at the heart of the protagonists' development throughout this new form of a "Bildungsroman."[7]

The narrator and his friends Heilmann and Coppi discover and debate works of art and literature. Visiting a museum in their home city Berlin, they are especially entranced by the fragmentary Pergamon frieze, which depicts an archaic mythological war. The three friends, surrounded by marching groups of the Nazi youth organization, discuss the ambiguities of Greek mythology. They draw parallels between conflicting ways of making sense of mythical stories and their difficulty making sense of their current political isolation. For them, ekphrasis, the process of describing a painting or a sculpture, and the analysis of oppression do not represent two separate projects, but rather form a necessary alliance. The courage to approach works of art slowly exposes both the artwork and the audience to probing questions that interweave technical, psychological, and political modes of thought. This process strengthens the protagonists' capability to endure their resistance to the Nazi regime as well as their doubts raised by the Stalinist show trials. Debating Dante and Rimbaud, they listen to each other and constantly question their own perspectives. Coppi is skeptical about Heilmann's insistence on the need for visionary prerational experiences and introspective speculations. Heilmann, on the other hand, warns the young activists about the danger of becoming dogmatic and indoctrinated followers of prescribed guidelines.

The Aesthetics of Resistance explores creative receptions of works of art that are received, discussed, and tried out as material for divergent responses and expectations.[8] Heilmann, Coppi, and the narrator engage in shifting and continuously retracting interpretations of many cultural products, including Dante's *Inferno*. The myth of Heracles plays a central role for their self-realization as human beings and resistance fighters in Nazi Germany, Spain, France, and Sweden. When the friends visit the Pergamon frieze in Berlin, they interpret the absence of the face of Heracles as an invitation to think and act without any role models or directives:

> [. . .] und Coppi nannte es ein Omen, daß grade er, der unsresgleichen war, fehlte, und daß wir uns nun selbst ein Bild dieses Fürsprechers des Handelns zu machen hatten. (I, 11)

The lack of a comforting closure and the painful but productive absence of a visible role model is addressed again in the novel's final passage:

> [. . .] und es würde kein Kenntlicher kommen, den leeren Platz zu füllen, sie müßten selber mächtig werden dieses einzigen Griffs, dieser weit ausholenden und schwingenden Bewegung, mit der sie den furchtbaren Druck, der auf ihnen lastete, endlich hinwegfegen könnten. (III, 268)[9]

Heilmann, who is too young to join the war against Franco's fascist troops in Spain, continues their discussion of the Heracles myth in a letter to the narrator, who has joined the Red Brigades. In his letter, which arrives in the Spanish town Denia two months later and via an exile route from Berlin to Warnsdorf, Prague, Paris, and Albacete, Heilmann suggests an alternative reading of Heracles, which questions his alleged courage and solidarity with the oppressed:

> Was aber wäre, schrieb Heilmann, [. . .] wenn wir sagen müßten, daß er von Furcht und Schrecken geplagt war und seine Handlungen nur dazu dienten, die eigne Schwäche und Vereinsamung zu überwinden. [. . .] Was waren die Ungeheuer denn, gegen die er kämpfte, andres als Träume, denen er sich immer wieder stellen mußte. (I, 314–15)

For Heilmann, who has studied a wide range of sources, the figure of Heracles becomes increasingly multifaceted and questionable (I, 314).[10] The man of action in the resistance group assumes the code name Stahlmann. He is often described with the same attributes as Heracles. Stahlmann reveals to the narrator, who has just joined the communist party, that he had suffered a traumatic temporary identity loss during a journey to Asia. As they take an extended walk through Stockholm, where they always have to hide from police, Stahlmann tells the narrator about his experience of sinking into madness during a visit at Angkor Wat, a Cambodian site of Hindu monuments (III, 93–108). The parallels between representations and discussions of the Stahlmann character and the Heracles myth in *Die Ästhetik des Widerstands* are discussed in more detail in a recent monograph by Berthold Brunner, whose careful and lucid comparison of these converging topical threads have become an indispensable new point of departure for scholarship on Weiss's summum opus.[11]

Heracles's absence in the Pergamon frieze is a central motif of the novel. Weiss engages this continuous topic for passionate debates among the protagonists in a rich intertextual dialogue with modern adaptations of the Heracles myth.[12] Heracles, the contradictory savior who figures prominently in Hölderlin's poetry as well as in Schelling's 1842 lectures on the philosophy of mythology, does not offer himself as an accessible, user-friendly commodity.[13] The protagonist in Frank Wedekind's dramatic poem *Herakles* (1917) refuses to accept the admiration and the divine status that is ascribed to him. Wedekind's Heracles skeptically responds that he has hardly succeeded in being human.[14] Heiner Müller's short piece "Herakles 5" (1964/66), which was initially planned as a satyr prelude to his Hölderlinian drama *Oedipus Tyrann,* emphasizes the corporeality of physical labor, desire, and disgust. Müller's Heracles envies Sisyphus because his stone at least does not smell like Augias' realm.[15] In "Herakles 2 oder die Hydra," a prose segment from Müller's play *Zement* (1974) whose dense descriptive style has been adopted in Weiss's *Ästhetik des Widerstands,* Heracles is imagined as hopeful for and simultaneously afraid of nothingness. His violent deeds leave him stuck between an animal existence and his a machine-like functioning.[16] The Canadian poet Anne Carson's "novel in verse" *Autobiography of Red* (1999) offers the most creative receptive retelling of the Heracles and Geryon myth in recent American literature.[17]

Creative production processes of writers and artists such as Théodore Géricault, Bertolt Brecht, and Pablo Picasso are described in detail. Likewise, Weiss minutely depicts inventive ways of reception that enhance the intellectual and emotional alertness of the protagonists. Picasso's ceaseless artistic production is understood by the narrator as a form of resistance. Picasso is characterized as using creative energy in the form of an active intervention in the fight against Franco's dictatorship. Fascism, Weiss emphasizes, directed its attack not only against the physi-

cal life of opponents and minorities, but also against the human mind
and its imaginative faculties:

> Das Zerstörerische, das sich über Spanien hermachte, wollte nicht nur
> Menschen und Städte, sondern auch die Ausdrucksfähigkeit vernichten.
> (I, 335)

The narrator emphasizes the alert mode of reception that Picasso's
painting *Guernica,* his response to the bombing of the Basque town
Guernica by German warplanes on April 26, 1937, both inspires and
requires:

> [. . .] den ersten Eindruck nur als Anlaß zu benutzen, das Gegebne
> auseinanderzunehmen und von verschiednen Richtungen her zu über-
> prüfen, es dann aufs neue zusammenzusetzen und es sich somit anzu-
> eignen [. . .] (I, 336)[18]

Bertolt Brecht's dialogical writing and research style is represented
as similar to Picasso's painting processes. According to the narrator, who
takes part in discussions of, and helps to prepare, Brecht's drama project
on the Swedish rebel Engelbrekt, both Brecht's composition and discussion style consist in the integration of ambivalent topics, in sudden shifts
of perspective, the pursuit of contradicting impulses, the constant
openness for new suggestions (II, 272).[19] As for Picasso, the process of
creative development is more important for Brecht than a finished result
(II, 272).[20]

Far from dismissing beauty as an outdated category, Weiss makes
ample use of an ethical and aesthetic physiognomical topos, the expres-
sive power and beauty of the resistance fighters' faces (I, 55; III, 198).[21]
At the end of the novel's last volume, the narrator points out that postwar Germany lacks a new face since most of those who could have helped
to provide it with one have been killed (III, 329).[22] In this context, it
remains an open question why the narrator calls himself "gesichtsloser
Fremdling" (II, 203). He might use this negative self-description as a
faceless foreigner in order to play down his own contributions to the
resistance movement or to ascribe anonymity to his identity. The accen-
tuated facelessness of the narrator, who after all also lacks a name allows
him to move seamlessly from plot layers to poetological reflections. The
process of narrating violence and resistance, which Müller compares to
slow camera movements, marks itself as being contingent on the narrating voice's desubjectivation.[23]

The protagonists insist on the explicability of reality. Its cognitive inaccessibility and their conceptual helplessness are described as only preliminary (III, 135).[24] Weiss proposes a hermeneutics of "not yet." Understanding, as his characters argue and put into praxis, is a cooperative work in progress. The first person singular and plural narrator commemorates the binding pledge of the small circle of young friends and resistance fighters always to subject the state of the world to rational examination and never to allow economic developments, methods of persecution, and the shift of warfare constellations to gain an overwhelmingly irrational and mythic dimension:

> Dies war für uns eine Grundbedingung, daß die Geschehnisse im großen Maßstab nie zu etwas Unverständlichem, Undurchschaubarem werden, daß wir unsre Isolation nie als ein Ausgeliefertsein ansehn durften. (I, 29)

Heilmann, Coppi, and the narrator share a pronounced disgust of educational privileges and institutionalized cultural hierarchies. Their goal is to abandon a state of passive acceptance of prefabricated pieces of officially sanctioned, authoritative knowledge. Like the German Romantics, they are both skeptical towards traditions and hierarchies and enthusiastically embrace the tradition of longing for epistemic oneness. The young friends enthusiastically agree on the necessity of spontaneously creating anew the whole realm of culture and science (I, 41; 55).[25] Eclectically searching for works of art that transgress perceptive limitations, the friends develop a distinct interest in creative techniques of avantgarde movements such as impressionism, surrealism, futurism, cubism, and dadaism. Rather than celebrating the irrational in order to escape from concrete reality, the friends are interested in making the real world's complexity accessible and in giving new solidity to the ungraspable (I, 68):[26]

> Eine solche Ausdrucksart, die sich über die Logik hinwegsetzte, die alles Fremdartige, Erschreckende gelten ließ, um vorzustoßen zu den Anlässen des eignen Verhaltens, mußte uns, auf unsrer Suche nach Selbsterkenntnis, entsprechen. Auch wir waren ja mißtrauisch gegenüber dem Bestimmten, dem Festgefügten, und sahn unter der Hülle von Gesetzmäßigkeiten die Manipulationen an denen viele von uns zugrunde gingen. (I, 57)

Welcoming modernist paintings because these forms of art overcome perceptive limitations, Heilmann, Coppi, and the narrator become well trained in observing aesthetic and technical differences. A recurring question in their debates is how a painter works toward new ways to expose the destructive drive of society:

> Wir sahn in den Bildern von Max Ernst, Klee, Kandinsky, Schwitters, Dali, Magritte Auflösungen visueller Vorurteile [. . .] Wir erörterten den Widerstreit in den Auffassungen, die es einerseits vorzogen, die Gegenwart in ihrer Vielschichtigkeit, Zerbrochenheit und Wirrnis zu schildern, andrerseits den Zerfall sachlich und genau wiedergaben, wie Dix und Grosz, die hier die vorhandne Wirklichkeit scharf zerlegten und ausmaßen, wie Feininger, und sie dort erhitzt aufflammen ließen, wie Nolde, Kokoschka oder Beckmann. (I, 57)

Having read Arthur Rimbaud's *Une saison d'enfer* to his friends, Heilmann suggests that far from being mutually exclusive, impulsive journeys into the unconscious and the need to recognize political crises can reinforce each other productively. The narrator elaborates on the necessary cooperation between rational acumen and imaginative courage:

> Beides ist richtig, meinte Heilmann, sowohl der Griff, der uns den Boden wegreißt unter den Füßen, als auch das Bestreben, einen festen Grund herzustellen zur Untersuchung einfacher Tatsachen. [. . .] Und so wie sich unsre politische Entscheidung aus Bruchstücken, Dissonanzen, Hypothesen, Resolutionen [. . .] zusammensetzte [. . .] so war auch die Kunst nicht in den Begriff zu bringen, ohne daß wir ihre Schwankungen, Brüche und Gegensätzlichkeiten hinzurechneten. Und wurde ihr das Widerspruchsvolle genommen, so blieb nur ein lebloser Stumpf übrig. [. . .] Immer gehörte das Zweckmäßige zur Kunst und das Eigenwillige, das streng Gebundne und der Sprung zum Überraschenden. (I, 58, 75)

Officially ordered amputation of creative work and political action are likewise deplorable and unacceptable. Neither art nor political engagement should become stagnant and subsumable under rigid categories. Not only the narrator, but many characters in the novel, including Heilmann, Stahlmann, Münzenberg, as well as most of the works of arts and artists discussed by the protagonists, work through traumatic experiences and memories of an endangered identity and try to reconcile their emotional worlds with the need for political analysis and praxis.[27]

The novel's protagonists engage in controversial discussions of censorship; the rigid regimentation of cultural politics in Stalin's U.S.S.R. provokes the question of why revolutionary art is persecuted in the country that declares that it is the home of revolution. Why, Heilmann asks, are innovative artists persecuted, when these individuals never stereotyped their literary characters and had even invented new universal languages, and why were their works replaced by those that reinstalled narrow-minded prescriptions (I, 66–67)?[28]

It is impossible for the protagonists to come to terms with Stalin's show trials, where many of Lenin's closest revolutionaries were sentenced for alleged treason and, due to torture and threats to their families, denounced themselves as criminals and accepted their verdicts in subservient humility. The identity loss of many of the proponents of the October Revolution has been the object of heated debates within communist movements. Weiss gives these discussions a feminist turn by having Marcauer argue that the show trials formed a stage for masculine obsession with power. In Marcauer's view, Stalin's murderous propaganda and sentencing machinery as well as its victims are mere manifestations of the masculine world of vanity and humiliation (I, 293).[29] Recently, some scholars have paid more attention to the feminist thread that runs through Weiss's literary works, and the role of women has been addressed in several insightful articles.[30]

Conceding that the fight against fascism bears a high physical and psychological risk, the social psychologist Max Hodann, the narrator's as well as the author's mentor, who joined the Red Brigades in the Spanish Civil War, adopts a Socratic notion of life when he insists, "untergehn aber müssen wir hellwach" (III, 132).[31]

> Die Gesamtkunst, fuhr er fort, die Gesamtliteratur ist in uns vorhanden, unter der Obhut der einen Göttin, die wir noch gelten lassen können, Mnemosyne. Sie, die Mutter der Künste, heißt Erinnrung. Sie schützt das, was in den Gesamtleistungen unser eignes Erkennen enthält. Sie flüstert uns zu, wonach unsre Regungen verlangen. Wer sich anmaßt, dieses aufgespeicherte Gut zu züchten, zu züchtigen, der greift uns selbst an [. . .] Die Mneme, beschützt von der Göttin Mnemosyne, leite uns zu den künstlerischen Handlungen an, und je mehr wir von den Erscheinungen der Welt in uns aufgenommen hätten, zu desto reichern Kombinationen könnten wir sie bringen, zu der Vielfalt eben, aus der sich der Stand unsrer Kultur ablesen lasse. (I, 77; III, 134)

Blending neurology and mythology and alluding to Hölderlin's poetic fragment *Mnemosyne* (1803/05), Heilmann and Hodann redefine culture as the social capability to share historical awareness and critical thinking, modes of reflection that do not exclude any perception, idea, or sense perception beforehand. Hodann strongly opposes any ideological instrumentalization of creative works. Art, he argues, could be a productive ally of progressive political endeavors, but it refuses to assume a subservient role for the sake of ideological purposes (I, 77):[32]

Dies war das Furchtbare, daß die Partei, deren Aufgabe es gewesen wäre, für die Befreiung der Kultur zu wirken, ihre schöpferischen Denker vernichtete und nur die Schablonen noch gelten ließ. (III, 151)

The narrator continues Hodann's claim that tolerance is a main criterion of the quality of culture by juxtaposing the German and the Soviet dictatorship's systematic destruction of the intellectuals (III, 151).[33] Willi Münzenberg, an undogmatic publisher who was lynched in France by either fascist or Stalinist killers, is characterized as somebody who effortlessly and with immense utopian energy embodies and works toward a nonviolent alliance of politics and creative thought:

> [. . .] daß die kommende Revolution total zu sein hatte, daß der ganze Mensch, von den Impulsen des Traums bis in die praktischen Handlungen, davon ergriffen werden mußte. [. . .] Seine Gedanken schienen ständig mit der Außenwelt zu korrespondieren, es war, als griffe er jedes Wort, jedes Bild aus einer Unbegrenztheit heraus, und doch war seine beiläufigste Bemerkung geprägt von einer starken innern Resonanz. (II, 55–56)

Far from viewing art and literature as mechanical tools for the sake of propaganda, Münzenberg welcomes them as opportunities to enhance one's ways to understand reality:

> [. . .] die visuelle Revolution bedeutete für ihn einen Weg zu reicher zusammengesetzten, mehr der Wirklichkeit entsprechenden Begriffen. (II, 67)

Heilmann, Coppi, and the narrator search for art that is disturbing and rebellious. Insisting that modernist writers, composers, and painters such as Joyce, Kafka, Schönberg, Strawinski, Klee, and Picasso have to be understood in connection with earlier cultural epochs, they study Dante's epos *Commedia,* especially its first part, the *Inferno* (I, 79).[34]

> Hier, aus dürren Andeutungen, aus übermittelten Wahrnehmungen andrer, aus Vergleichen und Gedankenverknüpfungen, Störungen ausgesetzt und der Gefahr des Überfalls, entstand in unsrer Vorstellung etwas von dem Gewebe, das uns umspann. (I, 135)

Théodore Géricault's painting *Le Radeau de Méduse* (1819, The Raft of the Medusa) forms another central object of creative reception in the novel. Immediate narrative shifts switch from the narrator's walks through Paris and musings about his personal creative freedom and political engagement to immersions in both Géricault's painting and the documented story that formed its basis. The narrator explores Géricault's working style, his meticulous preparations, and his obsessive attempts to gain physical closeness to the victims' experiences and corpses (II, 7–17, 119–21).

The narrator decides to become a writer and wants to embrace the project of searching for contexts across the boundaries of states and languages (I, 136).[35] But before he can begin to embark on a journey that transcends any national and linguistic confinements, the narrator has to overcome a deep sense of helplessness. He is far from certain whether the surrounding massive contingents of terror and dissolving contingencies of reality can be rationally processed in order to become more comprehensible and tangible:

> Und wie sollte das Schreiben für uns überhaupt möglich sein, fragte ich mich während des Berichts meines Vaters. Wenn wir etwas von der politischen Wirklichkeit, in der wir lebten, auffassen könnten, wie ließe sich dann dieser dünne, zerfließende, immer nur stückweise zu erlangende Stoff in ein Schriftbild übertragen, mit dem Anspruch auf Kontinuität. (I, 135)

Lotte Bischoff, whom Weiss interviewed while he worked on the novel and whom he called the most unassuming and courageous resistance fighter, usually does not participate in discussions. However, Weiss has her expressing a central argument for the bodily nature of art whose effect, she concludes, corresponds to the physical and emotional release that is brought about by breathing (III, 86).[36] Continuing their deliberations about the compatibility of free thought and directed action, the friends conclude that the experimental and preliminary character of a work of art, its complexity and self-reflexivity, do not have to undermine its usefulness, that is, its capacity to unmask oppressive systems:

> Wir stimmten darin überein, daß der Angreifer nicht in einem Vakuum bleiben durfte, sondern erkennbar geschildert werden mußte. Dies aber schloß nicht aus, daß mit den Medien der Kunst auf den Schwierigkeitsgrad, der das Verständnis entscheidender Vorgänge bestimmte, aufmerksam gemacht werden konnte. (I, 339)

Political analyses and aesthetic interpretations, they argue, are likewise useless and destructive if they are conducted impatiently and with either directives or prefabricated formulas in mind:

> Jeder Versuch, das Abgebildete unmittelbar zu erklären, würde zum Erlöschen des Werks führen. (I, 339)

What makes not only Dante's works durable and contemporary for the narrator as well as for Heilmann and Coppi, is their ability to inspire independent and diverse reflexive work (I, 82).[37] The young fellow readers and thinkers are convinced that culture and thought do not represent an elitist pastime, but can enable everyone to begin the truly democratic and universal praxis of survival and joy. They insist that working with literature, philosophy, and art was possible everywhere and that everybody was endowed with the gift of reflective thought (I, 338).[38] According to Hodann, a central character and mentor figure in the novel, the uncanny, far from consisting in nightmarish visions of excessive cruelty, rather must be located within the everyday social order with its claim to normalcy, and in the inability to recognize the compact yet unapproachable order of structural violence (III, 47).[39] Kafka's works become important to the narrator for their minute depictions of how distortions of consciousness have reached such an extent that they are not even recognized by those who have been subjected to it (I, 171). Survival is synonymous with the freedom of imaginative expression, and the intellectual task to render even the most obtuse oppressive conglomerations of power transparent is an act of resistance:

> Perseus, Dante, Picasso blieben heil und überlieferten, was ihr Spiegel aufgefangen hatte, das Haupt der Medusa, die Kreise des Inferno, das Zersprengen Guernicas. Die Phantasie lebte, so lange der Mensch lebte, der sich zur Wehr setzte. (I, 339)

The narrator becomes a member of the Communist Party as well as an independent writer. While walking through Paris, he enthusiastically envisions the contours of his twofold endeavors and commitments. He is convinced that aesthetic explorations and political straightforwardness do not weaken or negate, but necessitate and nurture each other:

> Der Gedanke an die Aufnahme in die Partei verband sich mit dem Begehren nach unbegrenzten Entdeckungen [. . .] in die geschloßne Organisation, in den kompromißlosen Kampf wollte ich mich begeben, und zugleich in die absolute Freiheit der Phantasie. [. . .] dies alles fügte sich zu einer Einheit zusammen. (II, 19)

The secondary literature on *Die Ästhetik des Widerstands* has sometimes tried to focus on unconscious conflicts and scenes of excessive violence while playing down the political fight, or vice versa.[40] It has to be maintained that thinking these divergent components and thematic undercurrents together rather than opting for an alleged topical hierarchy is not only an indispensable interpretive precondition but also the novel's performative and thematic vanishing point. Tarrying with a precarious cohabitation of dreams and concrete praxis, in other words, being a thinking and imaginative "zoon politikon" that dares to gather and differ is what the protagonists try to achieve. By rationalizing conflicting desires and by adding an unpredictable surplus of utopian emotionality to party discussions, the protagonists do not shy away from self-endangering questionings and transgressions of their own identities. Debates on resistance strategies are never separated from individual perceptions and projections. The group of characters in the novel consists of complex human beings who are not reducible to a phalanx of predictable figures.[41]

The risk of mental imbalances, unconscious visions, and madness are not excluded from the novel's project of rational inquiry.[42] The narrator's mother, who is haunted and silenced by her dreams and visions of the Shoah, embodies the limits of communicable rationalization. Her exposure to hallucinatory traumatic identifications with death camp victims has led to her cognitive retreat from her family and her surroundings. Her son notes that her petrified face reminds him of mythic facial features:

> [. . .] dieses Gesicht, groß, grau, abgenutzt von den Bildern, die sich darüber hergemacht hatten, eine steinerne Maske, die Augen blind in der Bruchfläche. Es war das Gesicht der Ge, der Dämonin der Erde [. . .] (III, 20)

The mother's abandonment of consciousness and retreat from communicability has a concrete historical reason. The vivid clinging of the mother to an imagined organism to Jewish prisoners causes her to give up rational discourse and conventional normalcy. Imprisoned with a group of Jewish men and women, she enthusiastically fantasizes an organic wholeness that she is afraid to leave (III, 12). Instead, she has repeated visions of, and identifies with, the Jewish Shoah victims (III, 130; I, 189). When the narrator concedes that a dialogue with her has become impossible and when he compares her to the earth goddess Ge and to Dürer's *Melencolia,* the mother is turned into an aesthetic, iconic object (III, 20).[43] In this context, Delisle suggests an aesthetic of an empty center.[44] The Swedish poet and dystopian novelist Karin Boye is characterized as a fragile comrade and nocturnal outsider. She befriends the narrator's mother. Boye also gives up rational thinking (III, 38).[45] She eventually commits suicide. Her inner conflicts are discussed sympathetically by Hodann, who later commits suicide himself. Boye, whose poem "Ogonen är vårt öde" (1935, translated as "Our eyes are our fate," 1994) discusses the fear of being imprisoned by a gaze and the desire to see, has been temporarily hypnotized by Goebbel's speech about a total war in Berlin's Sportpalast.[46] The main purpose of her stay in Nazi Germany, psychoanalytic treatment, causes permanent mental imbalance and reaffirms her feelings of guilt for choosing same-sex relationships (III, 33,

42). Hodann retrospectively comments that rationalization only intensifies Boye's suffering. She remains unable to break out of suicidal circles of compassion and dependence, of erotic addiction and disgust of sexuality (III, 39, 46–47).

In the middle of book three, the seemingly unproblematic conjunction "und" assumes a divisive role and works as a stumbling block, a zeugmatic "Widerstand" to any diegetically reductive reading. While leaving a bookstore that the narrator had entered upon seeing Rosa Luxemburg's face on a book cover in the display window, he witnesses the terror of visual violence:

> Mit den Knöpfen, die mir am Mantel fehlten, ging ich hinaus auf die Straße, wo mir einer entgegenkam, dessen Gesicht, in der Sekunde, da die Augen sich auf mich richteten, eingedrückt wurde und zu einer blutigen Masse. (III, 152)

The mesozeugma "eingedrückt wurde und zu einer blutigen Masse" allows for divergent readings and translations. It can be read as "I walked out on the street where somebody came towards me whose face, in the second in which the eyes were looking at me, was crushed and became a bloody mass." However, an alternative translation of the final part of the passage reads as follows: "and I walked towards a bloody mass." The observer, the victim, and the perpetrators are syntactically difficult to distinguish. "Blutige Masse" can be simultaneously understood as a bleeding lump or a bloodthirsty crowd. The syntactic and lexical ambivalence provides interpretive options for both unconscious impulses and historical events. The context leaves it open whether this passage refers to a dream segment or an actual experience of a man who is attacked by Nazis. While the passage identifies neither victim nor culprits, it can be read as a parallel to a previous passage where a retarded Jewish man is beaten and kicked to death by a group of teenagers (I, 189).

Horst Heilmann's fictional letter from his death cell in Berlin-Plötzensee Prison is addressed to an unknown future reader. This fictional letter, which provides one of the novel's most moving passages, also condenses Weiss's aesthetic and ethical project. The deliberations of this young resistance fighter who awaits his execution exemplifies the courage of facing one's world without clinging to prefabricated patterns of thought:

Heilmann an Unbekannt. Versuche, aus dem dichten Gewebe einiges hervorzuholen, von dem sich ablesen läßt, was uns widerfahren ist. Auch wenn ich glaubte, Einsicht zu haben in vieles, ist alles jetzt so ineinander verschlungen, daß ich nur winziger Fäden habhaft werden kann. Du, an deinem Ort, besitzt größern Überblick, kannst vielleicht einmal, wenn dich meine Zeilen erreichen sollten, die Zusammenhänge deuten. (III, 199–200)

These words of a young man shortly before his execution directly address the reader. Remembering discussions with Coppi, who is also hanged by the Nazis, and the narrator about Hölderlin's and Rimbaud's poetry, Heilmann advocates a utopian physiology of light and dreams:

[. . .] haltbar bleibt eigentlich nur, was aus diesen Visionen heraus geschrieben worden ist, zum Beispiel von Hölderlin, von Rimbaud. Wir sprachen über das Sehn im Traum. Fragten uns, wie in der vollkommnen Dunkelheit Farben von solcher Leuchtkraft in uns entstehn können. Sie werden hervorgebracht von unserm Wissen um das Licht. Das Licht sieht. (III, 204)[47]

In commemorating the failure of the European workers' movements to form a strong unity, Weiss is neither providing simplified patterns of guilt versus heroism, nor does he indulge in uncritical hagiography. *Die Ästhetik des Widerstands* does not ascribe unquestionable greatness to a selected group of resistance fighters. The protagonists, whose biographies Weiss researched by conducting interviews and studying archives, are for the most part characterized as unassuming human beings. They undergo phases of skepticism and mental as well as physical exhaustion, and some commit suicide.

Die Ästhetik des Widerstands postulates the necessity of finding transparent connections and of holding on to a rational and recognizable nexus in the midst of political and psychological confusion, "das, was in Fremdartigkeit untergehn wollte, in wiedererkennbare Zusammenhänge zu bringen" (III, 15). *Die Ästhetik des Widerstands* minutely examines possible alliances between art, the unconscious, and concrete actions against the Nazi dictatorship. The novel suggests a creative cooperation between concise documentation and multilayered dream sequences. For Weiss, art is neither reducible to propaganda nor to any conventionally assigned critical function. Literary, artistic, and mythological undercurrents inform the protagonists' desire to rationally understand the complexity of world politics without taking recourse to ideological binary thought systems. But mythologies and literatures are not only used as subtexts or objects of discussions in *Die Ästhetik des Widerstands*. In the novel itself, a new and open-ended mythology emerges from the coalescence of dreamlike journeys and the slow process of planning and communicating the detailed tasks of resistance.[48]

Reconfigurating inconsistencies into a story of loss that ends with a perspective on and from a precariously hypothetical horizon of a future hope, Weiss's aesthetic praxis resists the temptation to attempt comprehensive coverage or to provide harmonized versions of history that would unavoidably level off and explain away productive and necessary conflicts of writing and remembering. Weiss takes Walter Benjamin's formula of a necessary politicization of the aesthetic further by exploring what the political and the aesthetic might become. Brecht, Picasso, and other artists are inspiring to the narrator not because of their finished products but in their ways of beginning and constantly revising their works. Can the conflicts between imaginative experiments of the creative mind on the one hand and political coherence and partisanship on the other be brought into a precarious balance? Lenin's angry exclamation in the midst of a discussion on art and its regulations in Weiss's drama *Trotzki im Exil* identifies the common ground of diverse aesthetic convictions as the realization of the minute, imperceptible, and endangered status of thoughtful praxis.[49] Weiss's summum opus consists of manifold beginnings of responsible and free-floating thought by suggesting open and careful reading journeys along cultural history's friable fragments, which still preserve traces of utopian oneness.[50]

An antidote to ideological fossilizations of all convictions and a plea for creative alliances of artistic freedom and political courage, *Die Ästhetik des Widerstands* can be read as an irresistible introduction into creative thought as a work in progress. The novel reflects Weiss's personal oscillations between privileging condensed fragments and seeking refuge in coherent overviews of political and aesthetic contexts.[51] Weiss's literary works embody, as Caproni writes, a relentless search for an ethics beyond predictable prescriptions.[52] In the wake of, and in continuous reference to, Dante's, Géricault's, Hölderlin's, Rimbaud's, and Picasso's works of mourning and artistic transgression, *Die Ästhetik des Widerstands* invites the reader to explore possibilities of perceptive openness in the face of binary thought patterns and political pressure that, as Robert Musil writes in his novel *Der Mann ohne Eigenschaften* (1930), "alles Persönliche widerstandslos auslöscht."[53] Weiss's summum opus is nourished by the belief that an undogmatic joint effort of autonomous art and political action is possible. Throughout his literary works, Weiss insists that despite its conflicting connotations, "Widerstand" is possible and necessary. His textual worlds portray resistance as a process whose corporeal urgency can be "wahr genommen" that is perceived, thought through, and taken to its fragile and contingent, impossible, and indispensable realization.[54]

Notes

[1] Throughout this chapter, quotations from the novel refer to Peter Weiss, *Die Ästhetik des Widerstands. Roman.* In Peter Weiss, *Werke in sechs Bänden. Dritter Band,* edited by Suhrkamp Verlag in cooperation with Gunilla Palmstierna-Weiss (Frankfurt a.M.: Suhrkamp, 1991).

[2] The German writer Wolfgang Koeppen instantly recognized Weiss's opus magnum as one of the most important twentieth-century novels, see Wolfgang Koeppen, "Der Moralist glaubt an den Teufel," *Frankfurter Allgemeine Zeitung,* November 5, 1976. Also in Wolfgang Koeppen, *Gesammelte Werke in sechs Bänden. 6: Essays und Rezensionen,* edited by Marcel Reich-Ranicki (Frankfurt a.M.: Suhrkamp, 1986), 413: "Der Roman 'Die Ästhetik des Widerstands' ist für mich eines der erregendsten, mutigsten und traurigsten Bücher meiner Zeit." Koeppen refers to the first volume of the novel.

[3] On Dante's presence in *Die Ästhetik des Widerstands* and throughout Weiss's works see Jens Birkmeyer, *Bilder des Schreckens: Dantes Spuren und die Mythosrezeption in Peter Weiss Roman "Die Ästhetik des Widerstands"* (Wiesbaden: DUV, 1994). Peter Kuon, "'. . . dieser Portalheilige zur abendländischen Kunst. . .': Zur Rezeption der *Divina Commedia* bei Peter Weiss, Pier Paolo Pasolini und anderen," *Peter Weiss Jahrbuch* 6 (1997): 42–67. Martin Rector, "Sechs Thesen zur Dante-Rezeption bei Peter Weiss," in *Peter Weiss Jahrbuch* 6 (1997): 110–15. Klaus Scherpe, "Die *Ästhetik des Widerstands* als *Divina Commedia*: Peter Weiss künstlerische Vergegenständlichung der Geschichte," in *Peter Weiss: Werk und Wirkung,* edited by Rudolf Wolff (Bonn: Bouvier, 1987), 88–99. See also Klaus Scherpe, "10 Arbeitspunkte beim Lesen der *Ästhetik des Widerstands,*" in *Lesergespräche: Erfahrungen mit Peter Weiss' Roman "Die Ästhetik des Widerstands,"* edited by G. Dunz-Wolff, H. Goebel, and J. Stüsser (Hamburg: edition comtext, 1988), 168–74. Kafka's role in Weiss's work is negotiated in Andrea Heyde, *Unterwerfung und Aufruhr: Franz Kafka im literarischen Werk von Peter Weiss* (Berlin: Schmidt, 1997). On the central focal point of aisthesis, perception, in the novel see Birgit Feusthuber, "Die *Ästhetik des Widerstands* bleibt eine Zumutung," in *Widerstand wahrnehmen: Dokumente eines Dialogs mit Peter Weiss,* edited by Jens-F. Dwars, Dieter Strützel, and Mathias Mieth (Köln: GNN, 1993), 309–11. Here: 310.

[4] For more information about the resistance groups that figure prominently in the novel, see the following careful documentations: Regina Griebel, Marlies Coburger, Heinrich Scheel, *Erfasst? Das Gestapo-Album zur Roten Kapelle: Eine Foto-Dokumentation* (Halle: audioscop, 1992). Hans Coppi, *Harro Schulze-Boysen — Wege in den Widerstand: Eine biographische Studie* (Koblenz: Fölbach, 1993). Hans Coppi, Jürgen Danyel, Johannes Tuchel, eds., *Die Rote Kapelle im Widerstand gegen den Nationalsozialismus* (Berlin: Edition Hentrich, 1994). Hans Coppi, Geertje Andresen, eds., *Dieser Tod paßt zu mir. Harro Schulze-Boysen — Grenzgänger im Widerstand: Briefe 1915 bis 1942* (Berlin: Aufbau, 1999). Ursel Hochmuth, *Illegale*

KPD und Bewegung 'Freies Deutschland' in Berlin und Brandenburg 1942–1945: Biographien und Zeugnisse aus der Widerstandsorganisation um Saefkow, Jacob und Bästlein (Berlin: Hentrich & Hentrich, 1998). See also Elfriede Brüning's historical novel *Damit du weiterlebst* (Berlin: Neues Leben, 1949). Some of the resistance fighters who are protagonists in Weiss's novel also appear in Armand Gatti's drama *Rosa Collective* (Paris: Éditions du Seuil, 1973), 132–33 . For an overview of the literary critics' political bias that shaped the early reception history of the novel in the German press see Volker Lilienthal, *Literaturkritik als politische Lektüre: Am Beispiel der Rezeption der "Ästhetik des Widerstands" von Peter Weiss* (Berlin: Spiess, 1988).

[5] See Jost Müller, *Literatur und Politik bei Peter Weiss: Die "Ästhetik des Widerstands" und die Krise des Marxismus* (Wiesbaden: DUV, 1991), 150–51.

[6] *Notizbücher 1971–1980. 1. Band* (Frankfurt a.M.: Suhrkamp, 1981), 423: "Ästhetische Fragen sind immer politische Fragen."

[7] See Nana Badenberg, "Die *Ästhetik* und ihre Kunstwerke: Eine Inventur," in *Die Bilderwelt des Peter Weiss,* edited by Alexander Honold and Ulrich Schreiber (Berlin: Argument, 1995), 114–29. See also Nana Badenberg, "Kommentiertes Verzeichnis der in der *Ästhetik des Widerstands* erwähnten bildenden Künstler und Kunstwerke," in *Die Bilderwelt des Peter Weiss,* edited by Alexander Honold and Ulrich Schreiber (Berlin: Argument, 1995), 163–230. The importance of ekphrastic discussions and the opposition and confluence of painting and word/thought for the protagonists in *Die Ästhetik des Widerstands,* and in Weiss's work in general is analyzed in the following research contributions: Klaus Müller-Richter, "Bilderwelten und Wortwelten: Gegensatz oder Komplement? Peter Weiss' Konzept der Bildlichkeit als Modell dynamischer Aisthesis." *Peter Weiss Jahrbuch* 6 (1997): 116–37; Anton Philipp Knittel, *Erzählte Bilder der Gewalt: Die Stellung der "Ästhetik des Widerstands" im Prosawerk von Peter Weiss* (Konstanz: Hartung-Knorre, 1996); Stephan Meyer, *Kunst als Widerstand: Zum Verhältnis von Erzählen und ästhetischer Reflexion in Peter Weiss' "Die Ästhetik des Widerstands"* (Tübingen: Niemeyer, 1989); Rüdiger Steinlein, "Ein surrealistischer 'Bilddichter': Visualität als Darstellungsprinzip im erzählerischen Frühwerk von Peter Weiss," in *Peter Weiss: Werk und Wirkung,* edited by Rudolf Wolff (Bonn: Bouvier, 1987), 60–87.

[8] For a comprehensive list of and concise commentaries on the works of art that are discussed in *Die Ästhetik des Widerstands,* see Nana Badenberg, "Kommentiertes Verzeichnis der in der *Ästhetik des Widerstands* erwähnten bildenden Künstler und Kunstwerke," in *Die Bilderwelt des Peter Weiss,* edited by Alexander Honold and Ulrich Schreiber (Berlin: Argument, 1995), 163–230. See also Nana Badenberg, "Die *Ästhetik* und ihre Kunstwerke: Eine Inventur," in *Die Bilderwelt des Peter Weiss,* edited by Alexander Honold and Ulrich Schreiber (Berlin: Argument, 1995), 114–29.

[9] "Swinging" movements form a topos that the novel also employs to characterize Stahlmann, the "man of action" among the resistance fighters, whose "Schwungkraft" is predicated on an unwillingness to reflect on the past, see III, 93. His vivid gestures explicitly remind the narrator of Heracles, see III, 95: "Und mit weit ausholender Geste, als schwinge er einen Umhang, ein Löwenfell, um sich, wandte er mir sein gebräuntes Gesicht zu [. . .]"

[10] "Nun habe ich, schrieb Heilmann, nicht nur den Dodekathlos noch einmal, sondern andres noch, was von den Spuren des Herakles berichtet, studiert, und dabei ist seine Gestalt vielfältiger, auch fragwürdiger geworden."

[11] Berthold Brunner, *Der Herakles / Stahlmann-Komplex in Peter Weiss' "Ästhetik des Widerstands"* (St. Ingbert: Röhrig Universitätsverlag, 1999). Berthold Brunner, "Richard Stahlmann — zur historischen Person: Eine Textcollage und zwei hanschriftliche Lebensläufe," in *Peter Weiss Jahrbuch* 2 (1993): 118–53. See also Andreas Huber, *Mythos und Utopie. Eine Studie zur "Ästhetik des Widerstands" von Peter Weiss* (Heidelberg: Winter, 1990), 53–69, and Karl-Josef Müller, *Haltlose Reflexion: Über die Grenzen der Kunst in Peter Weiss' Roman "Die Ästhetik des Widerstands"* (Würzburg: Königshausen & Neumann, 1992), 158–59.

[12] In his final letter from his death cell, Heilmann even uses the Pergamon frieze as a metaphor for his personal life, see III, 200: "[. . .] ehe wir noch gemeinsam nach Herakles suchten, in unserm Lebensfries."

[13] See, for example, the last verse of Hölderlin's ode *Chiron,* which evokes a future return of Heracles: "Bis sie erscheinet, Herakles Rückkehr." See also Friedrich Wilhelm Joseph von Schelling, *Philosophie der Mythologie,* in F. W. J. Schelling, *Ausgewählte Schriften. Band 6: 1842–1852. Zweiter Teilband,* edited by Manfred Frank, 339–61 (Frankfurt a.M.: Suhrkamp, 1985). See also Stefan Meyer, *Kunst als Widerstand: Zum Verhältnis von Erzählen und ästhetischer Reflexion in Peter Weiss' "Die Ästhetik des Widerstands"* (Tübingen: Niemeyer, 1989), 176–77. For Heracles' incorporation into iconographic traditions, see "Herakles," in *Lexicon Iconographicum Mythologiae Classicae,* edited by John Boardman et al. (Zurich/Munich: Artemis, 1988), IV, 1: 728–838; IV, 2: 444–559.

[14] Frank Wedekind, *Herakles. Dramatisches Gedicht in drei Akten,* in Frank Wedekind. *Dramen 2. Gedichte,* edited by Manfred Hahn (Berlin/Weimar: Aufbau, 1969), 281–342, here: 342. A comparative study of twentieth-century German Heracles literature would have to include Rudolf Borchardt's poem *Der ruhende Herakles* (date uncertain), in which seeming scenic harmony is undermined by conflictual tensions, see Rudolf Borchardt, *Gedichte,* edited by Marie Luise Borchardt and Herbert Steiner (Stuttgart: Klett, 1957), 539–60.

[15] Heiner Müller, "Herakles 5," in Heiner Müller, *Werke 3. Die Stücke 1,* edited by Frank Höringk (Frankfurt a.M.: Suhrkamp, 2000), 397–409.

[16] Heiner Müller, "Herakles 2 oder die Hydra," in Heiner Müller, *Werke 2. Die Prosa,* edited by Frank Höringk (Frankfurt a.M.: Suhrkamp, 1999), 94–98. Here: 97–98: "[. . .] manchmal verzögerte er seinen Wiederaufbau, gierig wartend auf die gänzliche Vernichtung mit Hoffnung auf das Nichts, die unendliche Pause, oder aus Angst vor dem Sieg, der nur durch die gänzliche Vernichtung des Tieres erkämpft werden konnte, das sein Aufenthalt war, außer dem vielleicht das Nichts schon auf ihn wartete oder auf niemand [. . .] lernte er den immer andern Bauplan der Maschine lesen, die er war aufhörte zu sein anders wieder war mit jedem Blick Griff Schritt, und daß er ihn dachte änderte schrieb mit der Handschrift seiner Arbeiten und Tode."

[17] Anne Carson, *Autobiography of Red: A Novel in Verse* (London: Cape Poetry, 1999).

[18] This dialectical shift from analysis to synthesis, in conjunction with the reflexive verb "sich aneignen" to denote the positive work of appropriating segments of culture or nature as part of a nonviolent mode of productive reception, stands in close intertextual dialogue with passages by Goethe.

[19] "Im Aufnehmen zwiespältiger Themen, in den jähen Verschiebungen der Aspekte, dem Befolgen gegensätzlicher Impulse, der ständigen Offenheit für neue Vorschläge war etwas von Brechts Arbeitstechnik zu erkennen."

[20] "Im übrigen fesselte ihn das Experimentieren mehr als die Bemühung um ein abgeschloßnes Werk. Jedes Bruchstück, jedes Teilresultat hatte seinen eigenen Wert." In this context, it is instructive that Brecht titled his works as experiments, "Versuche," that are open for change and that do not assume or presume an ultimate and immobile status.

[21] "[. . .] ihre Gesichter [. . .] die Ausdruckskraft, die in ihnen verborgen lag [. . .] Hössler [. . .] Dieses offne, leuchtende Gesicht. Und die Gesichter der Hübners [. . .]" See also *Notizbücher 1971–1980. Band 2* (Frankfurt a.M.: Suhrkamp, 1981), 820: "Schönheit: sie ist zu finden in den Gesichtern des Widerstands."

[22] "Was sollte werden aus diesem Land, das jetzt fast aller beraubt worden war, die ihm ein neues Gesicht hätten geben können."

[23] Jost Müller, *Literatur und Politik bei Peter Weiss: Die "Ästhetik des Widerstands" und die Krise des Marxismus* (Wiesbaden: DUV, 1991), 174.

[24] "[. . .] wir besaßen für das, was das Offenkundige überstieg, nur noch keine Register, unsre Hilflosigkeit war eine vorläufige [. . .]"

[25] "Um zu uns selbst zu kommen, sagte Heilmann, haben wir uns nicht nur die Kultur, sondern auch die gesamte Forschung neu zu schaffen, indem wir sie in Beziehung stellen zu dem, was uns betrifft. [. . .] wir wollten keine Zuteilungen, kein uns zugemessnes Stückwerk, sondern das Ganze, und dieses Ganze sollte auch nichts Überliefertes sein, es mußte erst erschaffen werden."

[26] "[. . .] nicht, um wegzukommen vom Faßlichen, sondern um dem, was ungreifbar blieb, neue Festigkeit zu verleihn." In a similar vein, the protagonists' interest in and admiration for Dante is based upon their conviction that his work regains new terrain for thought by metrically mastering that which opposes and challenges rationality, see I, 80: "[. . .] das Chaotische, Weggleitende, absolut Ungewisse [. . .]"

[27] Gerlach's claim that most of the characters can be defined either as "rational and active" or as "emotional and passive" suggests an unproductive reduction of complex personalities to conveniently recognizable mosaic stones, see Ingeborg Gerlach, *Die ferne Utopie: Studien zu Peter Weiss' "Ästhetik des Widerstands"* (Aachen: Karin Fischer, 1991), 41.

[28] "Bei Gorki, Ostrowskij, Gladkow, Babel wurden die Charaktere nie zur Schablone [. . .] warum wurde eine Kunst, die revolutionär war, verleugnet und verfemt, warum wurden die Werke, die dem Experimentieren ihrer Zeit die Stimme verliehn [. . .] warum wurden diese kühnen mitrerißenden Gleichnisse des Aufbruchs ersetzt durch Fertigesm warum wurde eine enge Begrenzung der Aufnahmefähigkeit eingeführt, wenn ein Majakowski, Blok, Bednij, Jesenin und Bely, ein Malewitsch, Lissitzki, Tatlin, Wachtangow, Tairow, Eisenstein oder Vertow die Sprache gefunden hatten, die identisch war mit einem neuen universalen Bewußtsein."

[29] "Sie hätten selbst den Thron dessen einnehmen wollen, von dem sie sich züchtigen lassen, denn aus Eitelkeit und Hörigkeit, aus Hochmut und Erniedrigung besteht ihre Welt. Eure Ordnung, rief sie, zeigt sich dort in der Säulenhalle in ihrer letzten Konsequenz."

[30] The role of women in the novel is discussed in several recent articles. See Irene Dölling, "Frauen im Klassenkampf: Klassenkampf und Geschlechterfrage in Peter Weiss' *Ästhetik des Widerstands*," in *"Ästhetik des Widerstands": Erfahrungen mit dem Roman von Peter Weiss*, edited by Norbert Krenzlin (Berlin: Akademie, 1987), 45–63; Birgit Feusthuber, "Sprache und Erinnerungsvermögen: Weibliche Spurensuche in der *Ästhetik des Widerstands* von Peter Weiss," in *Ästhetik Revolte Widerstand: Zum literarischen Werk von Peter Weiss*, edited by Jürgen Garbers, Jens-Christian Hagsphil, Sven Kramer, and Ulrich Schreiber (Jena/Lüneburg: Universitätsverlag, zu Klampen, 1990), 207–37; Birgit Feusthuber, "Najaden und Sirenen: Weiblichkeitsbilder in der *Ästhetik des Widerstands*," in *Peter Weiss: Neue Fragen an alte Texte*, edited by Irene Heidelberger-Leonard (Opladen: Westdeutscher Verlag, 1994), 97–110; Bernd Rump, *Herrschaft und Widerstand: Untersuchungen zu Genesis und Eigenart des kulturphilosophischen Diskurses in dem Roman "Die Ästhetik des Widerstands" von Peter Weiss* (Aachen: Shaker, 1996), 120–23; Ursula Bessen, "Eine 'destruktive Gewaltfigur' oder Abschied von Mutter und Medusa," in *Peter Weiss Jahrbuch* 8 (1999): 89–96.

[31] "[. . .] untergehn aber müssen wir hellwach." Wolff's and Bergmann's recent biographical works provide more information about Max Hodann. See Wilfried Wolff, *Max Hodann (1894–1946): Sozialist und Sozialreformer* (Hamburg: von Bockel, 1993); Hans-Joachim Bergmann, "Max Julius Karl Hodann (1894–1946)," in *Berliner jüdische Ärzte in der Weimarer Republik*, edited by Bernhard Meyer and Hans-Jürgen Mende (Berlin: Edition Luisenstadt, 1996), 107–49.

[32] "Unverblümt bricht die Ideologie in ein Gebiet ein, das ihr wohl verbunden sein könnte, das sich ihr aber verschließen muß, wenn sie Unterordnung fordert."

[33] "[. . .] und so wie der Faschismus eingeschlagen hatte auf die differenzierten Leistungen von Kunst und Literatur, so war auch vom Zentrum des Kommunismus die Destruktion der Intellektuellen angeordnet worden."

[34] "Wir bestanden darauf, daß Joyce und Kafka, Schönberg und Strawinski, Klee und Picasso der gleichen Reihe angehörten, in der sich auch Dante befand, mit dessen Inferno wir uns seit einiger Zeit beschäftigten. Die Divina Commedia war ebenso beunruhigend, rebellisch und formal und thematisch scheinbar ebenso von allem Bekannten entfernt wie der Ullysses [. . .]"

[35] "Wohl konnte ich die Vorzüge, einem Land, einer Stadt anzugehören, einsehn, für mein Vorhaben aber gab es einen solchen Ausgangspunkt nicht, ich würde aus dem Formlosen, Ungebundnen heraus beginnen müssen und nach Zusammenhängen suchen über die Grenzen von Staaten und Sprachen hinweg." This emphasis on the artist's personal, transnational independence is reminiscent of several earlier works by Weiss, including *Fluchtpunkt*, in *Werke* 2, 294: "An diesem Abend, im Frühjahr 1947, auf dem Seinedamm in Paris, im Alter von dreißig Jahren, sah ich, daß ich teilhaben konnte an einem Austausch von Gedanken, der ringsum stattfand, an kein Land gebunden."

[36] "Die Kunst ist also etwas, das dem körperlichen Aufatmen ähnlich ist."

[37] "[. . .] denn das war es, was sie dauerhaft machte, daß sie unsre eignen Erwägungen weckten, daß sie nach unsern Antworten verlangten."

[38] "Wir aber gingen davon aus, daß die Beschäftigung mit Literatur, Philosophie, Kunst überall möglich war. Allen war die Fähigkeit gegeben nachzudenken."

[39] "[. . .] das Unheimliche sei nicht in den Schreckensgesichten zu sehn, diese könnten sich, in unendlicher Folge, bis zu immer unvorstellbarer werdenden Grausamkeiten variieren lassen, das Unheimliche sei vielmehr das ein für alle Mal Feststehende, diese riesige, unnahbare Ordnung, die kaum etwas Beunruhigendes von sich gibt, die einfach nur da ist, mit Selbstverständlichkeit fortwirkt und all das bestimmt, was uns dann schließlich, auf weit verzweigten Umwegen, erwürgt und vernichtet. Das Unheimliche [. . .] ist nicht das Grauenhafte [. . .] sondern unsre Unfähigkeit, das banale, kompakt Unverrückbare zu erkennen."

[40] While Bohrer emphasizes Weiss's alleged obsession with cruelty and violence and his poetological allegiance to Artaud and Genet, Hermand advocates the primacy of the political in Weiss's works. See Karl Heinz Bohrer, "Die Tortur — Peter Weiss' Weg ins Engagement — die Geschichte des Individualisten," in *Peter Weiss,* edited by Rainer Gerlach (Frankfurt a.M.: Suhrkamp, 1984), 182–207; Jost Hermand, "Das Floß der Medusa: Über Versuche, den Untergang zu überleben," in *Die "Ästhetik des Widerstands" lesen: Über Peter Weiss,* edited by Karl-Heinz Götze and Klaus R. Scherpe (Berlin: Argument, 1981), 112–20, here: 116.

[41] Shortly before his death, Weiss suggested that his novel should be understood from the perspective of "das Element des Traums." See Robert Cohen, *Bio-Bibliographisches Handbuch zu Peter Weiss' "Ästhetik des Widerstands"* (Hamburg: Argument, 1989), 164.

[42] Manon Delisle, *Weltuntergang ohne Ende: Ikonographie und Inszenierung der Katastrophe bei Christa Wolf, Peter Weiss und Hans Magnus Enzensberger* (Würzburg: Königshausen & Neumann, 2001), 158: "Das Andere der Vernunft [. . .] wird vielmehr in eine Form von Aufklärung integriert, die über ein eng rationales Erfassen der Welt hinaus geht."

[43] See Manon Delisle, *Weltuntergang ohne Ende: Ikonographie und Inszenierung der Katastrophe bei Christa Wolf, Peter Weiss und Hans Magnus Enzensberger* (Würzburg: Königshausen & Neumann, 2001), 161: "Zweimal wird die Mutter, die selber ihre inneren Bilder nicht mehr mitzuteilen vermag, von ihrem Sohn zum Bild gemacht. Diese Verwandlung vom stummen Subjekt innerer Bilder zum Objekt eines Deutungsvorgangs, der selber mit Bildern arbeitet, geschieht jedesmal gegen Ende eines Kapitels."

[44] See Manon Delisle, *Weltuntergang ohne Ende: Ikonographie und Inszenierung der Katastrophe bei Christa Wolf, Peter Weiss und Hans Magnus Enzensberger* (Würzburg: Königshausen & Neumann, 2001), 173–74: "Eine Ästhetik der Leerstelle [. . .]"

[45] "Boye, dieser zarte Mitsoldat, dieses nächtliche Ich [. . .]"

[46] See Karin Boye, *Dikter* (Stockholm: Bonniers, 1965), 187. English version in *Complete Poems,* translated by David McDuff (Newcastle: Bloodaxe Books, 1994), 125.

[47] This passage is reminiscent of Plotin's and Goethe's claim that the eye creates light.

[48] At times, Weiss makes use of historical coincidences that highlight the emergence of intertextual nexus, for example the historical fact that Horst Heilmann lived in the Hölderlin Street in Berlin.

[49] *Trotzki im Exil,* in *Werke* 6, 43.

[50] See the ekphrastic immersion into the Pergamon frieze at the beginning of the novel, I, 7: "[. . .] mürbe Bruchstücke, aus denen die Ganzheit sich ablesen ließ [. . .]"

[51] See Weiss's unpublished notebook entry from 1954: "Ich habe oft geglaubt, dass das Fragmentarische, Kaleidoskopische mir nahe läge, doch eigentlich suche ich eine Dichtigkeit, Ueberblick." Peter Weiss Archive, Academy of the Arts, Berlin, 76/86/6061.

[52] Attilio Mauro Caproni, *Tre Ipotesi Sceniche: Ionesco, Beckett, Weiss* (Roma: Manzella, 1975).

[53] Robert Musil, *Der Mann ohne Eigenschaften. Roman,* edited by Adolf Frisé (Reinbek: Rowohlt, 1988), 143. Compare Weiss's characterization of Hölderlin's and Rimbaud's achievements in *Notizbücher 1971–1980. Band 2* (Frankfurt a.M.: Suhrkamp, 1981), 788: "[. . .] beide haben [. . .] den Anlauf zum großen Sprung, den sie wagten, genau beschrieben."

[54] W. S. Merwin defines the work of translation as "impossible and indispensable." See W. S. Merwin, *East Window: The Asian Translations* (Port Townsend, WA: Copper Canyon Press, 1998), 12: "[. . .] an enterprise that is plainly impossible and nevertheless indispensable."

Works Consulted

Works by Weiss

Werke = Peter Weiss. *Werke in sechs Bänden*. 6 vols. Edited by Suhrkamp Verlag in cooperation with Gunilla Palmstierna-Weiss. Frankfurt a.M.: Suhrkamp, 1991.

"Die kleine Geschichte von 5 Seeräubern und einem Mädchen." 46 pages, with illustrations. Peter Weiss Archive, Academy of the Arts, Berlin. 76/86/6011. Written 1934.

"Günter an Beatrice. Bearbeitet und herausgegeben von Peter U. Fehér." 116 pages, with illustrations. Peter Weiss Archive, Academy of the Arts, Berlin. 76/86/6014. Written 1934.

"Bekenntnis eines großen Malers." Written 1935–37. Translated into Swedish in *Landskapen i drömmarna: Ur en ung författares arbetsböcker*. Hedemora: Gidlund, 1991.

"Fluch und Gnade oder Wolfgang Hungers kleine Chronik." 17 pages. Peter Weiss Archive, Academy of the Arts, Berlin. 76/86/6072. Written 1936.

"Ulule Schömgözewö, ein Fragment." 18 pages. Peter Weiss Archive, Academy of the Arts, Berlin. 76/86/6068. Written 1930s.

"Vom versunkenen Leben." 15 pages. Peter Weiss Archive, Academy of the Arts, Berlin. 76/86/6070. Written 1930s.

"Chloë. Aus Caspar Walthers hinterlassenen Aufzeichnungen." 60 pages. Peter Weiss Archive, Academy of the Arts, Berlin. 76/86/6027. Written 1937.

"Die Insel. Eine Art Flugschrift. Vor Augen geführt durch Skruwe. Herausgegeben von Peter Ulrich Weiss mit freundlicher Genehmigung des Bundesarchivs." 59 pages. Peter Weiss Archive, Academy of the Arts, Berlin. 76/86/6012. Three pages published in Peter Spielmann, ed. *Der Maler Peter Weiss: Bilder — Zeichnungen — Collagen — Filme*, 126–27, 162. Berlin: Frölich & Kaufmann, 1982. Written 1937. Translated into Swedish in *Landskapen i drömmarna: Ur en ung författares arbetsböcker*. Hedemora: Gidlund, 1991.

"Die Gezeiten. Eine Erzählung aus unseren Tagen." 127 pages, with illustrations. Peter Weiss Archive, Academy of the Arts, Berlin. 76/86/6010. Written 1938.

"Traktat von der ausgestorbenen Welt." 48 pages, with illustrations. Peter Weiss Archive, Academy of the Arts, Berlin. 76/86/6016. Partly published in Peter Spielmann, ed. *Der Maler Peter Weiss: Bilder — Zeichnungen — Collagen — Filme*, 51–61. Berlin: Frölich & Kaufmann, 1982. Written 1938. Translated into Swedish in *Landskapen i drömmarna: Ur en ung författares arbetsböcker*. Hedemora: Gidlund, 1991.

"Des Zaubervogels Lied." 14 pages. Peter Weiss Archive, Academy of the Arts, Berlin. 76/86/6067. Written 1938.

"Der Himmel über der Stadt." Written 1938.

"Glockenstadt und Scarabietta." Written 1938.

"Staube und bete dich an." 51 pages. Peter Weiss Archive, Academy of the Arts, Berlin. 76/86/6073. Written 1930s.

"Die Landschaften in den Träumen." 80 pages, with illustrations. Peter Weiss Archive, Academy of the Arts, Berlin. 76/86/6013. Written 1939. Translated into Swedish in *Landskapen i drömmarna: Ur en ung författares arbetsböcker*. Hedemora: Gidlund, 1991.

"Schmolk." 91 pages. Peter Weiss Archive, Academy of the Arts, Berlin. 76/86/6046. N.d.

Från ö till ö. Illustrated. Stockholm: Bonniers, 1947. Written 1944. Translated into German as *Von Insel zu Insel.* Berlin: Frölich & Kaufmann, 1984. In *Werke* 1, 7–52.

De Besegrade. Illustrated. Stockholm: Bonniers, 1948. Written 1947. Translated into German as *Die Besiegten.* Frankfurt a.M.: Suhrkamp, 1985. Also in *Werke* 1, 53–121. Translated into Japanese as *Yabureta monotachi.* Tokyo: Chikumashobo, 1987.

Articles in Swedish on Postwar Berlin for *Stockholms-Tidningen*. Written 1947. Translated into German as "Sieben Reportagen fuer Stockholms Tidningen." Frankfurt a.M.: Suhrkamp, 1985. Also in *Werke* 1, 122–43.

"Ur anteckningar." *Utsikt* 7/1948. Translated into German as "Aus Aufzeichnungen." In Annie Bourgignon. *Der Schriftsteller Peter Weiss und Schweden*, 285–88. St. Ingbert [Germany]: Röhrig, 1997.

"Den anonyme." *Utsikt* 5/1949. Translated into German as "Der Anonyme." In Annie Bourgignon. *Der Schriftsteller Peter Weiss und Schweden*, 289–90. St. Ingbert: Röhrig, 1997.

Der Turm. In *Werke* 4, 7–33. Written 1948. First published in *Spectaculum* 1963, 250–68 and 433. Stuttgart: Reclam, 1973. Translated into English as "The Tower." In *Postwar German Theatre*, edited by Michael Benedikt and George E. Wellwarth, 315–48. New York: Dutton, 1967.

Der Vogelfreie, published as *Der Fremde,* under the pseudonym "Sinclair." Frankfurt a.M.: Suhrkamp, 1980. Written 1948. In *Werke* 1, 145–219. Translated into Swedish as *Dokument I.* Stockholm: Private Edition, 1949.

"L. sass neben dem Kachelofen." Two pages. Peter Weiss Archive, Academy of the Arts, Berlin. 76/86/6061. Written 1951.

Der Schatten des Körpers des Kutschers. Mit sieben Collagen des Autors. In *Werke* 2, 7–56. Written 1952. First published Frankfurt a.M.: Suhrkamp, 1960 (latest edition 1991). Translated into Czech as *Stín vozkova tela.* Praha: Odeon, 1966; into Swedish as *Skuggan av kuskens kropp.* Stockholm, 1966; into Italian as *L'ombra del corpo del cocchiere.* Milano, 1968; into Spanish as *La sombra del cuerpo del cochero.* Barcelona: Seix Barral, 1968; into English as "The Shadow of the Coachman's Body." In *Bodies and Shadows.* New York: Delacorte, 1969, 1–57. Translated into Hebrew as *ha-Tsel shel gufo shel ha-'eglon.* Tel Aviv: ha-Kibuts ha-me'uhad, 1978; into Japanese as *Gyosha no karada no kage shoten.* Tokyo: Sanshusha, 1979.

Die Versicherung. In *Werke* 4, 35–87. Written 1952. First published in *Deutsches Theater der Gegenwart.* Edited by Karlheinz Braun. Band 1. Frankfurt a.M. 1967, 83–146.

Duellen. Illustrated. Private edition, Stockholm, 1953. Written 1953. Translated into German as *Das Duell.* Frankfurt a.M.: Suhrkamp, 1972. In *Werke* 1, 221–87. Translated into Spanish as *El duelo.* Barcelona: Lumen, 1973. Translated into Japanese as *Ketto; Aruiteiru sannin no kaiwa.* Tokyo: Hakusuisha, 1976.

"En glasdörr." 144 pages. Peter Weiss Archive, Academy of the Arts, Berlin. 76/86/6029. N.d.

Avantgardefilm Stockholm: Wahlström & Widstrand, 1956. Written 1955. Translated into French as *Cinéma d'avant-garde.* Paris: L'Arche, 1989; into German as *Avantgarde Film.* Frankfurt a.M.: Suhrkamp, 1995. Also as a short German essay version in *Akzente* 10 (2/1963): 297–320. Also in *Rapporte,* 7–35. Frankfurt a.M.: Suhrkamp, 1968.

Situationen. Written 1956. Translated into German as *Die Situation.* Frankfurt: Suhrkamp, 2000.

"Der große Traum des Briefträgers Cheval." In *Akzente* 5/1960. Written 1960. Also in *Rapporte* 2, 36–50. Frankfurt a.M.: Suhrkamp, 1971. Translated into French in *Du palais idéal à l'enfer ou Du facteur cheval à Dante,* edited by Günter Schütz. Paris: Kimé, 2001.

"Aus dem Kopenhagener Journal Herbst 1960." In *Jahresring* 62/63. Stuttgart, 1962, 224–39. Written 1960. Also in *Rapporte,* 51–71. Frankfurt a.M.: Suhrkamp, 1968. Translated into Swedish in *Rapporter.* 1968; into Italian in *Critica e lotta.* Milano: Feltrinelli, 1976.

Abschied von den Eltern. Erzählung. In *Werke* 2, 57–141. Written 1960/61. First published Frankfurt a.m.: Suhrkamp, 1961 (latest edition 1992). Translated into Swedish as *Diagnos.* Malmö, 1963; into French in *Point de fuite.* Paris: Éditions du Seuil, 1964; into Danish as *Afsked med foraeldrene.* Kopenhagen, 1964; into Dutch as *Afscheid van mijn ouders.* Amsterdam 1964; into Italian as *Congedi dai genitori.* Torino, 1965; into Polish as: "Uciecka z domu rodzinnego." In *Uciecka z domu rodzinnego. Azyl.* Warsaw, 1965. Also translated into Finnish as: *Jäähyväiset vanhemmille.* Helsinki, 1966; into Slovak in *Rozlucka srodicmi.* Bratislava, 1967; into English as "Leavetaking." In *Exile.* New York: Delacorte, 1968, 1–88. Translated into Spanish as: *Adios a los padres. Punto de fuga.* Barcelona: Editorial Lumen, 1968; into Japanese as *Ryoshin tono wakare.* Tokyo: Kawadeshoboshinsha, 1970.

Fluchtpunkt. Roman. In *Werke* 2, 143–294. Written 1960/61. First published Frankfurt a.m.: Suhrkamp, 1962. Translated into French as *Point de fuite.* Paris: Éditions du Seuil, 1964; into Dutch as *Einde van een Vlucht.* Amsterdam, 1964; into Swedish as *Brännpunkt.* Stockholm, 1964; into Danish as *Flugtpunkt.* Kopenhagen, 1965; into Polish as "Azyl." In *Uciecka z domu rodzinnego. Azyl.* Warsaw, 1965. Also translated into Italian as *Punto di Fuga.* Torino 1967; into English as *Vanishing Point.* In Peter Weiss. *Exile.* New York: Delacorte, 1968, 89–245; and into Spanish as *Adios a los padres. Punto de fuga.* Barcelona: Editorial Lumen, 1985.

"Gegen die Gesetze der Normalität." *Akzente* 4/1962. Written 1962. Also in *Rapporte,* 72–82. Frankfurt a.m.: Suhrkamp, 1968. Translated into Swedish in *Rapportre* 1968. Translated into Italian in *Critica e lotta.* Milano: Feltrinelli, 1976.

Das Gespräch der drei Gehenden. In *Werke* 2, 295–344. Written 1962. First published Frankfurt a.m.: Suhrkamp, 1963 (latest edition 1990). Translated into Swedish as *Vandring for tre röster.* Malmö 1964 into Finnish as *Kolmen kulkijan keskustelu.* Helsinki, 1965; into Norwegian as *Samtale mellom tre gående.* Oslo, 1965; into Czech as *Rozhovor trí chodcu.* Praha: MF, 1966; into Slovak in *Rozlucka srodicmi.* Bratislava, 1967; into Danish as *Samtalen mellem de tre gående.* Kopenhagen, 1967; into English as: "Conversation of the Three Wayfarers." In Peter Weiss. *Bodies and Shadows.* New York: Delacorte, 1969, 59–120. Other English version, "The Conversation of the Three Walkers." In Peter Weiss. *The Conversation of the Three Walkers and The Shadow of the Coachman's Body.* London: Calder & Boyars, 1972, 7–86. Also translated into Polish as *Rozmowa trzech idacych.* Warszawa: Panstwowy Instytut Wydawniczy, 1967; into Hungarian as "Harman mennek beszélgetnek." In *Mai nemet kisregenyek.* Budapest, 1968; into Italian as: *Colloquio dei tre Viandanti.* Torino, 1969; into Spanish as *La conversación de los tres caminantes.* Barcelona, 1969; into Japanese as *Ketto; Aruiteiru sannin no kaiwa.* Tokyo: Hakusuisha, 1976.

Nacht mit Gästen. Eine Moritat. In *Werke* 4, 89–111. Written 1962/63. First published in *Akzente* 10 (4/1963): 436–52. Translated into Swedish as: *Natt med gäster.* Stockholm, Staffanstorp, Cavefors, 1967; into English as "Night with Guests." In *The Best Short Plays 1968,* edited by Stanley Richards. Philadelphia, New York, and London: Chilton, 1968, 131–58. Also translated into Spanish as *De cómo el señor Mockinpott consiguió liberarse de sus padecimientos. Noche de huéspedes.* Hondarribia/Guipúzcoa: Argitaletxe Hiru, 1968; into Italian as "Notte con Ospiti." In *Cantata del Fantoccio Lusitano. Notte con Ospiti.* Torino, 1968; and into French as *La nuit des visiteurs.* In *Comment monsieur Mockinpott fut libéré de ses tourments.* Paris: Éditions du Seuil, 1970.

"Aus dem Pariser Journal." Written 1962. *Merkur* 17 (1/1963): 59–66. *Merkur* 17 (3/1963): 243–51. *Akzente* 11 (5–6/1964): 499–504. Also in *Rapporte,* 83–112. Frankfurt a.M.: Suhrkamp, 1968. Translated into Swedish in *Rapporter.* 1968. Translated into Italian in *Critica e lotta.* Milano: Feltrinelli, 1976.

"Diese Fenster, diese Tische." *Akzente* 10 (1/1963): 138–41.

"Anmerkungen zum geschichtlichen Hintergrund unseres Stückes." Written 1963. In *Materialien zu Peter Weiss' "Marat/Sade,"* edited by Karlheinz Braun, 7–11. Frankfurt a.M.: Suhrkamp, 1967.

Die Verfolgung und Ermordung Jean Paul Marats dargestellt durch die Schauspielgruppe des Hospizes zu Charenton unter Anleitung des Herrn de Sade. Drama in zwei Akten. In *Werke* 4, 155–255. Written 1962–1965. First published Frankfurt a.M.: Suhrkamp, 1963 (latest edition 1995). Translated into English as *The Persecution and Assassination of Jean-Paul Marat as Performed by the Inmates of the Asylum of Charenton under the Direction of the Marquis de Sade.* London: Calder, 1965; into French as *La persécution et l'assassinat de Jean-Paul Marat: représentés par le groupe théatral de L'hospice de Charenton sous la direction de Monsieur de Sade. Drame en deux actes.* Paris: Éditions du Seuil, 1965; into Danish as *Forfølgelsen af og mordet på Jean Paul Marat opført af skuespillertruppen på hospitalet i Charenton under ledelse af herr de Sade.* Kopenhagen, 1965; into Finnish as *Jean Paul Marat'n vaino ja murha Charentonin sairaalan näytteilijäryhmän esittämänä ja herra de Saden ohjaamana.* Helsinki, 1965; into Swedish as *Jean Paul Marat förföljd och mördad så som det framställs av patienterna på hospitalet Charenton under ledning av Herr de Sade.* Malmö, 1965; and into Czech as *Pronásledování a zavraždení Jeana Paula Marata predvedené divadelním souborem blázince v Charentonu za rízení markýze de Sada: Drama o 2 dejstvích.* Praha: Dilia, 1965. Also translated into Spanish as *Persecución y asesinato de Jean Paul Marat drama en dos actos representado por el grupo teatral del Hospicio de Charenton bajo la dirección del Señor de Sade.* México: Grijalbo, 1965; into Polish as "Marat/Sade." In *Dialog.* Warsaw, 1965; into Slovak as *Prenasledovanie a zavraždenie Jeana Paula Marata hrané hereckou skupinou Charentonského ústavu pod vedením pána de Sade.* Bratislava, 1966. Russian, 1966; into Norwegian as *Mordet på*

Marat — Forfølgelsen av og mordet på Jean Paul Marat fremstilt av pasienter på hospitalet Charenton under ledelse av herr de Sade. Oslo, 1966; into Hungarian as *Jean Paul Marat üldöztetése és meggyilkolása*. Budapest, 1966; into Italian as *La persecuzione e l'assassinio di Jean-Paul Marat, rappresentati dai filodrammatici di Charenton, sotto la guida del Marchese di Sade*. Torino, 1967. Also translated into Dutch as *De vervolging van en de moord de Jean Paul Marat opgevoerd door de verpleegden van hed krankzinnigengesticht van Charenton onder regie van de heer De Sade*. Amsterdam, 1965; into Arabic as *Idtihad wa-ightiyal Jan Bul Mara kama qaddamatuhu firqat tamthil Masahhat Sharnatun tahta ishraf di Sad*. al-Qahirah: Mashru' al-Maktabah al-'Arabiyah, 1967; into Japanese as *Mara no hakugai to ansatsu*. Tokyo: Hakusuisha, 1967, into Chinese as: *Cong Maha/Sade dao Maha Taibei*. Taibei Shi (Taiwan): Shu lin chu ban you xian gong si, 1988; and into Hebrew as *Marah / Sad: sipur redifato u-moto shel Z'an Pol Marah kefi she-hutsag 'al yede lahakat ha-sahkanim shel bet ha-marpe be-Sharenton be-hadrakhato shel ha-Markiz de Sad*. Ramat Gan: Bet Tsevi, 1992.

"Frankfurter Auszüge." *Kursbuch* (1/1965): 152–88. Written 1964.

"10 Arbeitspunkte eines Autors in der geteilten Welt." *Dagens Nyheter*, September 1, 1965. Written 1965. German version: "Notwendige Entscheidung: 10 Arbeitspunkte eines Autors in der geteilten Welt." *Konkret* (9/1965): 26–27. Also appears in the following two works: *Materialien zu Peter Weiss' "Marat/Sade."* Frankfurt a.M.: Suhrkamp, 1967; and *Rapporte* 2, 14–23. Frankfurt a.M.: Suhrkamp, 1971.

"Vater. Mutter. Ich." Peter Weiss Archive. Academy of the Arts, Berlin. 76/86/145. N.d.

Meine Ortschaft. Rostock: Volkstheater, 1965. Written 1964. Also in *Atlas. Zusammengestellt von deutschen Autoren*. Berlin, 1965. Later edition in Peter Weiss. *Rapporte*, 113–25. Frankfurt a.M.: Suhrkamp, 1968. Translated into English as "My Place." Also published in *German Writing Today*, edited by Christopher Middleton, 20–28. Harmondsworth: Penguin, 1967. Published in Swedish in *Rapporter*. 1968; in Italian in *Critica e lotta*. Milano: Feltrinelli, 1976; and in Catalan as *La meva localitat. Instrucció de sumari oratori en onze cants*. Tarragona: La Gent del Llamp, 1995.

Die Ermittlung. Oratorium in 11 Gesängen. In *Werke* 5, 7–199. Written 1964/65. First published Frankfurt a.M.: Suhrkamp, 1965. Translated into Swedish as *Rannsakningen*. Malmö, 1965; into Dutch as *Het onderzoek*. Amsterdam, 1965 into French as *L'instruction. Oratorio en onze chants*. Paris: Éditions du Seuil, 1966; into Czech as *Přelíčení: Oratorium o 11 zpevech*. Praha: Orbis, 1966; into English as *The Investigation*. New York: Atheneum, 1966. Also translated into Italian as: *L'istruttoria. Oratorio in undici canti*. Torino: Einaudi, 1966; into Japanese as *Tsuikyu: aushuvitsu no uta*. Tokyo: Hakusuisha, 1966; into Danish as *Forundersøgelsen*. Kopenhagen, 1965; into Hungarian as *A Viszgálat*. Budapest, 1966; into Norwegian as *Ransakingen*.

Oslo, 1967; into Spanish as *La indagación. Oratorio en 11 cantos.* Barcelona/México: Ediciones Grijaldo, 1968; into Bulgarian as *Sledstvieto.* Sofia, 1968; into Estonian as *Juurdlus. Oratoorium übeteistkümnes laulus.* Tallinn: Kirjastus "Perioodika," 1969; and into Catalan as *La meva localitat. Instrucció de sumari oratori en onze cants.* Tarragona: La Gent del Llamp, 1995.

"Vorübung zum dreiteiligen Drama divina commedia." *Akzente* 12 (2/1965): 100–111. Written 1965. Also in *Rapporte,* 125–41. Frankfurt a.M.: Suhrkamp, 1968. Translated into Swedish in *Rapporter.* 1968. Translated into Italian in *Critica e lotta.* Milano: Feltrinelli, 1976.

"Gespräch über Dante." *Merkur* 207, 6/1965. Written 1965. Also in *Rapporte,* 142–69. Frankfurt a.M.: Suhrkamp, 1968. Translated into Swedish in *Rapporter.* 1968. Translated into Italian in *Critica e lotta.* Milano: Feltrinelli, 1976.

Laokoon oder Über die Grenzen der Sprache. Hamburg: Kulturbehörde der Freien und Hansestadt Hamburg, 1965. Written 1965. Also in *Rapporte,* 170–87. Frankfurt a.M.: Suhrkamp, 1968. Translated into Swedish in *Rapporter,* 1968. Translated into Italian in *Critica e lotta.* Milano: Feltrinelli, 1976.

"I Come out of My Hiding Place." *The Nation* (May 1966): 652, 655. Written 1966. German version in *Über Peter Weiss,* edited by Volker Canaris. Frankfurt a.M.: Suhrkamp, 1970, 9–14, under the title "Rede in englischer Sprache gehalten an der Princeton University USA am 25. April 1966, unter dem Titel 'I Come out of My Hiding Place.'"

"Stockholmer Flüchtlingsgespräch." *Konkret* (4/1966): 28–29.

"Vietnam!" *Dagens Nyheter,* August 2, 1966. Written 1966. Translated into German as *Vietnam.* Berlin: Voltaire, 1967. Also in *Rapporte 2.* Frankfurt a.M.: Suhrkamp, 1971. 51–62.

Gesang vom Lusitanischen Popanz. Stück mit Musik in 2 Akten. In *Werke* 5, 201–65. First published in *Theater heute* 6/1967. Written 1966. Translated into Swedish as: *Sången om Skråpuken.* Stockholm/Staffanstorp: Cavefors, 1967. Translated into Hungarian as: "A Luzitàn Madàrijesztö." In *Nagyvilag.* Budapest, 1967. Translated into French as: *Chant du fantoche lusitanien.* Paris: Éditions du Seuil, 1968. Translated into Italian as: "Cantata del Fantoccio Lusitano." In *Cantata del Fantoccio Lusitano. Notte con Ospiti.* Torino, 1968. Translated into Czech as: "Zpěv o lusitánském hastrošovi." In *Divadlo.* 1968. Translated into Dutch as: *Gezang van de Lusitaanse Bullebak.* Amsterdam: Van Gennep, 1969. Translated into Portuguese as: *Canto do papão lusitano.* Paris: Ruedo Ibérico, 1969. Translated into English as: "Song of the Lusitanian Bogey." In Peter Weiss. *Two Plays.* New York: Atheneum, 1970. 1–63. Translated into Persian as: *Surud-i adamalk lujitaniya'i.* [Iran]: Nashr-i Nika, 1990.

"Che Guevara!" Swedish original *Dagens Nyheter,* November 14, 1967. German version in *Kursbuch* 11 (1968): 1–6. *Rapporte* 2, 82–90, Frankfurt a.M.: Suhrkamp, 1971. Written 1967. English version in *Notizbücher 1960–1971.* Band 2, 555–61, Frankfurt a.M.: Suhrkamp, 1982.

Rapporte. Frankfurt a.M.: Suhrkamp, 1968.

Translated into Swedish as *Rapporter.* 1968. Translated into Italian as *Critica e lotta.* Milano: Feltrinelli, 1976.

Wie dem Herrn Mockinpott das Leiden ausgetrieben wird. Spiel in 11 Bildern. In *Werke* 4, 113–53. Written 1963–1968. First published in *Theater heute.* 6/1968. Translated into Spanish as *De cómo el señor Mockinpott consiguió liberarse de sus padecimientos. Noche de huéspedes.* Hondarribia/Guipúzcoa: Argitaletxe Hiru, 1968. Translated into French as *Comment monsieur Mockinpott fut libéré de ses tourments.* Paris, Éditions du Seuil, 1969. Translated into English as "How Mister Mockinpott Was Cured of His Sufferings." In *The Contemporary German Theater,* edited By Michael Roloff. New York: Avon, 1972. 163–211.

Diskurs über die Vorgeschichte und den Verlauf des lang andauernden Befreiungskrieges in Viet Nam als Beispiel für die Notwendigkeit des bewaffneten Kampfes der Unterdrückten gegen ihre Unterdrücker sowie über die Versuche der Vereinigten Staaten von Amerika die Grundlagen der Revolution zu vernichten. In *Werke* 5, 267–458. First published Frankfurt a.M.: Suhrkamp, 1968. Written 1966–1968. Translated into French as: *Discours sur la genèse et le déroulement de la très longue guerre de libération du Vietnam. Illustrant la nécessité de la lutte armée des opprimés contre leurs oppresseurs ainsi que la volonté des États-Unis d'Amérique d'anéantir les fondements de la revolution.* Paris: Éditions du Seuil, 1968. Translated into Italian as: *Discorso sulla preistoria e lo svolgimento della interminabile guerra di liberazione nel Viet Nam quale esempio della necessità della lotta armata degli oppressi contro i loro oppressori come sui tentativi degli Stati Uniti d'America di annullare i fondamenti della rivoluzione.* Torino 1968. Translated into Japanese as: *Betonamu toron.* Tokyo: Hakusuisha, 1968. Translated into Swedish as: *Diskurs över det långvariga befrielsekriget i Vietnam dess förhistoria och förlopp som exempel på nödvändigheten av de undertrycktas väpnade kamp mot sina förtyckare likesa över Amerikas Förenta Staters försök att förinta revolutionens grundvalar.* Stockholm: Cavefors, 1968. Translated into Dutch as: *Gesprek over de voorgrschiedenis en het verloop van den langdurige bevrijdingsoorlog in Vietnam als voorbeeld van de noodzaak van gewapende strijd van de onderdrukten tegen hun onderdrukkers alsook over de pogingen van de Verenigde Staten van Amerika de grondbeginselen van de revolutie te vernietigen.* Amsterdam, 1969. Translated into Hungarian as: "Vitairat Vietnamról." In *Vitairat Vietnamról. A Luzitàn Madàrijesztö.* Budapest, 1969. Translated into English as: "Discourse on the Progress of the Prolonged War of Liberation in Viet Nam and the Events Leading Up to It as Illustration of the Necessity for Armed Resistance against Oppression and on the Attempts of the United States of America to Destroy the Foundations of Revolution." In Peter Weiss. *Two Plays*, 65–249. New York: Atheneum, 1970. Translated into Spanish as: *Discorso sobre los antecedentes y desarrolo de la interminable guerra de liberación del Vietnam.* Barcelona: Lumen, 1974.

Interview by Peter Limqueco. *International War Crimes Tribunal 1967: Stockholm, Sweden and Roskilde, Denmark.* London, Stockholm, Roskilde, International War Crimes Tribunal, 1967. Written 1967. Other English edition: *Prevent the Crime of Silence: Reports from the Sessions of the International War Crimes Tribunal Founded by Bertrand Russell.* London, Allen Lane, 1971. Translated into Swedish as: *Russelltribunalen. Från sessionerna i Stockholm och Roskilde.* Stockholm, PAN/Norstedt, 1968.

"Notizen zum dokumentarischen Theater." In *Werke* 5, 464–72. Also in *Rapporte 2*, 91–104. Frankfurt a.M.: Suhrkamp, 1971. First published in *Theater heute* 9 (3/1968): 32–34. Written 1968. Translated into English as "The Material and the Models. Notes towards a Definition of Documentary Theatre." *Theatre Quarterly* I/1 (1971): 41–43.

Trotzki im Exil. Stück in 2 Akten. In Werke 6, 7–106. First published Frankfurt a.M.: Suhrkamp, 1970. Written 1968/69. Translated into Spanish as: *Trotsky en el exilio.* Mexico: Grijalbo, 1970. Translated into Japanese as: *Bomei no torotsuki.* Tokyo: Hakusuisha, 1970. Translated into French as: *Trotsky en exil.* Paris: Éditions du Seuil, 1970. Translated into English as: *Trotsky in Exile.* London: Methuen, 1971. Translated into Welsh as: *Trotsci'n alltud.* Cardiff: Gwasg Prifysgol Cymru ar ran Cyngor Celfyddydau Cymru, 1979. Translated into Italian as: *Trotskij in esilio.* Torino: Einaudi, 1983. Translated into Czech as: *Trockij v exilu.* Praha: Dilia, 1990.

Interview by Gunilla Palmstierna-Weiss: *Rapport om Förenta staternas förstärkta angrepp mot Nordvietnam efter den 31 mars 1968.* Malmö: Solna, Cavefors, Seelig, 1968. Written 1968. Translated into French as: *Réponse à Johnson sur les bombardements limités ou l'Escalade U.S. Au Vietnam d'avril á juin 1968.* Paris: Éditions du Seuil, 1968. Translated into English as: *"Limited Bombing" in Vietnam: Report on the Attacks against the Democratic Republic of Vietnam by the U.S. Air Force and the Seventh Fleet, after the Declaration of "Limited Bombing" by President Lyndon B. Johnson on March 31, 1968.* London: Bertrand Russell Peace Foundation, 1969.

Interview by Gunilla Palmstierna-Weiss. *Notizen zum kulturellen Leben in der Demokratischen Republik Viet Nam.* Frankfurt a.M.: Suhrkamp, 1968. Written 1968. Translated into French as: *Notes sur la vie culturelle en République démocratique du Viet Nam.* Paris: Éditions du Seuil, 1969. Translated into Italian as: *Note politico-culturali dal Viet Nam.* Roma: Editori Riuniti, 1969. Translated into Swedish as: *Notiser om det kulturella livet i Demokratiska Republikken Viet Nam.* Staffanstorp 1969. English: *Notes on the Cultural Life of the Democratic Republic of Vietnam.* London: Calder & Boyars, 1970. Also New York: Dell, 1970.

"Die Luftangriffe der USA am 21.11.1970 auf die Demokratische Republik Viet Nam." In *Rapporte* 2, 132–51. Frankfurt a.M.: Suhrkamp, 1971. Short version in *Konkret* 25/1970, December 3, 1970. Translated into English as "The Air Attacks on the Democratic Republic of Vietnam by the USA on 21 November, 1970." In Malcolm Caldwell / Peter Weiss / Noam Chomsky. *American Presence in South East Asia.* Singapore: Island Publishers, 1971.

"Der Sieg, der sich selbst bedroht." Swedish original version in *Aftonbladet,* June 17, 1967. German version in *Rapporte* 2, 70–72. Frankfurt a.M.: Suhrkamp, 1971. Written 1967.

Rapporte 2. Frankfurt a.M.: Suhrkamp, 1971.

Rekonvaleszenz. In *Werke* 2, 345–546. Parts of it first published in *Notizbücher.* Written 1970–71. Translated into Swedish as: *Konvalescens dagbok.* Stockholm: Bonniers, 1993.

Hölderlin. Stück in zwei Akten. In *Werke* 6, 109–260. Written 1971/72. Translated into Swedish as: *Hölderlin. Skådespel i två akter.* Stockholm: Norstedt, 1972. Translated into French as: *Hölderlin. Théâtre.* Paris: Éditions du Seuil, 1973.

"Fünf Varianten des Epilogs." In *Der andere Hölderlin: Materialien zum "Hölderlin"-Stück von Peter Weiss,* edited by Thomas Beckermann and Volker Canaris, 133–41. Frankfurt a.M.: Suhrkamp, 1972. Written 1971/72.

"Notizen zum *Hölderlin*-Stück." In *Der andere Hölderlin: Materialien zum "Hölderlin"-Stück von Peter Weiss,* edited by Thomas Beckermann and Volker Canaris, 127–132. Frankfurt a.M.: Suhrkamp, 1972. Written 1971/72.

"Luis Corvalán." One-page poem about torture and resistance in Chile. Peter Weiss Archive, Academy of the Arts, Berlin. 76/86/7009. Written 1974.

Der Prozeß (nach Kafka). Strindberg-Übersetzungen: Fräulein Julie. Ein Traumspiel. Der Vater. Berlin: Henschel, 1979. Written 1961–1975.

Der Prozeß. In *Werke* 6, 261–336. First in *Spectaculum* 24. Frankfurt a.M.: Suhrkamp, 1976. Translated into Italian as: *Il processo.* Torino: Einaudi, 1977. Written 1975.

"Hugh Sattlefield zum Gedächtnis." Four pages. Peter Weiss Archive, Academy of the Arts, Berlin. 76/86/7014 and 76/86/7005. Written 1978.

"Verständigung." *Frankfurter Rundschau,* June 20, 1978.

"Arbeitsgespräche mit Brecht in Lidingö." *Kürbiskern* 13 (3/1978): 10–26.

Notizbücher 1960–1971. Frankfurt a.M.: Suhrkamp, 1982. 2 vols.

Notizbücher 1971–1980. Frankfurt a.M.: Suhrkamp, 1981. 2 vols.

Die Ästhetik des Widerstands. Roman. Erster Band. Frankfurt a.m.: Suhrkamp, 1975. *Zweiter Band.* Frankfurt a.M.: Suhrkamp, 1978. *Dritter Band.* Frankfurt a.M.: Suhrkamp, 1981. In *Werke* 3 (latest edition 1998). Written throughout the 1970s and finished in 1980. Translated into Swedish as: *Motståndets estetik.* Stockholm: Arbetarkultur, 1976–1981. Translated into French as: *L'Esthétique de la résistance.* Paris: Klincksieck, 1989 and *L'Esthétique de la résistance 2.* Paris: Klincksieck, 1992.

"Für Max Frisch." In *Begegnungen. Eine Festschrift für Max Frisch,* 217–18. Frankfurt a.M.: Suhrkamp, 1981.

Der neue Prozeß. Stück in drei Akten. In *Werke* 6, 337–407. First published in *Spectaculum* 35/1982. Written 1981/82. Translated into Swedish as: *Nya processen.* Stockholm: Arbetarkultur, 1982. Translated into English as: *The New Trial.* Durham, N.C.: Duke UP, 2001.

Interview by Jirí Mašín. *Endre Nemes. Výber z tvorby 1926–1981. Katalog výstavy.* Prague: Nár. Galerie, Kveten-cerven, 1982. (Essays on his friend, the painter Nemes, who appears in Weiss's novel *Fluchtpunkt* as Anatol).

"Wurzeln." *die horen* 27/2 (Summer 1982): 185–87.

Open Letters by Weiss

Letter to the editors of *Neue Kritik,* December 12, 1965 on *Marat/Sade. Neue Kritik,* 1965. Main passage of the letter quoted in Rector 1999, 82–83.

"Unter dem Hirseberg." In *Plädoyer für eine neue Regierung oder Keine Alternative,* edited by Hans Werner Richter. Hamburg: Rowohlt, 1965, 147–49. Also in *Rapporte* 2, 7–13. Frankfurt a.M.: Suhrkamp, 1971. Open letter to Hans Werner Richter, written 1965.

"Partisanen der Wahrheit." *Neues Deutschland,* May 21, 1965.

"Peter Weiss erklärt." *Frankfurter Allgemeine Zeitung,* October 27, 1965.

"Antwort auf einen Offenen Brief von Wilhelm Girnus an den Autor in der Zeitung *Neues Deutschland.*" In *Rapporte* 2, 24–34. Frankfurt a.M.: Suhrkamp, 1971. This letter, written on December 28, 1965, and sent to *Neues Deutschland,* was not published by this East German newspaper.

"Antwort auf eine Kritik zur Stockholmer Aufführung der 'Ermittlung.'" Original Swedish version in *Dagens Nyheter,* March 18, 1966. German version in *Rapporte* 2, 45–50. Frankfurt a.M.: Suhrkamp, 1971.

"Enzensbergers Illusionen." *Kursbuch* (July 6, 1966): 165–70. Also in *Rapporte* 2, 35–44. Frankfurt a.M.: Suhrkamp, 1971.

"Peter Weiss über die Inszenierung des 'Marat.'" *Neue Kritik* 7 (34/1966): 37–39.

"Antwort auf Kritiken zum 'Vietnam'-Aufsatz." Original Swedish version in *Dagens Nyheter,* September 7, 1966. German version in *Rapporte* 2, 63–69. Frankfurt a.M.: Suhrkamp, 1971.

"Ein Brief von Peter Weiss. An die Theaterbesucher und das Ensemble des Volkstheaters Rostock." *Ostsee-Zeitung,* November 8, 1966.

"Offener Brief an den Tschechoslowakischen Schriftstellerverband." Shortened version in *Die Zeit,* September 15, 1967 (Weiss also sent a copy to the East German newspaper *Neues Deutschland,* but they refused to publish it).

"Bemerkung über die Okkupation der ČSSR." *Theater heute* 9 (10/1968): 43.

"Ein Verlag der Autoren: Die Beschreibung einer Verfassung, ein Kommentar und zwei Erklärungen." *ZEIT,* February 28, 1969.

"Offener Brief an die *Literaturnaja Gaseta,* Moskau." Shortened version in *Süddeutsche Zeitung,* April 18, 1970, under the title "Offener Brief an Lew Ginsburg." Also in two essay collections: *Über Peter Weiss,* edited by Volker Canaris, 141–50. Frankfurt a.M.: Suhrkamp, 1970. *Rapporte* 2, 105–31. Frankfurt a.M.: Suhrkamp, 1971.

"Alle Zellen des Widerstands miteinander verbinden." *Kürbiskern* 9 (2/1973): 314–20.

"Der Autor als Ware. Zur Diskussion über das Drama." *Frankfurter Allgemeine Zeitung,* October 8, 1976.

"Peter Weiss zu Wolf Biermann." *Frankfurter Allgemeine Zeitung,* November 19, 1976.

"Absage an Sofia: Die Aufgabe des Schriftstellers ist die Einmischung." *Frankfurter Allgemeine Zeitung,* June 3, 1977.

"Ein Dialog, der in Sofia nicht stattfindet." *Frankfurter Allgemeine Zeitung,* June 8, 1977.

"In Sachen Humanität: Zur Lage in Vietnam." *Frankfurter Rundschau,* November 29, 1978. Reprinted in *Frankfurter Rundschau,* January 7, 1979.

"Zur Lage in Vietnam." *Deutsche Volkszeitung,* December 7, 1978.

"Die Hetze gegen Vietnam geht weiter." *Deutsche Volkszeitung,* December 14, 1978.

"Flüchtlinge aber setzen Verfolger voraus." *Frankfurter Rundschau,* August 16, 1979.

"Die unteilbaren Menschenrechte herrschaftsinteressiert verteilt." *Frankfurter Rundschau,* October 2, 1979.

"Noch ein Vietnam." *Kultur und Gesellschaft* 3 (10/1979): 3–6.

Fragments by Weiss

"Screw oder dreizehn Londoner Tage." *Peter Weiss Jahrbuch* 2 (1993): 9–19. Written 1937.

"Rörelser." Written 1950. Translated into German as "Bewegungen. Roman-fragment." *Peter Weiss Jahrbuch* 2 (2001).

"Bericht über Einrichtungen und Gebräuche in den Siedlungen der Grauhäute." In *Aus aufgegebenen Werken. Ein Lesebuch,* edited by Siegfried Unseld, 83–105: Frankfurt a.M.: Suhrkamp, 1968. Written 1953. Also in Peter Weiss, *In Gegensätzen denken. Ein Lesebuch,* edited by Rainer Gerlach and Matthias Richter, 119–35. Frankfurt a.M.: Suhrkamp, 1986.

"Gespräch in einem Raum." *Peter Weiss Jahrbuch* 7 (1998): 7–18. Written 1960.

"'Wäre ich schon in der Mitte meines Lebenswegs hier angelangt . . .' Aus einem Prosafragment." *Peter Weiss Jahrbuch* 1 (1992): 9–20. Written 1969.

Fragments of the Divina Commedia Project. In Christoph Weiss. *Auschwitz in der geteilten Welt: Peter Weiss und die "Ermittlung" im Kalten Krieg.* 2 vols. St. Ingbert: Röhrig, 2000, especially 60–87. N.d.

"Kafka und Henry Miller." In Andrea Heyde. *Unterwerfung und Aufruhr: Franz Kafka im literarischen Werk von Peter Weiss.* Berlin: Schmidt, 1997, 202–4. N.d.

"Skizzen zu einem Stück über Rimbaud." *Text + Kritik* 37 (1982): 1–4. N.d.

"Rimbaud: Ein Fragment." *Text + Kritik* 37 (1982): 4–10. N.d.

Interviews of Weiss

Interview by Simone Dubreuilh. *Lettres françaises,* January 30, 1958. Translated into German by Sepp Hiekisch-Picard and Dominique Picard in *Peter Weiss im Gespräch,* edited by Rainer Gerlach and Matthias Richter, 23–26. Frankfurt a.M.: Suhrkamp, 1986.

Interview by Thomas von Vegesack. *Stockholms-Tidningen,* September 3, 1963. German in *Die Welt der Literatur,* April 30, 1964. Also in *Peter Weiss im Gespräch,* edited by Rainer Gerlach and Matthias Richter, 27–30. Frankfurt a.M.: Suhrkamp, 1986.

Interview by Michael Roloff, in March 1964. *Partisan Review* 32 (1965): 220–32. Translated into German by Rainer Gerlach in *Peter Weiss im Gespräch,* edited by Rainer Gerlach and Matthias Richter, 31–43. Frankfurt a.M.: Suhrkamp, 1986.

Interview by Dieter Stér. *Theater heute* 5 (May 1964). Also in *Theater 1964. Jahressonderheft Theater heute*, 44–43. Also in *Peter Weiss im Gespräch*, edited by Rainer Gerlach and Matthias Richter, 44–49. Frankfurt a.M.: Suhrkamp, 1986.

Times, August 19, 1964.

Interview by Alfred Schüler. *Weltwoche*, October 30, 1964. Also in *Oberösterreichische Nachrichten*, August 27, 1965.

Interview by A. Alvarez, in November 1964. *New York Times*, December 26, 1965. Translated into German by Matthias Richter in *Peter Weiss im Gespräch*, edited by Rainer Gerlach and Matthias Richter, 50–60. Frankfurt a.M.: Suhrkamp, 1986.

Demokrat, March 30, 1965.

Interview by Wolfgang Gersch. *Theater der Zeit* 20 (9/1965): III. Also in *Peter Weiss im Gespräch*, edited by Rainer Gerlach and Matthias Richter, 61–62. Frankfurt a.M.: Suhrkamp, 1986.

Interview by "WMH." *Hamburger Abendblatt*, April 24, 1965.

Interview by Wilhelm Girnus and Werner Mittenzwei. *Sinn und Form* 17 (5/1965): 678–88. Also in *Peter Weiss im Gespräch*, edited by Rainer Gerlach and Matthias Richter, 63–76. Frankfurt a.M.: Suhrkamp, 1986.

Interview by Thomas von Vegesack. *Stockholms Tidningen*, June 4, 1965. German, partly shortened, in *Neues Deutschland*, June 5, 1965. In *Ostsee-Zeitung*, June 5, 1965. In *Frankfurter Rundschau*, July 15, 1965. In *Spandauer Volksblatt*, July 28, 1965. In *Sonntag*, August 15, 1965. Also in *Peter Weiss im Gespräch*, edited by Rainer Gerlach and Matthias Richter, 77–81. Frankfurt a.M.: Suhrkamp, 1986.

Interview by Ernst Schumacher. *Theater der Zeit* 20 (16/1965): 4–7. Also in *Peter Weiss im Gespräch*, edited by Rainer Gerlach and Matthias Richter, 82–93. Frankfurt a.M.: Suhrkamp, 1986.

Interview by "Ryman." *Dagens Nyheter*, September 20, 1965.

Interview by "Ninka." *Politiken*, October 10, 1965.

Interview by Ernst Schumacher. *Berliner Zeitung*, October 17, 1965.

Interview by Frederic and Boel Fleisher. *Falu-Kuriren*, October 19, 1965.

Interview by Wolfgang Ignée. *Christ und Welt*, October 22, 1965.

Interview by Per Olof Sundman and Tor-Ivan Odulf. In Christer Strömholm, *Till minnet av mig själv*. Stockholm 1965.

Interview by Hans Mayer, in October 1965. *Peter Weiss Jahrbuch* 4 (1995): 8–30.

In *Industria,* edited by Swedish Employers' Confederation. Stockholm, 1965, 58–60, 194–200. Translated into German by Matthias Richter in *Peter Weiss im Gespräch,* edited by Rainer Gerlach and Matthias Richter, 94–105. Frankfurt a.M.: Suhrkamp, 1986.

Interview by Hans Wachholz. *Ostsee-Zeitung,* February 14, 1966.

Interview by Wolfgang Neuss. *Sonntag,* March 13, 1966. Also in *Peter Weiss im Gespräch,* edited by Rainer Gerlach and Matthias Richter, 106–10. Frankfurt a.M.: Suhrkamp, 1986.

Interview by Jean Tailleur. *Les Lettres Françaises,* April 20, 1966. Translated into German by Sepp Hiekisch-Picard and Dominique Picard in *Peter Weiss im Gespräch,* edited by Rainer Gerlach and Matthias Richter, 111–16. Frankfurt a.M.: Suhrkamp, 1986.

Interview by Richard F. Shepard. *New York Times,* April 22, 1966.

Interview by Paul Gray. *Tulane Drama Review* 11 (1/1966.67): 106–14.

Interview by Peter Brook. *Theater heute* 7 (10/1966): 106–14.

Nouvel Observateur, September 28, 1966.

Interview by Oliver Clausen. *New York Times Magazine,* October 2, 1966.

Interview by Peter Dragadze. *Life,* October 28, 1966.

Interview by Walter Wager. In Walter Wager, *The Playwrights Speak.* New York 1967, 189–212.

Dagens Nyheter, January 14, 1967.

Dagens Nyheter, January 24, 1967.

Interview by Frederic Fleisher. *Variety,* February 8, 1967.

Interview by Henning Rischbieter. *Theater heute* 8 (3/1967): 6–7.

Interview by Herta Fischer. *Tagebuch* (April/May 1967): 21.

Interview by Sun Axelsson. *Ord & Bild* (5/1967): 364–70. Translated into German by Ruth Müller-Reineke in *Peter Weiss im Gespräch,* edited by Rainer Gerlach and Matthias Richter, 117–28. Frankfurt a.M.: Suhrkamp, 1986.

Interview by Ossia Trilling. *Times,* September 11, 1967.

Interview by Heinz Gundlach. *Ostsee-Zeitung,* February 7, 1968.

Interview by Giorgio Polacco, in February 1968. In *Gesang vom Lusitanischen Popanz. Mit Materialien.* Frankfurt a.M.: Suhrkamp, 1974, 87–92. Also in *Peter Weiss im Gespräch,* edited by Rainer Gerlach and Matthias Richter, 129–35. Frankfurt a.M.: Suhrkamp, 1986.

Interview by Rolf Dornbacher. *Abendzeitung,* March 4, 1968.

Interview by Arthur Joseph. *Frankfurter Allgemeine Zeitung,* March 8, 1968.

Interview by Bernt Engelmann. *Westfälische Rundschau,* March 9, 1968.

Interview by Hans Magnus Enzensberger and Martin Walser. *Theater heute* (3/1968): 3.

Interview by Manfred Müller and Wolfram Schütte. *Frankfurter Rundschau,* March 16, 1968. Also in *Peter Weiss im Gespräch,* edited by Rainer Gerlach and Matthias Richter, 136–42. Frankfurt a.m.: Suhrkamp, 1986.

Spiegel, March 18, 1968. Also in *Peter Weiss im Gespräch,* edited by Rainer Gerlach and Matthias Richter, 143–48. Frankfurt a.M.: Suhrkamp, 1986.

Interview by Claes Sturm. *Dagens Nyheter,* March 20, 1968. Translated into German by Michael Kanning in *Peter Weiss im Gespräch,* edited by Rainer Gerlach and Matthias Richter, 149–53. Frankfurt a.M.: Suhrkamp, 1986.

Interview by Wilm von Elbwart. *Die Tat,* March 22, 1968. Also in *Die Andere Zeitung,* March 28, 1968.

Interview by Peter Iden. *ZEIT,* March 22, 1968.

Interview by Otto Hahn. *L'Express,* April 1–7, 1968.

Interview by Günther Bellmann. *BZ am Abend,* May 2, 1968.

Dagens Nyheter, July 6, 1968. Translated into German by Michael Kanning. In *Peter Weiss im Gespräch,* edited by Rainer Gerlach and Matthias Richter, 154–57. Frankfurt a.M.: Suhrkamp, 1986.

Interview by Eugen Pop. *Lumea,* July 11, 1968.

Deutsche Volkszeitung, July 25, 1968.

Interview by Winfried Scharlau and Georg Wolff. *Spiegel,* August 5, 1968: 66–74. Also in *Peter Weiss im Gespräch,* edited by Rainer Gerlach and Matthias Richter, 158–69. Frankfurt a.M.: Suhrkamp, 1986.

Außerparlamentarische Opposition (2/1968).

Interview by Erich Fried. *Konkret* (10/1968): 12–14. Also in *Peter Weiss im Gespräch,* edited by Rainer Gerlach and Matthias Richter, 170–80. Frankfurt a.M.: Suhrkamp, 1986.

Discussion transcript, February 1968. In *Brecht-Dialog 1968: Politik auf dem Theater,* edited by Werner Hecht. Munich 1969.

Times, June 21, 1969.

Interview by Ossia Trilling. *Weltwoche,* July 4, 1969. Also in *Peter Weiss im Gespräch,* edited by Rainer Gerlach and Matthias Richter, 181–84. Frankfurt a.M.: Suhrkamp, 1986.

Interview by Hannes Schmidt. *Neue Ruhrzeitung,* December 20, 1969. Also in *Nürnberger Nachrichten,* December 27/28, 1969.

Interview by Bernd Lauscher. *Die Tat,* January 24, 1970.

Interview by Norbert Brügger. *Neue Ruhrzeitung,* April 7, 1971.

Interview by Disa Håstad. *Dagens Nyheter,* June 27, 1971.

Spiegel, September 13, 1971.

Interview by Thomas Petz. *Abendzeitung,* September 15, 1971.

Interview by Volker Canaris. *ZEIT,* September 17, 1971. Also in *Der andere Hölderlin. Materialien zum "Hölderlin"-Stück von Peter Weiss,* edited by Thomas Beckermann and Volker Canaris. Frankfurt a.m.: Suhrkamp, 1972, 142–48. Also in *Peter Weiss im Gespräch,* edited by Rainer Gerlach and Matthias Richter, 185–91. Frankfurt a.M.: Suhrkamp, 1986.

Interview by Alfonso Sastre, 1972. *Peter Weiss Jahrbuch* 6 (1997): 7–22.

Interview by Disa Håstad, December 1972. *Ord & Bild* (6/1976): 312–18. Translated into German by Michael Kanning in *Peter Weiss im Gespräch,* edited by Rainer Gerlach and Matthias Richter, 192–201. Frankfurt a.M.: Suhrkamp, 1986.

Interview by Jochen Reinert, December 1973. *Neues Deutschland,* January 9, 1974. Also in *Peter Weiss im Gespräch,* edited by Rainer Gerlach and Matthias Richter, 202–7. Frankfurt a.M.: Suhrkamp, 1986.

Frankfurter Allgemeine Zeitung, September 21, 1974.

Interview by Manfred Haiduk, August 1974. *Volkstheater Rostock. Programmhefte* 87 (1981/82). Also in *Peter Weiss im Gespräch,* edited by Rainer Gerlach and Matthias Richter, 208–15. Frankfurt a.M.: Suhrkamp, 1986.

Interview by Erwin Runge. *Unsere Zeit,* May 23, 1975. Also in *Ostsee-Zeitung,* May 31/June 1, 1975.

Interview by Jochen Reinert. *Neues Deutschland,* June 27, 1975.

Interview by J. Bondarev, et al *Voprosy literatury* 5 (1975): 155–83.

Interview by Rolf Michaelis. *ZEIT,* October 10, 1975. Also in *Peter Weiss im Gespräch,* edited by Rainer Gerlach and Matthias Richter, 216–23. Frankfurt a.M.: Suhrkamp, 1986.

Interview by Peter Sager. *ZEIT-Magazin,* November 12, 1976: 50–56.

Interview by Eva Adolfsson and Lars Bjurman. *Ord & Bild* (2–3/1977): 198–208.

Interview by Dorothea Behrend. *Sonntag,* May 22, 1977.

Interview by Barbara Heuss-Czisch. *Süddeutsche Zeitung,* August 4, 1977.

Interview by Michael Dultz. *Rheinische Post,* August 10, 1977.

Interview by Jacques Michel. *Le Monde,* October 5, 1977. Translated into German by Sepp Hiekisch-Picard and Dominique Picard in *Peter Weiss im Gespräch,* edited by Rainer Gerlach and Matthias Richter, 224–26. Frankfurt a.M.: Suhrkamp, 1986.

Interview by Peter Roos. In Peter Roos, *Genius Loci: Gespräche über Literatur und Tübingen*. Pfullingen 1978, 19–23. Also in *Peter Weiss im Gespräch,* edited by Rainer Gerlach and Matthias Richter, 227–30. Frankfurt a.M.: Suhrkamp, 1986.

Interview by Arne Ruth. *Expressen,* January 30, 1979. Translated into German by Michael Kanning in *Peter Weiss im Gespräch,* edited by Rainer Gerlach and Matthias Richter, 231–38. Frankfurt a.M.: Suhrkamp, 1986.

Deutsche Volkszeitung, January 18, 1979.

Interview by Günter Grasmeyer. *Norddeutsche Zeitung,* February 19, 1979. Partly identical to interview in *Deutsche Volkszeitung,* January 18, 1979.

Interview by Michael Opperskalski. *Rote Blätter* 9 (2–3/1979): 30–31. Also in *Peter Weiss im Gespräch,* edited by Rainer Gerlach and Matthias Richter, 239–42. Frankfurt a.M.: Suhrkamp, 1986.

Interview by Wend Kässens and Michael Töteberg, Spring 1979. In *Sammlung 2. Jahrbuch für antifaschistische Literatur und Kunst,* edited by Uwe Naumann. Frankfurt a.M. 1979, 222–28. Also in *Peter Weiss im Gespräch,* edited by Rainer Gerlach and Matthias Richter, 243–51. Frankfurt a.M.: Suhrkamp, 1986.

Interview by Harun Farocki. *Frankfurter Rundschau,* November 24, 1979.

Interview by Peter Roos. In *Der Maler Peter Weiss. Ausstellungskatalog Museum Bochum*. Bochum 1980, 5–37.

Interview by Harun Farocki. *Filmkritik* 24 (2/1980): 86–90. Also in *Peter Weiss im Gespräch,* edited by Rainer Gerlach and Matthias Richter, 252–58. Frankfurt a.M.: Suhrkamp, 1986.

Interview by Wolf Schön. *Rheinischer Merkur / Christ und Welt,* March 14, 1980. Also in *Peter Weiss im Gespräch,* edited by Rainer Gerlach and Matthias Richter, 259–62. Frankfurt a.M.: Suhrkamp, 1986.

Interview by Kerstin Vinterhed. *Dagens Nyheter,* August 5, 1980.

Interview by Harun Farocki. *Filmkritik* 25 (6/1981): 245–52.

Interview by Günter Grasmeyer. *Volkstheater Rostock. Programmhefte* 87 (1981/82).

Interview by Burkhardt Lindner. In *"Ästhetik des Widerstands" lesen*. Argument Sonderband AS 75, edited by Karl-Heinz Götze and Klaus R. Scherpe, 1981, 150–73. Also in *Peter Weiss im Gespräch,* edited by Rainer Gerlach and Matthias Richter, 263–89. Frankfurt a.M.: Suhrkamp, 1986.

Interview by Magnus Bergh and Birgit Munkhammar. *Bonniers Litterära Magasin* (6/1981): 374–78. Translated into German by Ruth Müller-Reineke in *Peter Weiss im Gespräch,* edited by Rainer Gerlach and Matthias Richter, 290–300. Frankfurt a.M.: Suhrkamp, 1986.

Interview by Heinz Ludwig Arnold, in September 1981. In *Peter Weiss. "Die Ästhetik des Widerstands,"* edited by Alexander Stephan, 11–58. Frankfurt a.M.: Suhrkamp, 1983.

Interview by Jürgen Lodemann. *Deutsche Volkszeitung,* September 17, 1981. Also in *linkskurve* (3/1982): 17–19.

Interview by Jacques Outin, in October 1981. In *Peter Weiss im Gespräch,* edited by Rainer Gerlach and Matthias Richter, 301–24. Frankfurt a.M.: Suhrkamp, 1986.

Interview by Jochen Reinert. *Weltbühne,* November 3, 1981. Also in *Die Neue,* December 3, 1981.

Interview by Sibylle Hoffmann-Rittberger. *Deutsche Volkszeitung,* February 11, 1982.

Interview by C. Bernd Sucher. *Süddeutsche Zeitung,* March 27/28, 1982. Also in *Peter Weiss im Gespräch,* edited by Rainer Gerlach and Matthias Richter, 330–34. Frankfurt a.M.: Suhrkamp, 1986.

Interview by Monika Keppler. *Kultur und Gesellschaft* (3/1982).

Interview by Andreas Wang. *die horen* 27 (125/1982): 177–80.

Interview by Gunilla Palmstierna-Weiss and Anita Brundahl. In *"Nya Processen": Dramaten Arbetsbok,* edited by Peter Weiss, Gunilla Palmstierna-Weiss, and Anita Brundahl. Stockholm 1982. Translated into German in *Der neue Prozeß.* Frankfurt a.M.: Suhrkamp, 1984, 109–19.

Interview by Elisabeth Sörensen. *Svenska Dagbladet,* March 2, 1982.

Interview by Ingela Lind. In *Dagens Nyheter,* March 7, 1982. Translated into German by Michael Kanning in *Peter Weiss im Gespräch,* edited by Rainer Gerlach and Matthias Richter, 325–29. Frankfurt a.M.: Suhrkamp, 1986.

Interview by Peggy Parnass. *konkret* (6/1982): 103.

Interview by Wend Kässens. *Theater 1982. Jahressonderheft Theater heute,* 90–92.

Weiss's Correspondence

"Brief an die Akademie." *Sinn und Form* 44 (1992/4): 596–603.

Three letters to Hans Bender, 1954–1963. In *Briefe an Hans Bender,* edited by Volker Neuhaus. Munich: Hanser, 1984. 26–28, 32, 72.

Briefe an Hermann Levin Goldschmidt und Robert Jungk, 1938–1980. Leipzig: Reclam, 1992.

"Briefe an Manfred Haiduk 1966–1982." *Peter Weiss Jahrbuch* 3 (1994): 7–41.

Correspondence with Hermann Hesse, 1937–1962 in Raimund Hoffmann. *Peter Weiss: Malerei. Zeichnungen. Collagen.* Berlin: Henschel, 1984. 162–69.

"In Sachen Solshenizyn." *Neues Deutschland,* May 17, 1991.

"Zwei Briefe an seine Eltern, Dezember 1938." *Peter Weiss Jahrbuch* 5 (1996): 7–18.

Translations of Other Authors by Weiss

Dagerman, Stig. "Der Verurteilte" ("Den dödsdömde"). *Neue Rundschau* (1948/10): 174–85.

Strindberg, August. *Fräulein Julie. Ein naturalistisches Trauerspiel.* Frankfurt a.M.: Suhrkamp, 1961. Other edition: St. Gallen: Stadttheater St. Gallen, 1993. Also in the following collections: *Der Prozess (nach Kafka). Strindberg-Übersetzungen: Fräulein Julie. Ein Traumspiel. Der Vater.* Berlin: Henschel, 1979. *Drei Stücke in der Übertragung von Peter Weiss.* Frankfurt a.M.: Suhrkamp, 1981.

———. *Ein Traumspiel.* Frankfurt a.M.: Suhrkamp, 1963. Also in the following collections: *Der Prozess (nach Kafka). Strindberg-Übersetzungen: Fräulein Julie. Ein Traumspiel. Der Vater.* Berlin: Henschel, 1979. *Drei Stücke in der Übertragung von Peter Weiss.* Frankfurt a.M.: Suhrkamp, 1981.

———. *Der Vater.* In *Der Prozess (nach Kafka). Strindberg-Übersetzungen: Fräulein Julie. Ein Traumspiel. Der Vater.* Berlin: Henschel, 1979. Also in *Drei Stücke in der Übertragung von Peter Weiss.* Frankfurt a.M.: Suhrkamp, 1981.

Paintings, Drawings, and Collages by Weiss

For information about the works that have survived, see the catalogues edited by Per Drougge (1976), Peter Spielmann (1982), Raimund Hoffmann (1984), and the volumes that were co-edited by Gunilla Palmsitena-Weiss (1983 and 1991), that are listed under secondary literature.

Films by Weiss

For more detailed information, see the catalogues by Hauke Lange-Fuchs (1986) and Gunilla Palmstierna-Weiss et al. (1991).

Studie I / Uppvaknandet (Waking Up, 1952).

Studie II / Hallucinationer (Hallucinations, 1952).

Studie III (1953).

Studie IV / Frigörelse (Liberation, 1954).

Studie V / Växelspel (Interplay, 1955).

Ateljéinteriör (The Studio of Dr. Faust, 1956).

Ansikten i skugga (Faces in the Shadow, 1956).

Ingenting Ovanligt (Nothing Unusual, 1957).

Enligt Lag (In the Name of the Law, 1957).

Vad ska vi göra nu da? (What Should We Do Now? 1958).

Hägringen (The Mirage, 1959).

Bag de ens facader (Behind the Facades, 1960).

Två Kvinnor (Two Women, 1960/61).

En Narkoman (A Drug Addict, 1960/61).

Anna Casparsson (1960).

Öyvind Fahlström (1960).

Book Illustrations for Other Authors by Weiss

Ekelöf, Gunnar. *Non Serviam*. Stockholm: Bonnier, 1945.

Hesse, Hermann. *Kindheit des Zauberers. Ein autobiographisches Märchen*. Frankfurt a.M.: Insel, 1974. (Handwritten and illustrated by Weiss, latest edition 1981).

———. *Der verbannte Ehemann oder Anton Schievelbeyn's ohnfreywillige Reissenach Ost-Indien*. Frankfurt a.M.: Insel, 1977. (Handwritten and illustrated by Weiss).

Lundkvist, Artur. *Sällska för natten*. Stockholm: Bonnier, 1965.

Literary Works Discussed in the Context of Weiss

Baraka, Amiri [Leroi Jones, pseud.]. *The System of Dante's Hell*. New York: Grove Press, 1963. A 1965 version is also published in *The fiction of Leroi Jones / Amiri Baraka*, 15–126. Chicago: Lawrence Hill, 2000.

Benn, Gottfried. *Sämtliche Werke. Band V,* edited by Gerhard Schuster. Stuttgart: Klett-Cotta, 1991.

Boye, Karin. *Dikter*. Stockholm: Bonniers, 1962.

Breton, André. *Oeuvres complètes III*. Paris: Gallimard, 1999.

Brüning, Elfriede. *Damit du weiterlebst*. Berlin: Neues Leben, 1949.

Duden, Anne. *Das Judasschaf*. Hamburg: Rotbuch, 1985.

Gatti, Armand. *V comme Vietnam*. Paris: Éditions du Seuil, 1967.

———. *Rosa Collective*. Paris: Éditions du Seuil, 1973.

Hamel, Peter Michael. *Kafka-Weiss-Dialoge für Viola und Violoncello. Musik zum "Neuen Prozess" von Peter Weiss für die Münchner Kammerspiele 1983.* Kassel / New York: Bärenreiter, 1987. [Musical score]

Hölderlin, Friedrich. *Sämtliche Werke und Briefe,* edited by Jochen Schmidt. Frankfurt a.M.: Deutscher Klassiker Verlag, 1992–94. 3 vols.

Lehr, Thomas. *Frühling.* Berlin: Aufbau, 2001.

Merwin, W. S. *East Window: The Asian Translations.* Port Townsend, WA: Copper Canyon Press, 1998.

Musil, Robert. *Der Mann ohne Eigenschaften. Roman,* edited by Adolf Frisé. Reinbek: Rowohlt, 1988.

Pepetela (Artur Pestana). *Mayombe.* Lisboa: edicões 70, 1980. English translation by Michael Wolfers, London/Ibadan/Nairobi: Heinemann, 1983.

Rilke, Rainer Maria. *Sämtliche Werke. Erster Band: Gedichte. Erster Teil,* edited by Ernst Zinn. Frankfurt a.M.: Insel, 1987.

Schmidt, Arno. "Herrn Dante Alighieri." In Arno Schmidt's *Wundertüte. Eine Sammlung fiktiver Briefe aus den Jahren 1948/49.* Edited by Bernd Rauschenbach, 6–9. Bargfeld, Zurich: Arno Schmidt Stiftung im Haffmans Verlag, 1989.

Secondary Literature

Badenberg, Nana. "Die *Ästhetik* und ihre Kunstwerke: Eine Inventur." In *Die Bilderwelt des Peter Weiss,* edited by Alexander Honold and Ulrich Schreiber, 114–29. Berlin: Argument, 1995.

———. "Kommentiertes Verzeichnis der in der *Ästhetik des Widerstands* erwähnten bildenden Künstler und Kunstwerke." In *Die Bilderwelt des Peter Weiss,* edited by Alexander Honold and Ulrich Schreiber, 163–230. Berlin: Argument, 1995.

Beise, Arnd. *Peter Weiss.* Stuttgart: Reclam, 2002.

Beise, Arnd, and Ingo Breuer. "Vier, fünf oder mindestens zehn Fassungen? Entstehungsphasen des *Marat/Sade* von Peter Weiss." *Peter Weiss Jahrbuch* 1 (1992): 86–115.

Bergmann, Hans-Joachim. "Max Julius Karl Hodann (1894–1946)." In *Berliner jüdische Ärzte in der Weimarer Republik,* edited by Bernhard Meyer and Hans-Jürgen Mende, 107–49. Berlin: Edition Luisenstadt, 1996.

Bertaux, Pierre. *Hölderlin. Essai de biographie intérieure.* Paris: Hachette, 1936.

———. *Hölderlin und die Französische Revolution.* Frankfurt a.M.: Suhrkamp, 1970.

Bessen, Ursula. "Eine 'destruktive Gewaltfigur' oder Abschied von Mutter und Medusa." *Peter Weiss Jahrbuch* 8 (1999): 89–96.

Birkmeyer, Jens. *Bilder des Schreckens: Dantes Spuren und due Mythosrezeption in Peter Weiss' Roman "Die Ästhetik des Widerstands."* Wiesbaden: DUV, 1994.

Birmingham, David. *Portugal and Africa.* Hampshire, London, New York: MacMillan / St. Martin's Press, 1999.

———. *The Portuguese Conquest of Angola.* London, New York: Oxford UP, 1965.

Bohrer, Karl Heinz. "Die Tortur — Peter Weiss' Weg ins Engagement — die Geschichte des Individualisten." In *Peter Weiss,* edited by Rainer Gerlach, 182–207. Frankfurt a.m.: Suhrkamp, 1984.

Bourgignon, Annie. *Der Schriftsteller Peter Weiss und Schweden.* St. Ingbert: Röhrig, 1997.

Boussart, Monique. "Zur Rolle Rimbauds in Peter Weiss' Werk: Vom Alter ego zur mythischen Figur." In *Peter Weiss: Neue Fragen an alte Texte,* edited by Irene Heidelberger-Leonard, 127–39. Opladen: Westdeutscher Verlag, 1994.

Breuer, Ingo. "Der Jude Marat: Identifikationsprobleme bei Peter Weiss." In *Peter Weiss: Neue Fragen an alte Texte,* edited by Irene Heidelberger-Leonard, 64–76. Opladen: Westdeutscher Verlag, 1994.

———. "Gestische Bilder im *Marat/Sade.*" In *Die Bilderwelt des Peter Weiss,* edited by Alexander Honold and Ulrich Schreiber, 37–47. Berlin: Argument, 1995.

Brunner, Berthold. "Richard Stahlmann — zur historischen Person: Eine Textcollage und zwei hanschriftliche Lebensläufe." *Peter Weiss Jahrbuch* 2 (1993): 118–53.

———. *Der Herakles / Stahlmann-Komplex in Peter Weiss' "Ästhetik des Widerstands."* St. Ingbert: Röhrig Universitätsverlag, 1999.

Brunse, Niels. "*Die Ästhetik des Widerstand* [*sic*] aus der Sicht des Übersetzers." In *Peter Weiss: Werk und Wirkung,* edited by Rudolf Wolff, 100–106. Bonn: Bouvier, 1987.

Bürger, Peter. "Über die Wirklichkeit der Kunst: Zur Ästhetik in *der Ästhetik des Widerstands.*" In *Peter Weiss: "Die Ästhetik des Widerstands,"* edited by Alexander Stephan, 285–95. Frankfurt a.M.: Suhrkamp, 1983.

Caproni, Attilio Mauro. *Tre Ipotesi Sceniche: Ionesco, Beckett, Weiss.* Roma: Manzella, 1975.

Carandell, José Maria. *Peter Weiss: Poesia y verdad.* Madrid: Taurus, 1968.

Cohen, Robert. *Bio-Bibliographisches Handbuch zu Peter Weiss' "Ästhetik des Widerstands."* Hamburg: Argument, 1989.

———. *Peter Weiss in seiner Zeit. Leben und Werk.* Stuttgart, Weimar: Metzler, 1992.

———. *Understanding Peter Weiss.* Columbia, S.C.: U of South Carolina P, 1993.

Coppi, Hans. *Harro Schulze-Boysen — Wege in den Widerstand: Eine biographische Studie.* Koblenz: Fölbach, 1993.

Coppi, Hans, and Geertje Andresen, eds. *Dieser Tod paßt zu mir. Harro Schulze-Boysen — Grenzgänger im Widerstand: Briefe 1915 bis 1942.* Berlin: Aufbau, 1999.

Coppi, Hans, Jürgen Danyel, and Johannes Tuchel, eds. *Die Rote Kapelle im Widerstand gegen den Nationalsozialismus.* Berlin: Edition Hentrich, 1994.

Delisle, Manon. *Weltuntergang ohne Ende: Ikonographie und Inszenierung der Katastrophe bei Christa Wolf, Peter Weiss und Hans Magnus Enzensberger.* Würzburg: Königshausen & Neumann, 2001.

Dölling, Irene. "Frauen im Klassenkampf: Klassenkampf und Geschlechterfrage in Peter Weiss' *Ästhetik des Widerstands.*" In *"Ästhetik des Widerstands": Erfahrungen mit dem Roman von Peter Weiss,* edited by Norbert Krenzlin, 45–63. Berlin: Akademie, 1987.

Drougge, Per, ed. *Peter Weiss: Måleri, collage, teckning = Malerei, Collage, Zeichnung = painting, collage, drawing = peinture, collage, dessin, 1933–1960.* Södertälje: Södertälje Konsthall, 1976.

Ellis, Roger. *Peter Weiss in Exile: A Critical Study of His Works.* Ann Arbor: UMI Research Press, 1987.

Falkenstein, Henning. *Peter Weiss.* Berlin: Morgenbuch, 1996.

Feusthuber, Birgit. "Sprache und Erinnerungsvermögen: Weibliche Spurensuche in der *Ästhetik des Widerstands* von Peter Weiss." In *Ästhetik Revolte Widerstand: Zum literarischen Werk von Peter Weiss,* edited by Jürgen Garbers, Jens-Christian Hagsphil, Sven Kramer, and Ulrich Schreiber, 207–37. Jena and Lüneburg: Universitätsverlag and zu Klampen, 1990.

———. "Die *Ästhetik des Widerstands* bleibt eine Zumutung." In *Widerstand wahrnehmen: Dokumente eines Dialogs mit Peter Weiss,* edited by Jens-F. Dwars, Dieter Strützel, and Mathias Mieth, 309–11. Köln: GNN, 1993.

———. "Najaden und Sirenen: Weiblichkeitsbilder in der *Ästhetik des Widerstands.*" In *Peter Weiss: Neue Fragen an alte Texte,* edited by Irene Heidelberger-Leonard, 97–110. Opladen: Westdeutscher Verlag, 1994.

Frisch, Christine. *"Geniestreich," "Lehrstück," "Revolutionsgestammel": Zur Rezeption des Dramas "Marat/Sade" von Peter Weiss in der Literaturwissenschaft und auf den Bühnen der Bundesrepublik Deutschland, der Deutschen Demokratischen Republik und Schwedens.* Stockholm: Almqvist & Wiksell International, 1992.

Gerlach, Ingeborg. *Die ferne Utopie: Studien zu Peter Weiss' "Ästhetik des Widerstands."* Aachen: Karin Fischer, 1991.

Griebel, Regina, Marlies Coburger, and Heinrich Scheel. *Erfasst? Das Gestapo-Album zur Roten Kapelle: Eine Foto-Dokumentation.* Halle: Audioscop, 1992.

Grimm, Christa. "'Und die einzige Rettung ist der Wundbrand der Wachheit.': Aspekte der Wahrnehmung und Erkenntnis im Werk von Peter Weiss." In *Peter Weiss: Leben und Werk. Peter Weiss: Liv och verk,* edited by Gunilla Palmstierna-Weiss and Jürgen Schutte, 110–19. Frankfurt a.M.: Suhrkamp, 1991.

Grimm, Reinhold, and Caroline Molina y Vedia. "Artaudsche Vollendung? Antonin Artaud und das Werk von Peter Weiss." *Peter Weiss Jahrbuch* 3 (1994): 135–49.

Haiduk, Manfred. *Der Dramatiker Peter Weiss.* Berlin: Henschel, 1977.

Hanenberg, Peter. "*Gesang vom Lusitanischen Popanz.*" In *Peter Weiss' Dramen: Neue Interpretationen,* edited by Martin Rector and Christoph Weiss, 155–75. Opladen and Wiesbaden: Westdeutscher Verlag, 1999.

Harmon, Maurice, ed. *No Author Better Served: The Correspondence of Samuel Beckett & Alan Schneider.* Cambridge, Mass. and London: Harvard UP, 1998.

Heidelberger-Leonard, Irene. "Jüdisches Bewußtsein im Werk von Peter Weiss." In *Literatur, Ästhetik, Geschichte: Neue Zugänge zu Peter Weiss,* edited by Michael Hofmann, 49–64. St. Ingbert: Röhrig, 1992.

Hell, Julia. "From Laokoon to Ge: Resistance to Jewish Authorship in Peter Weiss's Ästhetik des Widerstands." In *Rethinking Peter Weiss,* edited by Jost Hermand and Marc Silberman, 23–44. New York: Lang, 2000.

Herding, Klaus. "Arbeit am Bild als Widerstandsleistung." In *Peter Weiss: "Die Ästhetik des Widerstands,"* edited by Alexander Stephan, 246–84. Frankfurt a.M.: Suhrkamp, 1983.

Hermand, Jost. "Das Floß der Medusa: Über Versuche, den Untergang zu überleben." In *Die "Ästhetik des Widerstands" lesen: Über Peter Weiss,* edited by Karl-Heinz Götze and Klaus R. Scherpe, 112–20. Berlin: Argument, 1981.

———. "Obwohl. Dennoch. Trotzalledem: Die im Konzept der freien Assoziation der Gleichgesinnten aufgehobene Antinomie von ästhetischem Modernismus und sozialistischer Parteilichkeit in der *Ästhetik des Widerstands* und den sie begleitenden Notizbüchern." In *Peter Weiss: "Die Ästhetik des Widerstands,"* edited by Alexander Stephan, 79–103. Frankfurt a.M.: Suhrkamp, 1983.

Heyde, Andrea. *Unterwerfung und Aufruhr: Franz Kafka im literarischen Werk von Peter Weiss.* Berlin: Schmidt, 1997.

Heywood, Linda. *Contested Power in Angola, 1840s to the Present.* Rochester, N.Y.: U of Rochester P, 2000.

Hiekisch, Sepp. "Zwischen surrealistischem Protest und kritischem Engagement: Zu Peter Weiss' früher Prosa." In *Text + Kritik* 37 (1982): 22–38.

Hiekisch-Picard, Sepp. "Der Maler Peter Weiss." In *Peter Weiss,* edited by Rainer Gerlach, 93–115. Frankfurt a.M.: Suhrkamp, 1984.

———. "Der Filmemacher Peter Weiss." In *Peter Weiss,* edited by Rainer Gerlach, 129–44. Frankfurt a.M.: Suhrkamp, 1984.

———. "Weiss und Ekelöf: Anmerkungen zur Rezeption der poetischen Theorien Gunnar Ekelöfs im bildkünstlerischen, literarischen und filmischen Werk von Peter Weiss." In *Peter Weiss: Werk und Wirkung,* edited by Rudolf Wolff, 43–59. Bonn: Bouvier, 1987.

Hilton, Ian. *Peter Weiss: A Search for Affinities.* London: Oswald Wolff, 1970.

Hochmuth, Ursel. *Illegale KPD und Bewegung 'Freies Deutschland' in Berlin und Brandenburg 1942–1945: Biographien und Zeugnisse aus der Widerstandsorganisation um Saefkow, Jacob und Bästlein.* Berlin: Hentrich & Hentrich, 1998.

Hofmann, Michael. "*Die Versicherung.*" In *Peter Weiss' Dramen: Neue Interpretationen,* edited by Martin Rector and Christoph Weiss, 25–42. Opladen and Wiesbaden: Westdeutscher Verlag, 1999.

Hoffmann, Raimund, ed. *Peter Weiss: Malerei. Zeichnungen. Collagen.* Berlin: Henschel, 1984.

Holdenried, Michaela. "Mitteilungen eines Fremden: Identität, Sprache und Fiktion in den frühen autobiographischen Schriften *Abschied von den Eltern* und *Fluchtpunkt.*" *Peter Weiss: Leben und Werk. Peter Weiss: Liv och verk,* edited by Gunilla Palmstierna-Weiss and Jürgen Schutte, 155–73. Frankfurt a.M.: Suhrkamp, 1991.

Honold, Alexander. "*Wie dem Herrn Mockinpott das Leiden ausgetrieben wird.*" In *Peter Weiss' Dramen: Neue Interpretationen,* edited by Martin Rector and Christoph Weiss, 89–107. Opladen and Wiesbaden: Westdeutscher Verlag, 1999.

Howald, Stefan. "*Viet Nam Diskurs.*" In *Peter Weiss' Dramen: Neue Interpretationen,* edited by Martin Rector and Christoph Weiss, 176–92. Opladen and Wiesbaden: Westdeutscher Verlag, 1999.

Huber, Andreas. *Mythos und Utopie: Eine Studie zur "Ästhetik des Widerstands" von Peter Weiss.* Heidelberg: Winter, 1990.

Ivanovic, Christine. "Die Sprache der Bilder: Versuch einer Revision von Peter Weiss' *Der Schatten des Körpers des Kutschers.*" *Peter Weiss Jahrbuch* 8 (1999): 34–67.

Jens, Walter. "*Die Ermittlung* in Westberlin." *Über Peter Weiss,* edited by Volker Canaris, 92–96. Frankfurt a.M.: Suhrkamp, 1970.

————. Foreword to *Peter Weiss: Leben und Werk. Peter Weiss: Liv och verk,* edited by Gunilla Palmstierna-Weiss and Jürgen Schutte. Frankfurt a.M.: Suhrkamp, 1991.

Jungk, Robert. "Begegnung ohne Ende." In *Peter Weiss: "Die Ästhetik des Widerstands,"* edited by Alexander Stephan, 342–45. Frankfurt a.M.: Suhrkamp, 1983.

Karnick, Manfred. "Peter Weiss' dramatische Collagen: Vom Traumspiel zur Agitation." In *Peter Weiss,* edited by Rainer Gerlach, 208–48. Frankfurt a.M.: Suhrkamp, 1984.

Kleinschmidt, Erich. *"Der Turm."* In *Peter Weiss' Dramen: Neue Interpretationen,* edited by Martin Rector and Christoph Weiss, 9–24. Opladen and Wiesbaden: Westdeutscher Verlag, 1999.

Knittel, Anton Philipp. *Erzählte Bilder der Gewalt: Die Stellung der "Ästhetik des Widerstands" im Prosawerk von Peter Weiss.* Konstanz: Hartung-Knorre, 1996.

Köppen, Manuel. "Die halluzinierte Stadt: Strukturen räumlicher Wahrnehmung im malerischen und erzählerischen Werk von Peter Weiss." In *Peter Weiss: Werk und Wirkung,* edited by Rudolf Wolff, 9–26. Bonn: Bouvier, 1987.

Koeppen, Wolfgang. "Der Moralist glaubt an den Teufel." In Wolfgang Koeppen: *Gesammelte Werke in sechs Bänden. 6: Essays und Rezensionen,* edited by Marcel Reich-Ranicki, 410–13. Frankfurt a.M.: Suhrkamp, 1986. First published in *Frankfurter Allgemeine Zeitung,* November 5, 1976.

Kremer, Detlef. *"Der Prozeß / Der neue Prozeß."* In *Peter Weiss' Dramen: Neue Interpretationen,* edited by Martin Rector and Christoph Weiss, 235–64. Opladen and Wiesbaden: Westdeutscher Verlag, 1999.

Kuhn, Juliane. *"Nacht mit Gästen."* In *Peter Weiss' Dramen: Neue Interpretationen,* edited by Martin Rector and Christoph Weiss, 43–56. Opladen and Wiesbaden: Westdeutscher Verlag, 1999.

Kuon, Peter. "'. . . dieser Portalheilige zur abendländischen Kunst . . .': Zur Rezeption der *Divina Commedia* bei Peter Weiss, Pier Paolo Pasolini und anderen." *Peter Weiss Jahrbuch* 6 (1997): 42–67.

Lange-Fuchs, Hauke. *Peter Weiss und der Film: Eine Dokumentation zur Retrospektive der 28. Nordischen Filmtage Lübeck vom 30. Oktober bis 2. November 1986.* Lübeck: Nordische Filmtage Lübeck, Senat der Hansestadt Lübeck, Amt für Kultur, 1986.

Lilienthal, Volker. *Literaturkritik als politische Lektüre: Am Beispiel der Rezeption der "Ästhetik des Widerstands" von Peter Weiss.* Berlin: Spiess, 1988.

Lindner, Burkhardt. *Im Inferno. "Die Ermittlung" von Peter Weiss: Auschwitz, der Historikerstreit und "Die Ermittlung."* Frankfurt a.M.: Frankfurter Bund für Volksbildung, 1988.

————. "Der Widerstand und das Erhabene: Über ein zentrales Motiv der *Ästhetik des Widerstands* von Peter Weiss." In *Widerstand der Ästhetik? Im Anschluß an Peter Weiss,* edited by Martin Lüdke and Delf Schmidt, 28–44. Reinbek: Rowohlt, 1991.

Meyer, Marita. *Eine Ermittlung: Fragen an Peter Weiss und an die Literatur des Holocaust.* St. Ingbert: Röhrig, 2000.

Meyer, Stephan. *Kunst als Widerstand: Zum Verhältnis von Erzählen und ästhetischer Reflexion in Peter Weiss' "Die Ästhetik des Widerstands."* Tübingen: Niemeyer, 1989.

Müller, Heiner. "Erinnerung an Peter Weiss." In *Peter Weiss: Leben und Werk. Peter Weiss: Liv och verk,* edited by Gunilla Palmstierna-Weiss and Jürgen Schutte, 21–23. Frankfurt a.M.: Suhrkamp, 1991.

Müller, Jost. *Literatur und Politik bei Peter Weiss: Die "Ästhetik des Widerstands" und die Krise des Marxismus.* Wiesbaden: DUV, 1991.

Müller, Karl-Josef. *Haltlose Reflexion: Über die Grenzen der Kunst in Peter Weiss' Roman "Die Ästhetik des Widerstands."* Würzburg: Königshausen & Neumann, 1992.

Müller-Richter, Klaus. "Bilderwelten und Wortwelten: Gegensatz oder Komplement? Peter Weiss' Konzept der Bildlichkeit als Modell dynamischer Aisthesis." *Peter Weiss Jahrbuch* 6 (1997): 116–37.

Neumann, Michael. "*Hölderlin.*" In *Peter Weiss' Dramen: Neue Interpretationen,* edited by Martin Rector and Christoph Weiss, 210–34. Opladen and Wiesbaden: Westdeutscher Verlag, 1999.

Palmstierna-Weiss, Gunilla, Per Drougge, and R. Von Holten. *Peter Weiss: Bilder på papper.* Stockholm: Nationalmuseum, 1983.

Palmstierna-Weiss, Gunilla, and Jürgen Schutte, eds., *Peter Weiss.* Stockholm / Frankfurt a.M.: Moderna Museet / Suhrkamp, 1991.

Palmstierna-Weiss, Gunilla, Jürgen Schutte, Andreas Schönefeld, and Elisabeth Wagner, eds. *Peter Weiss: Målningar, teckningar, collage, film, teater, litteratur, politik.* Stockholm: Moderna Museet, 1991.

Pasinato, Antonio. *Invito alla lettura di Peter Weiss.* Milano: Mursia, 1980.

Philipsen, Bart. *Die List der Einfalt. NachLese zu Hölderlins spätester Dichtung.* Munich: Fink, 1995.

Rector, Martin. "Örtlichkeit und Phantasie: Zur inneren Konstruktion der *Ästhetik des Widerstands.*" In *Peter Weiss: "Die Ästhetik des Widerstands,"* edited by Alexander Stephan, 104–33. Frankfurt a.M.: Suhrkamp, 1983.

————. "Sechs Thesen zur Dante-Rezeption bei Peter Weiss." *Peter Weiss Jahrbuch* 6 (1997): 110–15.

————. *"Die Verfolgung und Ermordung Jean Paul Marats dargestellt durch die Schauspielgruppe des Hospizes zu Charenton unter Anleitung des Herrn de Sade."* In *Peter Weiss' Dramen: Neue Interpretationen,* edited by Martin Rector and Christoph Weiss, 57–88. Opladen and Wiesbaden: Westdeutscher Verlag, 1999.

Richter, Matthias. "'Bis zum heutigen Tag habe ich Ihre Bücher bei mir getragen': Über die Beziehung zwischen Peter Weiss und Hermann Hesse." In *Peter Weiss,* edited by Rainer Gerlach, 32–56. Frankfurt a.M.: Suhrkamp, 1984.

Rohrwasser, Michael. *"Trotzki im Exil."* In *Peter Weiss' Dramen: Neue Interpretationen,* edited by Martin Rector and Christoph Weiss, 193–209. Opladen and Wiesbaden: Westdeutscher Verlag, 1999.

Rump, Bernd. *Herrschaft und Widerstand: Untersuchungen zu Genesis und Eigenart des kulturphilosophischen Diskurses in dem Roman "Die Ästhetik des Widerstands" von Peter Weiss.* Aachen: Shaker, 1996.

Salloch, Erika. *Peter Weiss' "Die Ermittlung": Zur Struktur des Dokumentartheaters.* Frankfurt a.M.: Athenäum, 1972.

Sareika, Rüdiger. "Peter Weiss' Engagement für die 'Dritte Welt': *Lusitanischer Popanz* und *Viet Nam Diskurs.*" In *Peter Weiss,* edited by Rainer Gerlach, 249–67. Frankfurt a.M.: Suhrkamp, 1984.

Scherpe, Klaus. "Die *Ästhetik des Widerstands* als *Divina Commedia:* Peter Weiss' künstlerische Vergegenständlichung der Geschichte." In *Peter Weiss: Werk und Wirkung,* edited by Rudolf Wolff, 88–99. Bonn: Bouvier, 1987.

————. "10 Arbeitspunkte beim Lesen der *Ästhetik des Widerstands.*" In *Lesergespräche: Erfahrungen mit Peter Weiss' Roman "Die Ästhetik des Widerstands,"* edited by G. Dunz-Wolff, H. Goebel, and J. Stüsser, 168–74. Hamburg: edition comtext, 1988.

Schmitt, Maria C. *Peter Weiss "Die Ästhetik des Widerstands": Studien zu Kontext, Struktur und Kunstverständnis.* 2nd ed. St. Ingbert: Röhrig, 1990.

Schönefeld, Andreas. "Die filmische Produktion des multimedialen Künstlers Peter Weiss im Zusammenhang seiner künstlerisch-politischen Entwicklung in den späten 40er und 50er Jahren." In *Peter Weiss: Werk und Wirkung,* edited by Rudolf Wolff, 114–28. Bonn: Bouvier, 1987.

Schneider, Helmut J. "Der Verlorene Sohn und die Sprache: *Zu Der Schatten des Körpers des Kutschers.*" *Über Peter Weiss,* edited by Volker Canaris, 28–50. Frankfurt a.M.: Suhrkamp, 1970.

Schwerte, Hans. "Herakles und der Kentaur: Anmerkungen zu Peter Weiss *Die Ästhetik des Widerstands.*" In *Hinter jedem Wort die Gefahr des Verstummens: Sprachproblematik und literarische Tradition in der "Ästhetik des Widerstands" von Peter Weiss,* edited by Hans Höller, 1–20. Stuttgart: Akademischer Verlag Hans-Dieter Heinz, 1988.

Siegel, Eva-Maria. "'An ihrem Lachen kann man eine Frau doch erkennen': Dokumente und Anmerkung zum Verhältnis von Fiktion und Authentizität in Peter Weiss' *Ästhetik des Widerstands* am Beispiel Charlotte Bischoffs." *Peter Weiss Jahrbuch* 5 (1996): 37–69.

Soboczynski, Adam. "Von Schatten oder Schwarz auf Weiss: Überlegungen zu *Der Schatten des Körpers des Kutschers* von Peter Weiss." *Peter Weiss Jahrbuch* 8 (1999): 68–88.

Spielmann, Peter, ed. *Der Maler Peter Weiss: Bilde — Zeichnungen — Collagen — Filme*. Berlin: Frölich & Kaufmann, 1982.

Steinlein, Rüdiger. "Ein surrealistischer 'Bilddichter': Visualität als Darstellungsprinzip im erzählerischen Frühwerk von Peter Weiss." In *Peter Weiss: Werk und Wirkung*, edited by Rudolf Wolff, 60–87. Bonn: Bouvier, 1987.

Vogt, Jochen. *Peter Weiss*. Reinbek: Rowohlt, 1987.

———. "Treffpunkt im Unendlichen? Über Peter Weiss und Paul Celan." *Peter Weiss Jahrbuch* 4 (1995): 102–21.

Wandschneider, B. "Der Turm." In *Material zum Werk von 1978 bis 1998*, by Detlef Heusinger, 32–34. Bad Schwalbach: Edition Gravis, 1998.

Weinreich, Gerd. *Peter Weiss: Marat/Sade*. Frankfurt a.M.: Diesterweg, 1981.

———. Peter Weiss: *Die Ermittlung*. Frankfurt a.M.: Diesterweg, 1983.

Weiss, Christoph. "*Die Ermittlung*." In *Peter Weiss' Dramen: Neue Interpretationen*, edited by Martin Rector and Christoph Weiss, 108–54. Opladen and Wiesbaden: Westdeutscher Verlag, 1999.

———. *Auschwitz in der geteilten Welt: Peter Weiss und die "Ermittlung" im Kalten Krieg*. 2 vols. St. Ingbert: Röhrig, 2000

Wender, Herbert. "Entwicklungsstufen und Fassungen in der Textgeschichte des *Marat/Sade:* Anmerkungen zum Beitrag von Beise und Breuer in PWJ 1 (1992)." *Peter Weiss Jahrbuch* 3 (1994): 153–65.

Wolf, Ror. "Die Poesie der kleinsten Stücke." *Über Peter Weiss*, edited by Volker Canaris, 25–27. Frankfurt a.M.: Suhrkamp, 1970. First published in *Diskus* 2 (1961): 34.

Wolff, Wilfried. *Max Hodann (1894–1946): Sozialist und Sozialreformer*. Hamburg: von Bockel, 1993.

Index